ONE SUMMER'S GRACE

Libby Purves is currently the presenter of Radio 4 *Midweek* and is also a prolific journalist. The daughter of a British diplomat, she spent her childhood travelling with her family, attending school in Bangkok, France, South Africa and Britain. She was at Oxford University, and began sailing in the vacation when she was persuaded to abandon her duties as barmaid in the West of Ireland and join a cruising yacht on the way up the coast. After this, she attended evening classes in navigation and crewed on a dozen different boats before buying a part-share in a boat with Paul Heiney, then a colleague at *Today*.

Libby Purves is now married to Paul Heiney who is best known as a presenter on BBC TV's *That's Life*, and the hugely successful *In at the Deep End*, in which he was required to learn skills as diverse as sheepdog-handling, hairdressing and haute cuisine. He taught himself to sail after falling in love with the idea when he was sent to cover the Earls Court Boat Show as a reporter.

Nicholas Heiney made his first substantial cruise in Holland when he was two-and-a-half years old. He and his sister Rose had sailed extensively in the Mediterranean and from Lymington to Brighton before the Heiney family embarked on their voyage around Britain.

LIBBY PURVES

One Summer's Grace

A Family Voyage Round Britain

FONTANA/Collins

First published by Grafton Books in 1989

First published in 1990 by Fontana Paperbacks
8 Grafton Street, London W1X 3LA

Printed and bound in Great Britain by
William Collins Sons & Co. Ltd, Glasgow

To Valentine, Katharine and Mary Thornhill,
who first demonstrated to me, long ago,
that it is quite possible for small
children to go on great adventures.

The world is too much with us; late and soon,
Getting and spending, we lay waste our powers;
Little we see in Nature that is ours;
We have given our hearts away, a sordid boon!
The Sea that bares her bosom to the moon;
The winds that will be howling at all hours,
And are up-gathered now like sleeping flowers;
For this, for everything, we are out of tune;
It moves us not; Great God! I'd rather be
A Pagan, suckled in a creed outworn,
So might I, standing on this pleasant lea
Have glimpses that would make me less forlorn;
Have sight of Proteus rising from the sea,
Or hear old Triton blow his wreathéd horn.

WORDSWORTH
Miscellaneous Sonnets

ACKNOWLEDGEMENTS

Above all, thanks are due to my husband Paul Heiney. Without his seamanship and his meticulous planning and collecting of esoteric pilot-books, this voyage would have come to grief many times over. His task of collecting charts was made much easier by the help of Dr Stuart Ingram of the Royal Cruising Club, and the generosity of Christopher Thornhill in lending us his set of Scottish charts for the summer.

The co-operation of the London Weather Centre Offshore Desk meant a great deal to us, too; and we had altogether good reason to bless all the services of the Meteorological Office. The same goes for the Coastguards, particularly in Scotland where their willingness to give advice to individual yachts was admirable. The Yacht Clubs and their members around the coast are too numerous to list, but thanks to them all for their hospitality, and to the handful of people, often complete strangers, who correctly assessed our greatest need and gave us baths. Thanks also to the score of harbourmasters, lock-keepers and other professionals who – even in the busiest commercial harbours – showed great consideration for one small yacht. And to the Royal Mail and its employees for their ingenuity in finding us in unlikely places when we had our post addressed wrongly.

Our peace of mind was guaranteed by the presence of watchful friends and neighbours back home: without the attentions of Fran Gordon-Jones to our mail, we would have returned to find ourselves imprisoned for debt, tax offences, and failure to pay overdue parking-fines. And without Fran's efforts in typing up 100,000 words of rambling draft, this book would not be published today. Nancy Gildersleeves, Joyce Ash, Virginia Blackmore, Caroline Stevens, Roger and Cheryl Clark, and Dave Prutton, between them cared for our house, animals, and a field of growing crops. Thanks also to Coldfair Green First School for their encouragement and co-operation. And – although thanking a publisher in its own book seems a bit incestuous – it would be ungracious not to mention the service provided by Maggie Usiskin of Grafton Books who took on the terrible task of acting as an answering service and passing messages on to us. It is not every publishing office which would be prepared to take down complicated messages about dodgy water-softeners and horses' feet, let alone forward bundles of urgent page-proofs from rival publishers with such grace as her office did.

From May to August 1988 my husband and children and I stepped away from home, work and school to sail our boat *Grace O'Malley* round Britain. From Suffolk we went down-Channel, then north around Scotland and home again. We were not chasing any records or doing anything remarkable; people have been sailing these coasts for pleasure for a hundred years, and earning their living at it for thousands more. But to go round Britain all in one journey was our own vision of adventure and escape. We planned it for a year beforehand, dreamed of it on long winter drives as we sat in foggy roadhouses poring over the free maps, and became nervous about it whenever we saw the turbulent satellite pictures of Britain on the television weather forecast. Amid the duties of ordinary life, this trip was to be our escape, our sabbatical: one summer's grace.

This is the story of how it turned out.

LIBBY PURVES
Pattle's Farm, September 1988

1

At nine I woke, to sunlight dancing on the white cabin ceiling, and the gentle rhythmic creak of the gaff. It was an improvement; my dawn watch had been an endless, hypnotically boring session of steering under engine in a windless drizzle, looking out anxiously for the Elbow buoy at the southern edge of the Thames Estuary. I have never liked the estuary; it gives me the shivers. You can be ten miles offshore, with no land in sight, yet floating in a mere six feet of water; if you are unwary or confused, the banks wait like submerged crocodiles to grab your keel and pound you to pieces as the falling tide mercilessly withdraws its soft support. Paul has a certain tenderness for the place and likes threading through its invisible mazes, because it was here he had his first sailing adventures, heart-in-mouth between the Crouch and the Blackwater. Unfortunately, his rhapsodies on the subject have merely led me into an unreasonable conviction that he is somehow to blame for the whole place. Somewhere, deep in my heart, I regard the banks and currents of this offshore labyrinth as a kind of private indulgence of my husband's. The Thames Estuary, in short, *is all his fault*. If we had not lived in Suffolk, and resolved to sail round Britain clockwise to catch the best winds, nothing on earth would have persuaded me to begin a season's pleasure by groping across this nightmare stretch of water.

This quaking mood of mine partly explained the absence, on this peaceful morning, of children's strident voices from the quarter-bunks. Our family journey round Britain was beginning to daunt me more than a little: a year of preparation, clearing the decks at home, finishing last-minute commissions, collecting charts, and finally stowing the boat with everything from lamp-oil to Postman Pat jigsaws had worn us both out physically and emotionally. I had a bad cough, which frequently doubled me up in helpless convulsions; Paul had an assortment of minor rashes and ailments of the sort that make GPs tell people to Take it Easy. The strain was increased, if anything, by the natural interest shown by friends and occasional local newspapers: several weeks of making confident, happy pronouncements about the wisdom of taking children of five and three in a small boat around two thousand miles of hazardous coastline had drained me of all the confidence I had originally felt. The process was similar to the way a Hollywood couple can be driven to divorce (so I have always suspected) by nothing more than the pressure of giving interviews to Hollywood reporters about their wonderful caring marriage. As Paul wrote in his intermittent journal:

> Two children, four months, and only thirty feet of boat. No nanny. Only Mummy and Daddy to turn to and the *Grace O'Malley* wanting attention too. But in many ways, we've had insufficient time for our children in the past. On this cruise we will have no excuses. No phones to interrupt, no important calls to make. No excuses!

So we decided to make a virtue of our attack of nerves. We could get our shakedown sail, our first seasickness, and the horrors of the Thames Estuary all over with in one fell swoop, without the children. They could be ferried down to join us at Brighton, and leaving Ipswich we would ship as crew the infinitely more robust and reassuring figure of our friend Michael Devenish.

Michael was crooning snatches of opera to himself on the helm as I lay watching the sunlight on the boatyard's deep chestnut varnish. Paul lay heavily asleep, rolled in a blanket in Rose's bunk. Michael, as I stumbled up into the cockpit, pointed out the latest piece of coast with the typical pride of a helmsman ending his watch: rather as if he had built it himself. 'White cliffs of Dover.' So they were. We were round both the Forelands and pointing West at last. I shivered down below again, and put the kettle on; it was newly polished, and reflected my face as it swung cosily on its gimbals. There was a nice symbolism, I thought, in this way of beginning the cruise. It was right that children should only come along after an adult interlude. Long before they were born, Paul and I had sailed together in our old *Barnacle Goose*, a twenty-six-foot Contessa, making fifty-six-hour crossings to the West of Ireland, rounding the Fastnet, sailing to Southern Brittany and landing on Ushant. And in turn, long before I knew Paul, I had sailed with Michael Devenish on an eventful, risky, delightful journey through the Outer Hebrides and to St Kilda aboard an ancient Brightlingsea oyster-smack called *Kathleen*, captained by our beloved friend Christopher Thornhill: a man of such charm, uncertain temper, and adventurously romantic attitude to cruising that nobody has sailed with him without forever afterwards bearing his mark. Even Paul, who spent only two short weekends aboard *Kathleen*, shows the Thornhill influence: there is something in his eye when he approaches a rocky cleft with pilot book in one hand and tiller in the other, crying 'If I get through this hole I'll have a whisky!' which is authentically Christopher in origin.

I am more timid: but any spark of courage I have now, any determination to explore, any sense of risk well taken and any romantic devotion to traditional boats, was kindled by that fortnight under *Kathleen*'s rusty old sails. I was twenty-four and young for my age, a local radio drudge; Christopher had recruited me on an impulse to cook for him, for Michael, and for another man he didn't know very well but who was universally known as 'Stoker' from the foulness of his language and the depth of his stubble (I believe Stoker later went into the City, but everyone is entitled to adopt a romantic persona on their holidays). Alone with these odd strangers, I learned a great deal about how to steer a heavy, wilful old gaffer in a big sea and about how to cook haggis (in the oven, to let the fat run out). I thought Michael, in particular, was wonderfully adult and debonair, and became so devoted to him that I would even hold the torch and mirror in the dark cabin while he shaved (an obligingness which brought only hoots of derision from Christopher and Stoker). For the three men, the fortnight was merely another good cruise on the old boat. To me, it was one of the more significant events in my confused, late-adolescent life. I lay in my bunk on that first wild night passage out to Barra, hearing the wind's shriek and the waves' tumble close around me, and looking past the wildly swinging paraffin cabin-lamp at Michael or Christopher hauling the tiller with all their strength as we bore down on the distant lighthouse. And I discovered with a small shock of recognition that I was, for the first time since childhood, utterly happy. I was proud, too: Stoker was lying sick, but while Christopher and Michael kept watch about, I climbed in and out of my bunk all that night keeping the bilges pumped, and lashing down various objects and furnishings which had crashed awkwardly around the cabin. Once I felt desperately sick myself, and went for a pill to the first-aid box; it was fastened down in the forepeak, right on top of the box of forty Loch Fyne kippers which were essential to *Kathleen*'s victualling. Even then, while I fiddled sweatingly with unfamiliar knots in the reek of kippered herring, the pride and happiness never left me for a moment.

In this flat grey patch of Channel fifteen years later, Michael and I – both older now, both of us parents – remembered all these things as we drank our early tea aboard this newer, lighter, easier modern gaffer. *Grace O'Malley* owes a lot to my early devotion to the old oyster-smack, but it must be admitted that she is a sort of *Kathleen*-and-soda: a less richly atmospheric and considerably less hazardous version of the old boat. The slow, creaking, gentle watch went by under sail, and we passed the mouth of Dover Harbour with more ease than ever before, thanks to the seamen's strike. Usually it is like crossing a motorway on a tricycle, as the ferries thunder in and out. We rounded the low, gloomy shape of Dungeness and made for Beachy Head as dusk fell again.

It is an odd bit of coast, this: inhospitable now, but haunted by the ghosts of old harbours. There were seven of the Cinque Ports once: now Hythe is nothing but a bland, straight beach; Sandwich is sandy, Romney is marsh, Winchelsea is gone, Hastings is a haven only for beach-fishermen and fairground swingboats; and even Rye, great port of the sixteenth century, is silty and problematical, struggling to remain a harbour at all. The sea has risen, rivers have abandoned their old beds, storms and floods have hurled tons of shingle on to the hideous, hissing, promontory of Dungeness; there never has been and never can be anything safe or permanent about this shifty coast. Dover remains a port, but an entirely artificial one, its harbour walls enclosing a mile of English Channel: one Edwardian seaman inveighed furiously against this interference with nature, on the grounds that the narrowing of the twenty-one-mile strait caused the tide to flow even faster than before. Myself, I prefer an ancient rock harbour; you know where you are with rock. The south-east of England, rather appropriately, is more inconstant and fickle in its ways than the Celtic kingdoms of the West.

Still, I have had some fun here. On my first night watch under full sail, watching the Royal Sovereign blinking serenely ahead of me, I had happy memories to examine. For two or three years after the *Kathleen* voyage I sailed as crew aboard another old boat based at Newhaven. She was a small Itchen Ferry, eighteen feet long, seventy years old, but with a bowsprit and paraffin sidelights which reminded me sentimentally of *Kathleen*. I was in an energetic phase of sailing, having put a small-ad in *Yachting Monthly* offering myself as crew: I was introduced to little *Sheltie* by an obsessive young surveyor called Richard Hayward, whose life was devoted to fussing over the diminutive and somewhat mildewed shape of his little boat. He had a mania for detail and completeness: for an eighteen-foot boat to have a full Admiralty-sized chart table is admirable, if unusual; the drawback on *Sheltie* was that when unfolded, his home-made chart table occupied most of both bunks, and rendered cooking, engine maintenance, and access to the lavatory bucket in the fo'c'sle utterly impossible (sometimes the bucket was full of anchor-chain, anyway, so male or female, one clung to the tarry shrouds for natural functions). There were periodic scares during the years I sailed on *Sheltie*; not only such understandable maritime alarums as the time the exhaust pipe set fire to the floorboards off Portland Bill, but more esoteric crises like the time the boat was – according to its furious, demented owner – invaded in his absence by marauding feral mink, who left seagulls lying around in the cabin with their heads bitten off. After this alleged invasion, Richard manufactured a pair of minkproof screens out of perforated aluminium, which we solemnly fitted across the cockpit whenever we left it. Personally, I never quite believed in the mink; but I grew fond of the boat, in an exasperated sort of way, through three winters of painting her chubby bottom and hammering tarred hemp into the roomy gaps between her planks.

I have never been able to enthuse anybody else, least of all Paul, about *Sheltie*: although Richard and I drifted apart long ago, the one thing that unites us is that we know what a fine adventure it can be to sail a tiny, rather smelly, highly vulnerable old boat to new harbours by sheer determination and incurable optimism. On fire off Portland, or lost in Lyme Bay, we had only our own skins to worry about, and a conviction that there was probably no need to do so. Life changes: today, with children, I would not sail any less staidly than aboard the *Grace O'Malley*, with her twenty-seven horsepower auxiliary engine, her liferaft, her Decca navigator and comfortable chart table. But I defiantly remember my reckless salad days, and always will.

In the small hours we tied up in Brighton Marina. It is a yachtsmen's Dover, a miniature version of that utterly artificial harbour. It is, I suppose, the ring-road hypermarket of yachting;

but we had plenty of characterful slimy old harbours and wild anchorages to look forward to, and decided we had earned a night in Brighton. Besides, I happened to know that *Sheltie* was there, and hoped for a sneaky visit to her.

After several self-congratulatory whiskies we all slept, to awaken to a brilliantly sunny day, a rising south-west wind we were glad to have avoided, and the smell of bacon drifting from the café. At eleven, Michael's wife Belinda appeared with small Harry and Lucy, contemporaries and great mates of Nicholas's and Rose's. We looked at these two with sudden alarm, wakened from our complacent adult world to remember how very small children are, and how apparently unsuited to wobbling pontoons and narrow decks. Almost simultaneously Richard Hayward arrived, having spotted us on one of his weekend forays to the Marina to renew some unspeakable part of *Sheltie*; then our own children trotted down the pontoon with their nanny Virginia. The wind was so fierce by now that the 'little sail' we had promised Lucy and Harry was commuted to a run as far as Brighton pier with the jibs up only, and a motor back again against the wind; twenty minutes at sea was long enough for all of us. Once again, Paul and I exchanged glances, worrying, wondering whether we were a bit silly to commit these nursery children to three or four months of strenuous cruising.

Then suddenly the afternoon became surreal. We tied up again, the sun came out, and I sought to entertain the children further. 'Shall we go and see a boat called *Sheltie*?' I asked brightly. Richard, keen to show off his beloved to a new generation, led the way to the East Pontoon where she lay, stumpy and defiant with her little bowsprit and neat pinrails and home-made square cockpit. The four children climbed on to the narrow side-deck and peered into the windows as her owner groped confidently for the key on its hook under the stern-deck. 'I may – have dropped it – ' he panted – 'in the rush to get away in the rain with Claire and the new baby – she was getting a bit – urrgh – anyway, didn't have time for the mink-screens . . .' He groped furiously while Michael and Paul watched from the pontoon, and we two mothers hovered fussily over the entranced, balancing children. 'Is this a small boat? Is it the one the mink once got into?' asked Nicholas eagerly. 'Are they in there now?' 'No, no, darling,' I said with soothing maternal blandness. 'Of course not – '

Then Richard, with a face of thunder, emerged from his dark

16

oubliette, 'I can smell them,' he hissed. 'They're jolly well BACK!' He brandished a section of seagull-corpse. A leg and thigh, ending in a dark caked bloody mass. Michael, an incurable hunter, stiffened like a pointer. 'What, they're here now?' 'Yes – listen – scrabbling . . .' In the confused minutes that followed, delight piled upon delight: the mink had not only returned to their old haunt, they had actually *stolen the key*, on its tasty cork float, and therefore locked the owner out. The children jumped and crowed at the news. An invading animal, furry to boot, which eats messily and locks grown-ups out of their own boats was more than anyone could have expected on a bland day in bland Brighton Marina. Eventually Michael, who had leapt from the pontoon quivering with bloodlust, made a long arm and got the key from the cockpit locker where the mink, bored with the taste of cork, had dropped it. Hatches slid back; and moments later, all seven of us had our heads over, peering into the gloom at the remarkable sight of one small, sleek, insolent creature sitting on the chart table looking at us with bead-bright eyes, and another darting in and out of the engine-box. They had that surly, arrogant look of rats caught in an old pantry; they were not particularly scared of us, but resented our letting the light in to what was patently their home. 'Do they ever bite?' asked Lucy. 'Very much so,' snarled Richard. 'Savagely.' Belinda and I withdrew our children prudently before the mink got tough, and retired to *Grace O'Malley* for a riotous nursery tea. Harry was busy inventing 'a poisoning-machine for mink' (Just Like His Father, muttered Belinda) while Rose fell wholeheartedly into the role of 'a dear little furry mink that's friendly'. The two older children ate steadily, quietly satisfied by the drama they had witnessed. When the three men returned for their tea, Paul looked distinctly green, but the other two had the swaggering gait of the successful hunter. What had happened to the mink? asked the children in chorus. 'We – er – chased them back into the sea,' said Michael diplomatically, under his wife's stern eye. 'Got 'em with a stick,' muttered Richard. In a furious aside, he confided that he was indignant at his failure to interest the marina authorities in his furry corpses. 'They just said that nobody else had ever complained of mink getting in. Well, I said . . .' Paul passed up cups of tea through the hatch, and hissed inhospitably: 'Don't let either of those two below decks, for God's sake. They stink of it.'

* * *

The next morning, with our friends gone, Paul and I suffered something of a crisis of confidence. The mainspring of our treasured Zeiss barograph broke, necessitating a daredevil ride on the folding bicycle up the pontoons to telephone for spares to be sent on to us ('It'll take a week' – 'Make it Falmouth, then'). That was quite fun. Then the plastic handlebars of the folding bicycle shattered dramatically, necessitating an even longer trudge back to the phone box to ring the makers and suggest they did the same. ('We'll get them off today,' they said more helpfully. 'Make it Portsmouth, then, please' – our voyage, as yet unmade, was beginning to be shaped by these forwarded artefacts. I had lost the aerial of my new portable phone, and that was on its way to Poole.) Such marginal gadgets are nothing to get emotional about; but the third blow was worse. Both batteries were entirely, irredeemably, flat. Clearly, our newly bought charging system did not work at all. And there were two days of Bank Holiday ahead, and the children bratty and discontented from the day's excitement, and the wind still hard out of the south-west. We had promised ourselves to be cheerful and optimistic about setbacks, but we had hoped for rather more glamorous setbacks – being galebound in Islay, or becalmed amid flocks of puffins – rather than being stuck in Brighton Marina with a duff alternator. But we passed the time with school lessons for Nicholas, pothooks for Rose, rowing-lessons and rattly journeys on the ancient Volks Electric Railway along the Brighton prom.

Meanwhile Paul unearthed a quiet, serious middle-aged electrical engineer called Neville Preston, who became quite a member of the family over the Bank Holiday, limping up and down the pontoons with his bad hip to try out one theory after another. On Tuesday lunchtime he raised his head at last from the smelly recesses of the engine compartment and triumphantly announced that the regulator was wired up back to front. 'You can see why. Look at that diagram – tell me, how would *you* wire that?' Craftsmen are always courteously unwilling to believe in the depths of a client's ignorance; I did not like to say that under no circumstances would I even attempt to wire up a regulator. Paul, who in his youth worked for Bernard Miles as a theatrical electrician, and boasts of having personally wired the gents' lavatory at the old Mermaid Theatre, tried a few wise nods. Mr Preston nimbly reconnected everything, and at four o'clock *Grace O'Malley* was fit for sea.

The wind was still in the south-west, so we decided on a short fifteen-mile leg westwards to Littlehampton before striking out round Selsey Bill and its tricky offlying rocks towards Portsmouth, our next major goal. The children – or at least Nicholas – seemed as keen as we were to escape the concrete embrace of Brighton Marina. At five fifteen, we set our sails inside the harbour wall, and motored out into an unfriendly, reflected loppy swell off its wall. The real voyage, the family voyage, had begun.

Wind and sea were brisker than we had expected. *Grace O'Malley* tore ahead, and while the children solemnly ate their hot dogs on deck in their harnesses, I went forward to pull down a reef and reduce the size of the mainsail. Much to my pleasure, although we had hardly ever had to reef *Grace O'Malley* in her short life, the actions came back to me in the right sequence: topping-lift tightened, peak let down, throat hauled down enough to engage the eyelet on its hook on the boom, tighten up, wind the reefing-line to draw the new tack of the sail down on to the far end of the boom, peak up again, topping-lift off. Everything fell easily to hand, and the wide, generous decks felt safe even at this steep angle of heel. *Grace O'Malley* is a comfortable boat to work: she is not descended from daft, skittery racing yachts but from proper working craft: boats fit for fishermen, or traders, or pilots.

Or mothers. Nicholas watched the manoeuvre with big, clouded eyes, cautiously confident in his parents' capacity to make the giant brown sail grow and shrink for the wind. As I lurched back along the deck, soaked with spray, I was able to slide comfortably down next to the perching children on the coaming; they immediately demanded their pudding, and I proudly produced two individual cheesecakes and spoons previously stowed in my wet oilskin pocket. The combination of nursery treats and seriously necessary reefing of sails made an odd, poignant contrast with the earlier sailing days I had been dreaming of; and for the children, no doubt, it made a faintly disturbing contrast to the sedate little routines of tea at home. They should have been under the familiar oak beams of the kitchen now, with dusk falling and Nelson the cat prowling under the chairs for tit-bits; yet we had brought them out here among the grey breaking Channel seas, with dark clouds obscuring the last sun, and the wet bunt of mainsail canvas flogging overhead. I resolved in that moment that, on this strange rash family journey, the wet and windswept Mummy who struggled back from the mast in a rising wind would always have (metaphorically at least) a treat and a spoon stowed in her pocket. And an explanation for it all. 'We had to make the sail smaller, to make *Grace O'Malley* more comfy in the wind,' I said. 'All right,' said Nicholas doubtfully. Rose sat giggling, faintly excited, faintly bewildered, swaying in her miniature oilskin suit on the increasingly wet deck.

Perhaps we should have stopped at Littlehampton. But by now it was clear that if we kept going we could actually steer a direct course for the Looe Channel, the short-cut through the reefs off Selsey Bill. We would be hard on the wind and heeling mightily, but there was no full gale forecast, and we knew that without children we would certainly have pressed on and reached Portsmouth wet, tired, and triumphant in the small hours, having skipped a harbour and won a day's progress. We would even catch the fair tide through the narrow gut of rocks at the Looe. It made sailing sense to go on. We did not spend too long asking ourselves whether it made family sense, on the children's first night at sea, to commit ourselves to a night passage in such a wild sea; for one thing the forecast was for an eventual decline in wind, and more importantly, I suspect that we both felt that if we funked this small passage now because the children seemed so very tiny and vulnerable, we would never actually make it round 2000 miles of unpredictable coastline. We would end our journey in ignominy, defeated by the forces of nursery inertia. So on we pressed into the gloom.

The children, tired of perching, weary of the whitening sea-crests and the strange new pounding of their small world against the unremitting south-westerly, opted for bed. I put them in their nightclothes, Rose very small in her red nightdress, and tucked them up in sleeping-bags in the wide quarterberths under the cockpit. Ten minutes later, Rose was sick. I bundled her up tighter, in a saloon berth with the leecloth fastened to stop her rolling out, and lay down myself for half an hour leaving Paul alone with the darkness and the wind. It dropped slightly at dusk, and we shook out the reef.

But through my fitful sleep, it rose again to a shriek, reminding me shudderingly of all the other times I have lain below on a yacht trying to ignore the new sounds and movements of the boat which mean that out there, in the wet and howling night, a sail must be reefed or changed. Then Rose was sick again, sadly and copiously, so that I was glad not to have taken off my oilskin suit. Lurching around the cabin by the swinging paraffin lamplight, I managed the mopping, the reassurances, the jokes, the firm promise of 'feeling better now'. She fell asleep instantly on receipt of a clean muslin comforter, her ubiquitous 'duster'. On deck Paul called for a hand on the helm while he took in a reef; he looked so sick that I went forward myself to do it. We had left it late, and there was no smug self-satisfaction this time: the sail was too strong for me, and it was fully ten minutes before I succeeded in getting the eye into its hook in the dark, and winding down the foot. I came shuddering back into the cockpit, confidence in rags, conscious of the two children asleep below me. 'Littlehampton? Turn back?' Again we thought briefly, and feared for our whole journey. 'No,' said Paul. 'We've got the Decca, we can pinpoint the Looe Channel, and we'll be there in three hours at this rate. Then we can turn a bit off the wind, and it will be quieter.'

The hours grew worse and worse. Once, Paul attempted a sleeping watch below; but gave up when the fitful little cries came from Rose; he opted to return pea-green to the helm while I went below by the light of the wildly swinging paraffin lantern to hold her damp, trembling little head over the pot. On deck, the wind seemed to rise even further, although we could still hold our course; we thought of taking down the second reef, and maybe we should have done so; but we opted for speed, just to get out of this unpleasant mess. Whichever of us was off the helm would alternate between keeping a lookout for unlit lobster-pots from the cockpit, and checking and re-checking our position both with the old-fashioned log and compass reckoning, and with the electronic navigator box – a new acquisition last season, and one of our few concessions to the age of the microchip. On one of these trips below, I found the cabin floor awash, and all the vegetables floating dismally in seawater in their plastic bins: we had forgotten to close the sink drain seacock, and the galley basin had been filling up and spilling into the food bins. It was no danger to the ship, the leak being instantly stoppable simply by turning the seacock off as we should have done in the first place, but it depressed us. I mopped the swaying floor with Rose's damp, discarded red nightdress, and wondered again how wise we were to be doing this.

Still, reason prevailed. We were taking a dusting, and the sea was one of the roughest we had met in years, but it was not dangerously high; merely uncomfortable. Nicholas was fast asleep, warm and dry, and Rose was taking enough sips of water to avoid the only real danger of seasickness, dehydration. Their ordeal, and ours, would not last more than another eight or nine hours at worst; probably the worst would be over in two or three. It does not do to be melodramatic, even when you are crawling around on a soaking cabin floor under a wild, leaping paraffin light, mopping up seawater with your baby's nightdress. We had, after all, made plenty of rough two-handed passages before, and knew what it was like. Paul was sick again.

Then two things happened. A visit to the chart table convinced me that we were being set too far north by the tide, close to the Mixon rocks, unlit in the dark; and when I went on deck to tell Paul, a loud distressed bleeping behind me signified that the Decca was out of order. ANTENNA FAIL, it flashed. The aerial had never been quite the same since my sister-in-law sat on it the previous summer. Things were now bleaker; we were charging into a ring of rocks, with only one weakly-lit route out of it, and this route was one which we could no longer be certain of finding. Especially since it had begun to rain. We tacked the boat (wails of protest from below as Rose was overcome by sickness at her new angle) and spent the next hour making efforts to get a decent position from the old-fashioned but reliable system of holding up a hand-compass and getting a bearing on two distant lighthouses, Owers and Nab. It is a horrible job in a rough sea; the compass-card seems as if it will never stop spinning and settle, and when it does you have lost sight of the light behind a tall wave; then, reciting your bearings in your head, you stumble below (pausing to sort out sick children), and plot them on the chart, which is disintegrating under repeated soakings from your wet sleeves. In the end we got a position, laid off a course for Looe Channel, and within another half-hour were rewarded by a weak green flash on the horizon: the Looe Channel buoy.

Nicholas awoke, below, and lay looking up with sad brown eyes. 'What's the matter?' I asked. He had not cried out. 'I'm waiting,' he said. What for? 'I'm waiting to feel better.' Ten minutes later his waiting was over; he threw up in his pillow and felt much better. I took one look at the pillow and robustly hurled the whole lot overboard, to be lost in the foam-capped waves which gleamed green under our starboard side-light. We both felt better, then. 'Wow,' said Nicholas reverently, and sank back to sleep.

The calmer water we should have found after the Looe did not materialize. Days of south-easterly winds followed by this south-westerly had stirred up a vicious sea which lasted all the way to Spithead. Paul was still being sick right up to the harbour entrance, and Rose well inside it. Within Portsmouth Harbour, our navigation lights mysteriously failed and as we struggled to get the mainsail down (it was jammed), the harbour police roared up and played a spotlight on us with much officious hailing and a quite unfounded accusation that we had come in, unlit, too near the car ferry (we had been ten minutes ahead of it, and had gone a good distance out of the main channel to fight the sail down). Bad-temperedly, we tied up at Camper & Nicholson's Marina, put the children under clean duvets with a drink of water, and tidied the boat.

And so it was that from three to four on that wet, windy May morning I was rinsing and drying vegetables individually, and picking soggy biscuits out of the holes in saucepan-handles. But we were safe in port, with forty-five miles of nasty coast behind us. 'We shan't have to go round Selsey Bill again,' I murmured to Paul as we drifted off to sleep. 'We get back to Harwich by way of Cape Wrath, instead.' I didn't know whether it was an encouraging thought or not. This was half-past four; Rose awoke at six, crying and fretful. With an enormous effort of will I woke and reminded myself that we had taken these children away from everything normal – school, friends, garden, toys, dry land itself – and were only offering them in return our constant company and extra love. I crawled into the wide bunk beside her, and we cuddled and whispered and dozed companionably together, tired and doubtful and glad to be in harbour; all of us in the same boat.

2

Sailing small yachts around Britain – piecemeal or wholesale – is no new pastime. Yachting may have begun as a rich man's racing sport, but by the end of the nineteenth century there was plenty of evidence that some few maverick yachtsmen, at least, were attempting voyages instead of contests and doing it in yachts far humbler and less comfortable than the floating palaces of the wealthy. The folding pipe-cot, the smelly paraffin-stove and bucket lavatory were emerging as the norm of yachting, quite independently of the polished Edwardian elegances that lay off Cowes. Of the early cruising yachtsmen, the singlehanders are the best known, because – having various bizarre axes to grind – they tended to write the books. John MacGregor (of the yawl *Rob Roy*) made a muscular-Christian pilgrimage in the 1860s with a boatful of improving tracts; he in turn inspired E. E. Middleton to make and write *The Cruise of the Kate*, a circumnavigation of England (not Britain: he nipped through the Forth and Clyde Canal and missed out most of Scotland). MacGregor was a bit of a hearty bore, and Middleton a misfit of the gloomiest type: everywhere he went, he found the natives 'surly and insolent', and since he was a splenetic and opinionated flat-earther, one can see their point. A few years later R. T. McMullen wrote one of the most famous early yachting books, *Down Channel*, and became celebrated even more in yachting legend for being found dead and rigid at the helm; though scarcely more rigid than he was in life. McMullen was the kind of skipper I used to dread in my small-ad sailing days: preoccupied with tight reefs and neat coils, apoplectic about 'slovenliness' and deeply suspicious of women.

All these men were formidable and brave seamen, sailing an extremely difficult coast without engines and – more awesome by far – without weather forecasts; but between them they have given early yachting a regrettable image of heavy, dull masculinity and imperial authoritarianism. Then along came Hilaire Belloc, with his magnificent descriptions of coastal sailing in *The Cruise of the Nona*;

more readable, more a complete and lovable man than the rest put together; but his book is oddly marred by perverse ramblings about parliamentary government and by his deeply embarrassing affection for good old Mussolini. All these, largely thanks to a modern literary convert to cruising, Jonathan Raban, author of *Coasting*, are enjoying something of a revival today; but the effect of the revival, we found, was mainly to make people at parties draw back nervously from anyone announcing a projected voyage round Britain in a yacht. 'Wonderful,' they would say, wondering what hideous political or religious insight we were chasing across the waves. 'You'll really, er, find out a lot about yourselves.' In vain we protested that we only wanted to find out a bit about the coast and a lot about the boat, to take a summer's grace from our jobs, and to show the children something different to the bland comforts of middle-class country life. Nobody believed us. Thanks to Middleton and MacGregor and Belloc and Raban, friends persisted in suspecting us of having seen some lurid, antisocial Light.

The antidote to all this, and the work we had brought with us to illuminate our way with a gentler glow, was Frank Cowper's *Sailing Tours*, a series published between 1892 and 1895 with the modest aim of helping the emerging breed of cruising yachtsmen to find their way into new harbours without running into anything. Cowper was a peaceful, scholarly chap, an Oxford classicist whose hobby was pottering around in small river and estuary boats until he bought his first cabined yacht, *Undine*, and began making Channel crossings. Far-sightedly, he predicted a need for a real yachtsman's guide to British waters; there was no such thing extant, as witness Daniel Defoe's abandoning of his plan to circumnavigate Britain one hundred years earlier for want of a pilot-book. In a forty-eight-foot converted fishing lugger, *Lady Harvey*, Cowper began a remarkable three-year voyage around the coast. He toured almost the entire coastline, including all of Scotland and Orkney, and made many detours up the Bristol Channel and the Clyde. The books are a delight: in alternate chapters, he offers first 'Sailing Directions' and then 'Anecdotes', relishing the latter with the glee of a true gossip. As a seaman, Cowper must have been remarkable, handling his big boat either alone or with a series of inexperienced local lads taken on around the coast: he was not driven by any of the sad, complicated devils that urged on the better-known single-handers. His is a simple, joyful, spirit of curiosity:

As the rash mouse contemplating the tasty cheese ignores the dangers surrounding it, so I, with equal recklessness, enamoured of the glorious sport of amateur cruising, incurred lightly many risks . . . And yet perhaps it was this very innocence that enabled me to carry out my purpose so successfully.

He had a theory that one should never read in detail about the rocks and currents and storms of a region before setting out, but 'start first and read about the dangers afterwards'; and he keeps the inevitable Victorian outbreaks of heroic patriotism about 'little ships breeding a nation of hardy seamen' well under control. Nor does he waste space in abasing himself with philosophical tremblings before the Eternal Might of the Sea; he merely relays every eddy and every oddity of specific stretches of water in a way so lastingly accurate that in wild places, we frequently found as much help and sense in Cowper as in our modern pilot-books. His work breathes decency and the kindly, sentimental spirit which has pervaded many mild and gentlemanly yachting writers since – Maurice Griffiths, Frank Carr, Alker Tripp, and today Michael Richey and J. D. Sleightholme: appreciative, amiable, innocent, self-deprecating chaps whose more or less unworldly joy was to wander the coasts and oceans, putting up with considerable hardship and danger; not to test their tiresome virility or to build up the British Empire, but to find more sights and places to observe and enjoy. It is hard to think of Cowper at the end: in his seventies and infirm, moving alone into a sheltered hostel far from the sea in Winchester. He died there on 29 May 1930 at the age of eighty-one, thinking himself forgotten and his books outdated; but he sailed again beside us in 1988 and his four volumes became part of the fabric of our voyage. We would rather have thrown all the electronics overboard than been without them.

I had a brief glance at Cowper that morning in Portsmouth; he speaks disparagingly of the difficulties of mooring a yacht in amongst the naval busyness of the place, and relates an incident from 1844 when two divers engaged in blowing up the *Royal George* had a fight, during which 'Corporal Jones kicked out the glass eye of Private Girvan's diving dress'. Thus refreshed, I turned back to Rose's interminable monologue on how Jingle the teddybear had been very sick in the night, and so had Otter and Peter Colony (her tiger). But they were all, she said, much better. I marvelled at her recovery after the night's gastric horrors, and her keenness to eat a hot breakfast as soon as possible on the shore.

I had promised myself, and Paul, to stop maundering on about my old sailing voyages and concentrate on making this one; but fate was against me. Walking up the pontoon, I was a little startled to see a sad-looking steel yacht called *Makahiki*; ten years earlier I sailed from the Canary Islands to Barbados on *Makahiki*, as crew to a couple I had barely met – another aberration of my small-ad phase of sailing. It was eerie to see that deck again where the flying fish had landed, that wheel at which I had stood in the sunlight, steering through blue waves for three weeks. This was a grey morning in Portsmouth, and she was tethered by grubby ropes in Camper and Nicholson's utilitarian marina behind the warships; but this same *Makahiki* had once carried me gaily through a Christmas morning, with the sunrise reddening the puffy trade wind clouds and the Queen crackling calm goodwill to us on the World Service. I stood feeling odd for a few moments, haunted by an ocean; then the children dragged us off for bacon sandwiches in a steamy Gosport café.

By lunchtime we were all walking a wider, grander deck. HMS *Warrior*, the huge Victorian ironclad warship, half frigate, half modern battleship, had come home at last to Portsmouth as a permanent memorial to – well, to herself, really. *Warrior* never fired a shot in battle; she was nothing but a state-of-the-art unbeatable ship created to upstage the French. She was and is an astonishing hybrid: a steamship with a mass of squaresails, a wooden ship plated in inches of iron. She had a figurehead unsuitably placed on her slender bow because the Admiralty thought the sailors would be unhappy without one ('Jack likes a figurehead'), yet she had an armoured conning-tower like any World War I battleship (the officers, it is said, thought it ungentlemanly to hide inside a steel cage, and continued to pace the open deck like Nelson). *Warrior* ushered in the modern age: she was the ultimate deterrent, the nuclear submarine of her day, the vessel that made war pointless because, for the moment, she could beat anything. She and her French rival, *La Gloire*, were the beginning of the international arms race. At *Warrior*'s launching in 1860, an observer said that she looked, among the frigates which had hardly changed since HMS *Victory*, 'Like a black snake among the rabbits.' When her day was done, she spent an inglorious few decades as a floating fuel-jetty in Milford Haven, her decks buried deep in concrete.

I had last seen the black snake at Hartlepool, just before she was towed south, away from the redundant north-east shipwrights who miraculously had this intriguing job dropped into their laps by the fad for restoring historic ships. They had done well: she was glorious in her transformation, with her shipshapeness, neatness, completeness, her pleasant tarry smells and wide spaces. The children ran and whooped on the long, scrubbed deck, and I roamed happily around. This was my kind of warship: the first ship of the line ever to have a dedicated drying-room for sailors' clothes, a battleship that never saw a battle. A big, domesticated, purring black cat: deterrent, not aggressor. Wisely, the Maritime Trust had decided not to label anything: 'You must wander around,' said Captain Wells, her historian, with dreamy pleasure, 'and think that the sailors have just left her, hammocks slung, mess-table laid.' We revelled in *Warrior*, and the next morning Paul took Nicholas on his own to HMS *Victory* and to the Tudor warship *Mary Rose*. Quite accidentally, this interlude of tourism gave Nicholas the clue to history: every tale of castle or Armada, Jacobite or inventor, that we told him throughout the rest of the voyage would be met by a stern enquiry 'Was that before or after Nelson's *Victory*? Well, was it as old as *Mary Rose*? Was that when *Warrior* was still sailing?' Tudor, eighteenth-century and Victorian periods were branded forever in his mind as shapes of ships; later, he added Viking, and had as useful a key to chronology as any child could get before his sixth birthday. *Victory* also set off a difficult discussion about civilized values: he and Paul were most intrigued that in Nelson's day, when battle was about to be joined, a warship would put a cannon into the captain's quarters and remove all his fine gilded furniture into a small boat, which was towed astern out of danger. There was an agreement between the French, English, and Spanish that they would not fire on one another's furniture-boats. Very civilized. On the other hand, deep in the bowels of these picturesque ships lived children of six, bought from orphanages or indigent parents, employed to fill sacks with gunpowder in quarters too small for adult men. Nicholas was very thoughtful about these. 'I aren't six yet, are I?' he asked repeatedly, 'I wouldn't have go on the orlop deck where they painted it red so you couldn't see the blood, would I?'

Our own two powder-monkeys were fast recovering their health and spirits after their bad night. The main fear was that Rose would balk at going to sea again. So we grasped the nettle and motored out of Portsmouth harbour with brisk, optimistic dispatch. It was calm; rather than fuss our wary daughter with sails, we went on under engine across the Eastern Solent, reading Peter Rabbit stories in a syrupy, soothing manner. Nicholas climbed astride the boom and rode it like a horse, shrieking with macho delight; his sister lay in my arms silently for a while, then, surprised at not feeling ill, ate six Jaffa cakes with mounting confidence. We snaked up the Beaulieu River, admiring the irony of Lord Montagu's immaculate capitalist conservation of its woods and sands and birds, as set against the democratically attained and revoltingly tacky development of the Hamble and Southampton Water, a botch-up of hideous marinas and slick 'prestige' developments. We were at ease on long-familiar waters, the children were happy to be on this short recreational trip, and the sun began to shine on our voyage again. The only moment of panic came – to poor Nicholas – when he asked what RCC meant on his father's cap. 'Daddy and I belong to the Royal Cruising Club,' we explained. We are fond of the RCC: it is a club whose mildest-looking members at monthly dinners generally seem to be fresh back from Greenland or Patagonia, but listen with great courtesy to your florid account of a daring passage to Calais. But Nicholas fastened, alarmed, on one word of the answer. 'You belong to the Royal Cruising Club? What, so you don't belong to us?' He was so worried that even as we were tying ourselves to the pontoons at Buckler's Hard, I had to continue assuring him in embarrassingly loud shouts that he and Rose had first call on us, the RCC making do with the residue only of our attention.

Buckler's Hard is a shamelessly picturesque and faintly twee tourist trap in the high season, but on this fresh May afternoon, with the forested banks of the river glinting in the low sunlight, the clean grass, the deserted hill to roll down, and the few yacht masts swaying on the blue river, it was a joy to see. Nicholas found a model of HMS *Victory* in the maritime museum and identified the very porthole he had peered out of that morning, in Portsmouth. At dusk, my brother Andrew and his girl-friend Lindsay arrived for supper, and we hauled Andrew up the mast to change the navigation light-bulb, followed by the children in the bosun's chair in turn, rising a giddy three or four feet above the deck before demanding to be let down.

29

It was a convivial evening, with topics ranging rather loosely and alcoholically from sex education to the fact that RAF socks are so rough that middle-aged airmen have no hair left below the knee; and as we talked and drank, the children fell asleep. Afterwards, however, when we were alone, Paul became suddenly sunk in gloom. 'I just don't think we can do it. Not all the way round Britain, with all those open-water passages, and Rose so small. She's so little, and so demanding, such a pest . . .' He was unwilling to talk it out, unwilling to speak at all, beyond the bald statement of his lack of faith in the voyage.

I was feeling better about it all, excitedly optimistic in a way that had something inexplicably to do with all the old ships: with *Victory* and *Warrior*, with the risen *Mary Rose* and rusty old *Makahiki*; even with *Sheltie*. With a few drinks inside me, it seemed that if other ships had overcome invasion by rodents, being sunk in the Solent mud for four hundred years or written off as concrete fuel-jetties for thirty; if accommodation could be found for rococo furniture in naval battles, and for seamen's drying-rooms in the middle of an arms race, *Grace O'Malley* and her adult crew could surely get a temperamental three-year-old round Britain by hook or by crook.

With reasonable confidence we set sail next day down the beautiful Western Solent. I sang 'My Name is Captain Kidd, Many wicked things I did' in the required *basso-profundo* for Rose until I succumbed to prolonged, convulsive bronchitic coughing, which infuriated Paul the whole way across Christchurch Bay. By the time we tied up at Poole Town Quay, we were all a little frayed, but the children were allowed to peep up and see that we had moored right outside a model railway exhibition. Paul and I sat on deck enjoying the vulgar and rorty character of Poole on a Friday night.

We had moved well away from the dignified naval traditions of the Solent: Poole was a great haunt of smugglers in its day, with networks of stone passages between the mischievous citizenry's cellars, and it has turned now to cheerfully piratical tourism for its living. There is no chic nonsense about Poole Town Quay: girls in tarty short leather skirts shrieked at loafing boys, couples entwined purposefully in alleyways above the glimmer of the dock, the chip-shop blared old Beatles' tunes. Content in my bunk, I awarded myself a treat I had been saving, and deep into the noisy night I lay and re-read *Moonfleet*.

3

There are some books which if encountered in childhood can so powerfully capture and colonize the imagination that it is impossible later to separate literature from experience. Did one actually live in a house with a tangled kitchen-garden path, or was that in *Peter Rabbit*? Was it one's own adult companions who were so abrupt and oddly-spoken, or was that mainly the White Queen? Certainly when I was a young adult I had at one point forgotten about *Moonfleet*, J. Meade Falkner's Victorian adventure story set among the smugglers and revenue men of the Dorset coast in the eighteenth-century; yet the first time I saw the chalky shores of Christchurch Bay from the sea and heard the sweep and suck of the Chesil Bank shingle, I knew that for some reason they were familiar. More than familiar, disturbing. Then the first time I saw Portland Bill, from the deck of *Sheltie*, I said, 'Wasn't that once called the Snout?' – and knew quite clearly that in onshore gales in the days of sail, sailors had seen its shape to windward through murk and driving rain, known themselves embayed and looked upon their death. The boy hero John Trenchard and his protector Elzevir Block did so, in the last adventure in the slave-galley which would wreck them on their own home beach of Moonfleet:

> . . . We were in a bay, for there was the long white crescent of surf reaching far away on either side, till it was lost in the dusk, and the brig helpless in the midst of it. Elzevir had hold of my arm, and gripped it hard as he looked to larboard. I followed his eyes, and where one horn of the white crescent faded into the mist, caught a dark shadow in the air, and knew it was high land looming behind . . . and we saw a misty bluff slope down into the sea, like the long head of a basking alligator poised upon the water, and stared into each other's eyes, and cried together, 'The Snout!'

The alligator still basks: it could be no other head than Portland Bill. I remembered the story when I uttered the word 'Snout', and

31

went back to my ancient Puffin paperback, which was still safe on my mother's shelves. In 1962 they were still putting: 'For all readers from nine upwards, especially boys', on the cover; I saw it again, and felt again the full force of my tomboyish resentment. *Moonfleet* turned out to be almost alarmingly full of familiar mental furniture, of descriptions and information which I had lugged around for twenty years, their origin entirely forgotten. The motto of the wicked Mohunes, *Ita in vita ut in lusu alae pessima jactura arte corrigenda est* (As in life, so in a game of hazard, skill will make something of the worst of throws), I had quoted to myself for years, thinking I must have learned it at school. I had always thought that I must have visited the deep well at Carisbrooke Castle as a child; re-reading *Moonfleet*, I understood that I had never been there at all, except when I was lowered in imagination next to John Trenchard, to pull Blackbeard's diamond in its crackling packet out of the damp well-wall. As for the night he spent in the church vault, hiding crushed next to a black-bearded skeleton in a rotten coffin, I had thought it was a nightmare of my own: yet there it was in Chapter Four. If the test of good prose is to be such a clean windowpane that you forget style and see only the content, Meade Falkner must have been a master: I had forgotten not only the words but the existence of the book itself, yet absorbed forever the chalky scenery, the deep well, the fear, the blue flare lit on the beach to guide desperate ships on to soft ground, the glimmer of a candle in a window and the deadly hiss of the under-tow. Reading it yet again in rackety Poole Harbour that night, I fell asleep forgetting everything else; and awoke refreshed and ready for anything.

A hundred years ago, when Meade Falkner was still working on the phrases which were to colonize my mind so comprehensively in the 1950s, Frank Cowper sailed south-westwards from Poole Harbour and rounded Anvil Point just as we did on that May morning. We approached the towering mass of St Alban's Head with a joy identical to his. Nothing has changed:

Promontory on promontory, peak on peak, the varied coastline wanders away to the golden west. Headlands of many shapes, tossing their summits to the sea like wild waves driven before the roaring blast, grow fainter and fainter in the mellow light, sinking gradually to the lowland where Melcombe and Weymouth shimmer under the westering sun. But again, away in the South-West, far out like a giant wedge, the long ridge of Portland rises like some half-submerged monster in the western sea.

My own tired fears forgotten, I steered down towards Bishop Aldhelm's headland in the brisk, bounding swell, watching the children assiduously trying to stick triangles of coloured paper into patterns, and rejoiced in the boat's easy movement, in our commanding wind and the unchallenging landfall ahead of us (if you can't find Weymouth pier on a clear day you ought not to be let out alone. There are not many landfalls like this). The children, meanwhile, grew bored with sticking: Nicholas, who shows glimmers of the true romantic cruising spirit, showed a decent interest in the white spikes of Old Harry and observed that 'Rocks are more friendly when sailors give them names.' Rose opted for the more obvious stimulation of the Laughing Policeman tape, played repeatedly so that the boat rolled and lurched westwards with Charles Penrose's laughter booming manically from her belly.

I have adored Weymouth ever since I was eighteen years old, and sold into slavery by my mother as temporary nanny to the children of her friends' children while the latter were participating in Weymouth dinghy week. The children were four years old and eighteen months; the parents, a couple whose relationship put me off marriage for years afterwards, consisted of a bullying, big, blond son of the minor aristocracy and his nice, rather terrified wife. They had muddled their hotel bookings, and we ended up for the first two days in a boarding-house so traditional that occupants were thrown out at 9 a.m., rain or shine, and not allowed back until 5 p.m. I grew wearily familiar with every petal on the floral clock, every grain of sand on the windswept beach, every carriage of the model railway. Mostly I sat with the other nannies, exchanging stultifying chat about our stultifying employers. The Hon. Bullyboy would get back in the evening, trailing his ineffectually smiling young wife in tousled wet hair and rubber wet-suit, and would bait my sullen youthful awkwardness throughout supper; the children would scream and create at the sight of their parents as if I had beaten them up and tethered them foodless all day to the bandstand. Never have I been so glad to see a railway station as on the last afternoon. Yet I came out of it loving Weymouth; it is so aristocratically insouciant beneath its top-dressing of seaside tat.

The first bathing-machine in the land rolled down to the sea here, and in 1789 King George III lit the torch for our modern-day beachwear royalty by taking his famous public bathe on the Melcombe side (Cowper claims that the National Anthem was played by the town band as, 'with such dignity as it is possible for a shivering, podgy old gentleman of very commonplace appearance to assume, the King of Great Britain, France and Ireland descended the chilly steps'). Weymouth, especially at dusk in the off-season when the Georgian promenade domineers haughtily over the humbly shuttered ice-cream kiosks, remains the sort of town where a ghostly band might still play around the phantom of a stout royal bather.

I took the children to find R. C. Darrington, Sand Artist, on the front. He was still there on his pitch at the age of seventy-seven; told us he had a fine Last Supper vandalized the previous year, but was still producing delicate horses with flowing manes, realistic cottage loaves and giant crabs in bas-relief, still bearing the proud sign: 'Sea water, sand and powder paints my only tools'.

We had a rest day on the beach, a calm, hazy, warm Sunday with a good supply of other children to join in various screaming, splashing, digging, earnest games. Ours adopted two in particular, overdressed misses called Tamsin and Janet; when their Dad (beer gut, gold chains, 'Jus' back from Spain, thass the place, narmean?') turned up, the four parted with real regret. 'Is there any point making friends,' asked Nicholas crossly, 'if I never see them again?' I told him an old, perfectly true, tale of how I had once made a beach friendship in France when I was nine, and met the boy again fifteen years later as an old friend: he was much impressed, if not convinced that such lightning could strike twice. Back on board, he forgot his frilly friends and worked hard at his self-appointed job of being Ship's Poet. It had begun with a desire to write a poem about sailing (imagine our fond delight), and had commuted itself into the following surreal work:

The lion and the walrus

The sea was rough but the walrus and the lion went paddling
Then they saw the sun coming out
And they made a sandcastle
But in the moonlight they saw a shark
And they saw a minesweeper sweeping up the bombs

34

All this had to be written out by hand, and illuminated in the margin with pictures; which, since he had forgotten what the poem was about in the effort of copying it, were mainly dragons. The children seemed now entirely settled in the curious ways of cruising, although each night, preparing for bed, they would ask, 'Do we sail all night?' – clearly a little apprehensive of a repetition of the Selsey Bill experience, of flying pillows, lurching, retching, darkness and confusion and tense adults pushing past their beds dripping with water and babbling of lighthouses. Not tonight, we told them thankfully. Tomorrow night we'll catch the tide around Portland, and make the great leap westward across Lyme Bay. Tonight, harbour and sleep.

Paul and I took turns at wandering around Weymouth. Already I was living at a different pace and with different attitudes to normal life; I felt less suspicious, less threatened, less critical. Approaching human life from the neutral sea was beginning to make me more appreciative. I stopped and chatted to the sort of hulking teenage boys who in bigger cities seem so alien and dangerous (a most kind skinhead directed me to the launderette, and a bunch of leather-clad bikers mourned the absence of teenage discos in Weymouth). I listened benevolently to the suspiciously raucous laughter from the upstairs rooms of the Harbour Café, admired the festive look of the trawlers with their bundles of balloon-like pink buoys, and read the legend in the art gallery window: 'YOU CAN'T SEE THE PICTURE YOU WANT? LET US PAINT IT' – an approach to fine art which, in my mellow mood, I could only applaud. Good old Weymouth.

Euphoric, with my fat clean sack of laundry, I slipped into the Church of the Trinity to find it a haven of Mothers' Union exhibits, bells and smells and bustling, earnest-pressing-forward community Anglicanism. There was one window with a text from the Magnificat, and I knelt to gaze at it for a long time. Our Lady, Queen of Heaven, is holding up the small baby Jesus. Both look serene. But they are in a small boat, on a tossing glass sea. So we must have been right, I thought hazily, a little sunstruck from the long day on the sand. We must have been right to bring the children to sea. From that day, through all adventures and misadventures, I never doubted it again.

4

At half past three on our third day in Weymouth we finally slipped out of the river, mainsail reefed, to make southward for the tip of Portland Bill and west across Lyme Bay. Portland is an awesome lump of stone, despite all the chipping and quarrying it has suffered over centuries: from its wharfs have sailed great pale stone buildings, Buckingham Palace and St Paul's, Broadcasting House and countless solid London offices. Up on its cliff convicts used to hew the Portland stone, helpless to escape across the narrow shingle spit and constantly tantalized by the sight of fishing-boats passing freely below them. Today, submarines move silently in and out of the vast naval harbour south of Weymouth, breaking the surface like steel crocodiles.

There is a clear passage of quiet water round the Bill itself, if you pass very close inshore during a certain magical period on each tide; woe betide the small boat that reads the tide-table wrongly, for it will be set dramatically southward right into the Portland Race. Even with a fair tide, your options are strictly limited: once across that narrow tip of land, you are entirely committed to Lyme Bay with no chance of returning to Weymouth if the wind strengthens or your hearts fail. We could sail up to Lyme Regis and risk not getting in because of low tide; we could make across to Exmouth or Teignmouth, fifty miles away, or head for Torbay. Our forecast was not too bad, no winds over Force Five and that mainly in the north; we stifled our apprehensiveness about the children. Rose, knowing that it was to be another sea-night, lay in the cockpit curled in my arms, whispering jokes but not entirely happy; Nicholas ate his seasick pill with concentrated care. Once clear of the edges of the Race, but still in very lively waters with the sails reefed down and the boat jumping excitably forward on a close reach, I put the pair of them to bed and lay down myself. In the interests of a broader, easier course and less heeling, we had finally decided to make straight for Salcombe, round Start Point sixty miles to the west of us. Later in the voyage, we were to cover sixty-mile stretches almost absent-mindedly, but at this early stage it seemed a long way to go at four or five miles an hour; I frowsted in my bunk trying to ignore the sea, and tranquillized myself not only by listening to 'The Archers' on the radio, but by stealing Paul's tiny television (used normally for looking at the satellite weather map on the news) and watching 'Coronation Street', as well. Feeling better, I came on deck, officiously took out the reef, and prepared to stand the 8.00 to 10.00 watch.

We had, at last, rigged up our self-steering gear. Why we never got round to clipping the thing on for that grim passage from Brighton to Portsmouth, I cannot think; we had hung on to the helm then, turn and turn about, clinging to the tiller like a pair of drowning monkeys and unable to let it go for a second to check the navigation or turn a child over without calling up the other watchkeeper. This time, with the machine purring to itself, my duties were confined to keeping lookout, updating the navigation in the dusk, and making calm decisions about what the boat needed next. Very shortly, I decided she needed either the topsail – which would have entailed waking Paul up for half an hour's tangling and cursing – or resorting to what fishermen used to call the iron topsail, all twenty-seven horsepower of it. *Engine on 2100*, says the log. Then, miraculously, *Engine off 2200*; the wind returned and lifted the evening mist. Within ten minutes the world changed. It was like winning the football pools: from chugging meanly along in the mist, craning anxiously for entangling lobster-pots, I had become the rich possessor of a fine sailing breeze, a good-tempered, bounding boat, and best of all a view of Berry Head lighthouse on the starboard bow. I sang it a verse or two of its own hymn (Berry Head inspired Newman's 'Lead, Kindly Light'). In minutes more, the twinkling coast of Torbay became visible; then, dead ahead, Start Point itself. I took full credit for all these lights, and for the stars above, as if I had lit them up myself with matches. When I jubilantly called Paul up for his night-watch I was able to lay a whole basketful of riches at his feet: two lighthouses, a confirmed position, an easy course to sail, a fast breeze, and a cup of tea.

Up to windward lay Torquay, Brixham, the black cliffs around Dartmouth; ahead of us the bigger, blacker hulk of Start Point, beginning of the true West. Up a cleft in this great promontory, between Prawle Point and Bold Head, lay Salcombe; meanwhile, we had the night, the glimmer of the sidelights on the red and green bow-wave, and the sluicing cleaving speed of *Grace O'Malley* on a broad reach. I hardly slept for pleasure; the next watch from midnight till two was a rare delight, a reminder of why we spend so much effort and money on going sailing in the first place. I was alone; Lyme Bay lay broad and dark around me with ships' lights to avoid and roguish waves to slide over; that was my task, but the boat herself was my private joy: a perfect thing gracing a perfect night, carrying my sleeping family; a world complete. And so I bore down on the black cliffs and blinding flashes of Start Point in perfect happiness.

Sailing these Western Channel waters, even in worse weather than this, has always thrilled me. They are beautiful, deep, and they are timeless; there is none of the nagging historical uncertainty, the *memento mori* of the shifting Eastern Channel and east coast, where great harbours vanish like great reputations, to become silted, muddy villages of no import. Down here, down-Channel, Dartmouth and Plymouth and Falmouth and Torbay are more confident places: they were havens four hundred years ago when the Armada sailed up-Channel to its defeat, and they were probably havens too four thousand years ago, when men in flimsy craft fished perilously outside their harbours and fled back before southerly gales. Seamen are bred here: from Stoke Gabriel came John Davis, the explorer who in the sixteenth century discovered the Davis Strait in the Arctic Circle; Raleigh grew up in the Dart Valley. *Drake he was a Devon man, and ruled the Devon seas*, I murmured, hauling the boat up a point to round the lighthouse more closely, *Capten, art tha' sleeping there below?* The wind freshened, and the boat heeled sharply, surging forward as I recited to the stars,

But if the Dons sight Devon, I'll quit the port o'Heaven
And drum them up the Channel as we drummed them long
   ago . . .

Well, 1588, Armada Year, was going on all around us, dominating the tourist industry just as the 1988 seamen's strike was ironically dominating every news bulletin; and although the Maritime Museum and other authorities were repeatedly telling us that it wasn't Drake at all who should get the credit, but some chap in a suit called Howard of Effingham, and that the weather did most of the work for them anyway, I resolved to tell the children the full, blood-and-thundering, bowling-green version from my own childhood the next day, and let them see Start and Prawle, Bolt and Lizard and the deep cleft of Salcombe from which the fireships sailed, in the same way that I once did: by the same old deceptive light that never was on sea or land. Balder and more balanced history could come later. Meanwhile, *Drake he was a Devon man, and ruled the Devon seas*. I thumped the hatch, swaggering to myself alone in the night, growing sleepy.

Eventually, the euphoria faded and we merely longed to be still, and asleep. Salcombe was there for us. You do not appreciate a harbour until you use it seriously. People say, 'Oh, Devon, simply ruined, tourist traps, coaches everywhere'; but the sailor coming in never sees the cream teas and car parks until he has given thanks for the shelter, the clear leading lights and the calm water. A harbour is eternal, and offers the same solace to a plastic yacht as to trawler, smack, or galleon. We thankfully picked up a mooring at 4 a.m., and fell into our bunks to sleep sweetly.

5

Salcombe, in any case, was off-duty as a tourist trap. So early in the season had we arrived that the teashop had not laid in one single scone or clot of cream, and the chic, vapid little boutique where I bought a shirt was empty of tourists and shrill summer residents, containing only a bored assistant and one old lady searching for sixty denier hose. 'Unseasonal weather,' she confided chirpily. 'It's so hot I've taken my spinal jacket off, dear.'

The sailors were already out, though: Des Sleightholme, former editor of *Yachting Monthly*, sailed past us and hospitably lobbed a packet of home-grown asparagus on to our stern-deck; and we received clear evidence of the character-building power of sailing (although not quite in a direction that the Victorian empire-builders would have approved of) when another launch came by and disgorged our old friend Christian and his girl-friend Marie. Christian was about to set off for Scotland on the Island Cruising Club's communal schooner *Hoshi*, in the hideously demanding role of 'cook-mate'. If they had wanted a reference, we could have given them a dozen: he had sailed with us as a novice, and we had many happy memories of Christian sitting on the cabin steps in East Cowes on a freezing Easter Sunday morning, picking out 'For all the Saints' on a musical pocket calculator; Christian making endless sandwiches on a dreadful thirty-six-hour beat against a rising gale towards the Fastnet Rock (I was six months' pregnant; it was not thrilling to have liver-sausage-and-cucumber sandwiches posted into my damp bunk at 4 a.m.); Christian steering down a wild rolling sea, discussing the future of religious television. But in those days Christian had never been entirely with us; he was a restless, nervous, driven man; harassed almost into insanity by a job directing 'Songs of Praise' and other BBC religious programmes, and morbidly (we thought) obsessed with restoring a huge house in Cricklewood where he lived a solitary, gloomy life among DIY materials and clouds of rising damp. He talked more about arris-rails and RSJs than seemed healthy in a young bachelor. On the

Irish trip, he came for the passage but barely stayed for a single pint because, he explained nervily, 'I've got a skip booked.' We worried about him. But in Salcombe, he told us the good news: he had given up the BBC (and, for the moment, all forms of paid work) sold the house, moved in with Marie, and now spent the entire summer afloat, helping out on the ICC training boats and frying onions on *Hoshi*. We stopped worrying about him.

Salcombe was good for us all. Sitting on East Portlecombe beach making sandcastles, I reflected with surprise on how much the pattern of family relationships had already changed in ten days. The best change was the growing confidence and affection from Nicholas to Paul: 'my Daddy' had always been his main hero in the world, but things are never all easy between a shy, chippy, self-conscious boy child and his affectionate, bearish, slightly short-tempered father. On the boat, passing tools to Daddy, consulting Daddy on the navigation and getting – on the whole – a mild and sympathetic response instead of a rushed, distracted one, Nicholas grew in status in his own eyes, and ours. Correspondingly, he seemed to need Mummy less: at home, he padded into my bed at dawn every day, unable to face the world without an hour's cuddling. On the boat, he was beginning to get up silently before the rest of us, dress, and sit colouring or navigating by himself at the chart table, always remembering to put the pencils back in the rack with tidy little clucking noises.

As for Rose, her cheek, high spirits, tantrums, and impromptu poetry recitals continued much as they had at home, only in rather different proportions. If anything, there were fewer tantrums (although they seemed worse, since it was impossible to walk more than five feet away from them). She was unimpressed, as yet, by the actual sailing – unlike Nicholas who has always been deeply stirred by taut sails, bow-waves, and tales of the great Armada – but enjoyed the play-house aspect of the boat, and the newness of each harbour. Nor was she much troubled by homesickness for her regular friends and minders; at three years old, the present counts for more than even the recent past. Nicholas, on the other hand, grew quiet sometimes, and thought things over. 'It's funny living on water,' he would say. 'But water does interesting things. It goes to beaches and throws up shells, and it goes to harbours and rivers . . .' he would tail away, looking longingly towards the solid shore. We made shore excursions a priority.

It was a hot unseasonal early summer: that night we wallowed up the deep romantic chasm of the River Yealm, where shoals of aggressive mullet banged into our dinghy, furiously seeking nourishment from its rubber flanks. Wild geese honked overhead in groups of three and five. There were too many moorings: too much uninhabited white plastic afloat on the Yealm, but there is still a certain peacefulness even in these over-used, honeypot West Country harbours. Maybe one of the reasons why yachtsmen, as a body, have been too slow to take up the cudgels for conservation of wild places is that our own untamed wilderness is always waiting for us outside the harbour mouth, and so wild is it out there that a yachtsman yearns – more than most outdoor people – for the security of buildings, teashops, launderettes, and telephone boxes. It is not a laudable trait, but it is hard to suppress. Once, after a week of not seeing another boat and barely another soul, galebound in a great open bay called Smerwick in the far west of Ireland, Paul and I fled southward under storm jib longing with indecent passion for the small port of Dingle. 'There might be cinemas!' we cried. 'Traffic-lights! Tarmac!' We had overdosed on grey rock and gannets, surf and terror. We wanted to wrap a city around us, warm and frowsty as an old dressing-gown.

In Newton Ferrers, we were not yet at that stage by far. I did notice from Paul's journal that he felt a particular pull towards the Yealm Hotel: 'Mahogany doors, marble mosaic, smell of cabbage on the boil. Soft chairs, meals brought . . .' But then he was shamed when he rowed downriver and met an aged singlehander, well into his eighties, who was on his way from the Solent to the Scillies to pick up his crew, 'a young man of eighty-one'. Old Dick Stevens refused our offer of a drink aboard *Grace O'Malley* because, 'After a drink I do rather tend to fall in the sea,' but we kept seeing him again on our passage down-Channel, usually anchored outside a harbour to save trouble getting in, always with his RCC burgee fluttering aloft and the old cabin-lamp hissing warmly below.

News had reached us in Salcombe of a nephew: Jonathan Grant Purves, my eldest brother's first child, born with some difficulty at the precise moment when we were rounding Portland Bill. We knew all about the difficulty, because my mother (not an habituée of the ship-to-shore VHF radio call) had broadcast the most scarifying gynaecological details to the entire Western Channel, and then failed to put the phone down, thus rendering us powerless to interrupt or end the transmission of a further broadcast, relayed across her sitting-room and interwoven with the television, in which she told her friend Janet all about it too. Paul, head in his hands with embarrassment, finally managed to contact Start Point Radio on another VHF channel and beg them to cut off this merry obbligato of forceps and afterbirths. Anyway, I thought I had better see this baby before we got any farther west, and it was decided that I would make a flying day-trip back to Suffolk while Paul took the children off to the Shire Horse Centre at Yealmpton (the first sign, this, of withdrawal symptoms from his normal occupation with all things hairy, harnessed, and highly-bred).

But only a new baby, nothing less, could have been worth that grimy journey. The train rolled out of Devon sunshine back into Home Counties mist, taking me back into winter and into the old life. At the Suffolk railway station only ten miles from my home, I saw a woman in a Husky jacket putting a couple of small children into their safety seats in the back of a Volvo, calling out to them in strident country tones, and loading in some piece of tasteful antique tat from the Campsea Ashe auction rooms; and I actually shuddered, as if someone had walked upon my grave. A fortnight had blown sand into my life's old rut, filled it in until barely a trace remained: a thousand wild horses could not have dragged me back prematurely into our perfectly comfortable, cheerful, cosy, rural middle-class life. I did not want the children back there, either, not until they had opened their eyes on some new scenes and new people. As for London, its sights and smells filled me with such horror that I was ashamed of ever having thought Newton Ferrers crowded. Late that night, tired and chastened, I blew three blasts on a lifeboat whistle for Paul to fetch me across the soft black water: *Grace O'Malley* had never felt so much like home.

The next day, still with no wind, we made across a heaving, glassy sea towards Polperro, upon which piskeyfied, tourist-jammed, sickeningly picturesque little harbour Paul had stubbornly set his mind. I was most unkind about this ambition, but this was a ritual visit. Young and poor, as a Radio 4 'Today' reporter, Paul had been sent here on a job and had vowed one day to sail his own boat in. So we did. The children thought the Smuggling Museum superb, and longed (vainly) for a Joan the Wad china ornament. The small strand was filthy, and there was nothing to be gained from looking at the fishing harbour which could not be gained equally easily by looking at a postcard of it; after lunch, we both agreed heartily to get out of Polperro and head up St Austell Bay to have a crack at Charlestown.

We were, in fact, restless. Two motoring passages and a succession of holiday paradises and yacht-harbours had begun to make us feel like a coach party. Poole, Weymouth, Salcombe, Newton Ferrers, are the motorway service areas for obvious-minded yachtsmen heading west. Paul and I had had one of our periodic arguments about buns: he buys terrible, dense, rock-solid things that only he could eat, I buy sponge cake which he considers too soft. We bickered: deprived of adversity and character-building storms and rain, we were falling to pieces like sponge cakes ourselves in the hot, enervating holiday sun. It was deeply ungrateful of us to scorn this West Country beach holiday, but we longed for adventure.

Nicholas had his own problems. He suddenly became quiet that afternoon. Suspecting homesickness, I resolved to bring it to a head. A casually shown photograph of home finally brought on the expected onslaught. He cried on my shoulder for ten minutes, huge tearing sobs, and finally said, as if it were terrible news, that 'sometimes, I even want you to send me home to Pattle's Farm'. I could not stop his crying; tritely, I said that we all had moments of homesickness – and this fearful truism dried the tears in seconds. 'Really? Even my Daddy?' Yes, yes, I said, he misses his horses. But he knows he'll see them again. And you miss your friend Matthew, but I miss Matthew's Mummy and all my other friends. He beamed. Just why companionship in adversity should be so stimulating I do not know, but within minutes Nicholas was wriggling and singing in his bunk, kicking his legs in the air; in half an hour he and Rose were playing trains in the cabin, ignoring the unpleasant roll of the boat across St Austell Bay under engine, and giggling helplessly. I took much longer to recover from the scene than he did.

Across the blue bay, the tall chimneys of the clay-works at Par rose among the curious moon-mountain cones of clay tips; ahead lay Charlestown. I fancied Charlestown as a destination, partly because it is a village in transition. Charles Rashleigh, a local mine-owner, built it at the very beginning of the last century as a china-clay port: the houses line up neatly around a miniature harbour designed by Smeaton, builder of the Eddystone Light. The family have owned the place ever since, and now have sold it off. A leisure consortium bought this tempting slice of old Cornwall in the month before we arrived there, and reports were that the inexorable process had begun: they were selling off the cottages for gentrification and holiday use instead of letting them off at controlled rents to working locals. But so far, of all villages in Cornwall, Charlestown had reason to be the least touched by the imbalances, the frivolities, the leisure ethos of the late twentieth century.

Social anthropology, however, has to take a back seat when it is far from certain whether you are going to get into your untouched Georgian harbour in the first place. Even the author of our pilot-book admitted to never having actually taken a yacht into Charlestown. Little coasters come in and out on the high tides, carrying china clay for papermills; the harbour is private and incomers have to ask permission by radio. This we failed signally to do, not for want of trying; the nearest we got was the harbourmaster of Par, just along the coast, who informed us rather to our dismay that there was no longer a Charlestown Harbourmaster to ring, but Somebody's Leisure Inc. We tried the number he offered us, but got no reply. Picturing a thoroughly modern 'Harbour Facilities Executive', too busy punching a computer screen and planning Jacuzzi complexes to let ships in and out any more, we ploughed on despondently towards this mysterious harbour without much clue as to what we should do when we got there.

As we circled outside the stone piers, peering hopefully in, a big coaster registered in Limassol appeared suddenly from round the curled stone fist of Smeaton's breakwater; it looked very rusty, very workmanlike, and absolutely nothing to do with the Leisure Industry. A pilot launch appeared behind it, and the bare-chested lads on board this craft told us that 'Harbourmaster was aboard the coaster, and might be ashore in ten minutes.' We edged in behind the piers and circled a bit more, watched by half a dozen anglers, and admired the plain, dour cottages and solid stone piers of this miniature port. By now we wanted to stay very much indeed. Eventually, a middle-aged, shock-headed Cornishman appeared, startled by our repeated request for a berth for the night. 'You'll go aground,' he said. 'There's no water at all when the tide goes down, you know.' 'We know. We have legs,' said we proudly. Indeed we had, huge wooden beams which got in everyone's way on the side-deck. They had never been tested, but we had the bolts for them, and we had faith. Slowly the harbourmaster thawed, and placed us in the outer basin by a stone pier, with worried exhortations to brace ourselves away from the wall when we touched the ground, and not to allow the boat to drift back because although the harbour floor was level underneath us, 'a big hole' gaped in the bed just behind our rudder. Picturing ourselves dangling over a ravine, we hauled nervously forwards. Mr Brabyn, the harbourmaster, watched impassively. Then the children popped up through the hatch in striped jerseys like small burglars and began to flirt with him, having a great penchant for harbourmasters. He thawed further, and told us his name was Graham. Interested Charlestown residents and tourists came and looked at us; we looked back at them.

While the tide was high, we walked up through the village, past the deserted Visitors' Centre with its robot smuggler in a cage outside, shouting recorded 'Ha-hars!' to the empty square; despite him, there was a sort of quiet dignity about the place, the sense you get in a place that may be overrun with visitors by the day, but which remains inhabited by its own people, with every house-light lit at night and no weekend cottages to lie dark and silent all week like gaps in a row of teeth. The harbour itself was bedecked with stern notices saying THIS IS A WORKING PORT; but it is a miniature doll's house of a port: a little jewel, barely three coasters'-lengths long, beautifully built, barely modernized, with wild flowers growing down to the water at the head. It is still the little Georgian harbour Smeaton built, still takes china-clay ships now as it has since they came in under sail. In the museum the next day we found an 1899 photograph showing the very steps by which *Grace O'Malley* lay; and paintings from a hundred years before, showing the same pier unchanged. On the other hand, one should not be over-sentimental about the past: the villagers of the now vanished hamlet of West Polmear may not have been too pleased at the nasty modern development imposed by Charles Rashleigh on their fishing-village. As for the picturesque bustle of sailing-ships and early steamers, we later found a contemporary writer describing operations at Charlestown in the 1880s as a 'Little Hades':

The smoke of its torment ascended in heavy clouds of black and white dust as we scrambled down the steep hill-side into the gruesome pit, where a crowd of undistinguishable beings

46

are for ever emptying and loading an inexhaustible fleet of schooners. What the natural features of Charlestown originally were it is impossible to say, for everything is coated with white or black dust, and sometimes with both together, the result being a most depressing grey, as of ashes . . . at first we could see nothing, but gradually our eyes accustomed themselves to the murk, and we made out that on one side of the harbour vessels were being loaded with china clay, and their crews were as white as millers. On the other side, coal was being discharged and the crews were as black as Erebus. The villagers were black and white, according to which side of the port they resided on, while some were both black and white, like magpies.

Even allowing for the fastidious Victorian gentleman's approach to industry – a modest, mutton-chop-whiskered aesthetic shrinking of this sort had been apparent in contemporary descriptions of the building of HMS *Warrior*, too ('Imps with red-hot pincers') – Charlestown was clearly no Disneyland then. Yet today, in the last days of its commercial decay, with peaceful, unhurried coasters rusting gently in the dock among the dandelions, Charlestown has a charm it will never have again, and was never originally intended to have. What is this love affair between the British and decay? Why do we appreciate it so, why so resent the touch of fresh paint and the bustle of investment? Almost the worst thing, when we contemplated the selling of the small houses in the town, was to think of the stylish Laura Ashley and Colefax and Fowler curtains that would soon be up, the pine kitchens and the designer tricycles; but on what grounds, for heaven's sake, did we feel so hostile to pleasant chintzes?

At dusk, the few tourists gone, the water began to gurgle from under us; our confidence in the legs which would hold us upright was revealed to be the puny thing it really was. We sat terrified as *Grace* transferred her great weight from sea to land, groaning horribly. The children refused to sleep. At ten thirty there was silence, and the last of the tide was swilling around the two galvanized iron socks at the base of our legs. A shock-headed silhouette peered down from the wall now fifteen feet above our deck. 'Okay?' said Mr Brabyn. He took his responsibilities seriously. 'Are the children asleep, then?' No. They popped

47

up instantly and insisted on presenting him with one of our ship's supply of lucky bears (manufactured by my mother, each in a miniature Aran sweater): 'He should have a bear because he's kind, isn't he Mummy?' He was; never have I met a harbourmaster so worried about a visiting yacht, fussing like a hen with one chick.

He had, I suppose, reasonable cause. Not only is a yacht a rarity in Charlestown, but legs – those baulks of heavy timber bolted to a traditional boat's sides to enable it to settle levelly on the seabed at low water – are far less popular than they were in the days of regular sail. Many – probably most – modern single-keel yachts never dry out unless propped against a harbour wall or stout wooden piles designed for the purpose. Sitting on a beach like a fat contented duck is reserved for twin-keeled boats and centreboard dinghies. We had never owned, let alone used, a pair of legs; our experience was enlarged that night. We discovered that the slightest movement of the water, the merest suggestion of a swell, is enough to cause creaking of the legs against the boat; amplified by the hollow hull, the sound is unimaginably loud, as if the boat is being wrenched apart. Going down, we had had a sense of our helplessness in the face of this tremendous transfer of weight from water to wood, and sat working out what we would do if the boat simply fell over sideways. Going up, at least, we knew she would float within the hour.

Rose, unfortunately, had a bunk next to a particularly hyperactive leg, and woke in the small hours crying with cross fright. I crawled in with her and helped her block her ears for the twenty minutes that the racket lasted, and then left her; we all slept until nine o'clock, by which time we had to check that the legs were still bolted on securely for the next exciting descent. Then the children and I had the great satisfaction, before lunch, of strolling in through the harbour mouth itself on the firm sands, with only a trickle of water to wet our bare feet. There is something very pleasing about strolling around in a completely dry harbour. 'The bed of the very sea,' said Nicholas reverently. We visited an astonishingly good, little-advertised diving museum in the Visitors' Centre, which further inflamed the children's new love-affair with the seabed, and a school fête where the band's rendering of 'Eleanor Rigby' was all but drowned by the steam organ's version of 'I do like to be beside the seaside', despite furious gestures from the organizers. 'She do have to finish the roll, see,' said the steam-organ man tranquilly under the racket.

Fortified by all this, we eased out of Charlestown harbour on the last of the afternoon high tide, and came out into a brisk north-westerly wind and bright continuing sunshine. So we ran down past the dark and light, the rolling and billowing, craggy and sublime Cornish land until we rounded up into Falmouth at evening.

Falmouth is the Piccadilly Circus of the coast. Stay here long enough, tied up to the town pontoons under the Custom House, and friends will appear, expected or unexpected, from land or sea. Yachts coming up from Brittany and Biscay, in from the Atlantic, down from the Solent, round from Ireland and the North, come in to Falmouth; it is the first safe all-tide harbour after Land's End, has the best shelter and the best chandler's shop. People who love boats drop out to Falmouth and its hinterland, to live with sea close on three sides of them, in small cottages on precipitous hills; we had barely tied up before one lot of friends was aboard drinking whisky, and bringing news of another lot. Even so far west, my network of pre-marital acquaintances seemed to be working well: out of the gloom of the town pontoons a patriarchal white-bearded figure hailed me and turned out to be an extrovert Irish doctor, Felix MacHenry, who had sat in the desk next to me twelve years before in the Oxford College of Further Education evening classes on navigation. Our teacher was an eccentric ex-merchant officer turned architect, and to this day, faced with a knotty tidal calculation, I echo his cheerful cry: 'Near enough for Nellie, near enough for Nelson.' Nor shall I forget his astro-navigation practice out of the college window with a sextant, which proved conclusively that we were in Dundee, or his Morse Code tests which invariably turned out to be the titles of ancient Bing Crosby songs. This was unfair on us younger pupils: Felix MacHenry's generation, once they had decoded 'WHERE THE BLUE – ' had no trouble in filling in ' – OF THE NIGHT MEETS THE GOLD OF THE DAY', but those of us under twenty-five had to work out every single letter, with puzzled frowns.

So there was more whisky drunk, on Felix's boat, while he gaily dispatched his young sons Felix and Ian to babysit for us on *Grace O'Malley*. What exactly went on I cannot say, but shreds of evidence keep emerging to this day ('Felix made Rose put her finger in a limpet' . . . 'Ian shut Felix in the lavatory' . . . 'We learned a rude poem, listen . . .'). So successful was the relationship that by ten thirty the next morning, with us meant to be at the launderette and Felix meant to be fixing his halyards, the three adults were drinking black coffee aboard our boat, and the four children doing more unspeakable things together on theirs. ('Oh, good, Nicholas and Rose have come to babysit us this time. Do you know what I've got in this bucket?')

In Falmouth I had a severe attack of my great failing, mother-hood-fatigue. Sometimes, quite suddenly, I can no longer tolerate the slow maundering pace, the endless questioning, the constant need to uplift your small companions' morale. I want to stride out, lift my eyes to far horizons without people stepping off pavements to their doom beside me, and to answer no questions but my own. In this mood I snap, the children play up, and I am no help to them. On the beach I sat staring moodily out across the azure bay at the darker, troubled water ruffled by the offshore wind. Penden-nis Castle was high and fine, St Anthony Head lighthouse a brave sight in the sunshine; ahead of us, to the south, lay the great mass of the Lizard, last and fiercest headland of the Western Kingdom. If I am honest, the Lizard was probably the root of my trouble anyway: neither Paul nor I had been west of it, except across to Ireland; the coast of North Cornwall and South Wales is notoriously bleak and short of emergency havens, and we had to round that headland next and move on into unknown country, away from Falmouth, friends, and shelter. And all this, I thought bitterly, with children in tow who made a drama out of walking a mile and a half to the beach on a sunny day. It was unfair of me: they would not have made a drama out of it if I had not been so snappy.

Paul was tense, too. He had ignored Cowper's good advice not to read too far ahead, and been stricken with gloom by the words of Mark Fishwick in *West Country Cruising* about what lay around Land's End:

There is, sadly, little to recommend the North Cornish coast. In the prevailing winds from a westerly quarter it presents an exposed and rugged lee shore with just a few drying harbours that cannot be guaranteed as places of refuge – an unwhole-some combination and a natural deterrent for pleasure boating.

However, with Falmouthian serendipity, the author himself then turned up on the pontoon, a slight, bearded, cheerful man, and announced himself as a fellow member of the RCC. He and his girl-friend Vicki had sailed around Britain in the opposite direction to ours two years earlier, and pronounced it, 'Fine, but not relaxing. Not easy in one summer, unless you go through the Caledonian Canal.' They bore us off to dinner in their cottage up on the hill, its tiny garden perched above the chimneypots of the houses below, and fondly recalled the high and low moments. The image which stuck in my mind was of 'Vicki, lying on her bunk all day in Grimsby Number One Fish Dock watching the Royal Wedding of Fergie and Prince Andrew on a miniature television with a picture the size of a dog-biscuit.' The cruise had been Mark's somewhat thorough method of 'introducing Vicki to cruising, the easy way' – easy, he explained, because there were so few long passages and so many nice harbours. Vicki, an artist, smiled serenely and made no reference, glowing or otherwise, to her private feelings that day in Grimsby Number One Fish Dock.

Mark had made the journey partly to research more memories of his boat, *Temptress*, a 1910 yawl built in Cornwall. The boat was owned by Edward Allcard, who wrote books about his ocean voyages in the 1940s and created a national newspaper sensation when he discovered a beautiful Portuguese girl stowaway in his fo'c'sle on leaving the Azores. Mark showed us the actual fo'c'sle the next day, and I must admit I could understand a certain note of ribald disbelief in some of the press reports; it is not the most likely place for a full-sized beautiful stowaway to stay hidden for twenty-four hours. Nonetheless, he lent me the book *Temptress Returns*, and I found myself entirely convinced by Allcard's account of his surprise, of the stowaway's gradual adaptation to life on the open sea, and of their half-pleased, half-strained relationship. Equally convincing are the excerpts from poor Otilia's journal:

> I have a feeling of non-existence in mid-ocean in a boat only a hand and a half long, which is taking me to a far-away land with an unknown man. I must say that in spite of his most unattractive beard I feel far more reassured when he is by my side . . . He must be sound asleep: otherwise my jerky steering would have disturbed him.

The children had widened their yachting acquaintanceship, too. Aboard the *Caroline-Emma* opposite us on the pontoon was a family cutting itself more thoroughly adrift than us: the father was a trawler skipper, the mother had just been made redundant, and after some consideration they had decided to buy the boat and sail off, complete with children from eighteen years to eighteen months, down the trade winds to the Caribbean. The younger ones played board games with Nicholas and Rose, and we listened rather proudly to the conversations our children were beginning to have about their new life: 'Will you be going tomorrow? We're off to Mousehole. We don't make very early starts because Rose gets so grumpy in her bed. We might put the sails up if there's a wind. The weathercast man said northerly, Mummy says.' They were struggling nobly to make sense of it all.

On the last evening in Falmouth I walked along the waterfront alone on the pretext of posting a letter. I really wanted a last look at the Killigrew Monument. Martin Lister Killigrew was the son-in-law and last of the Killigrew family, Cornish aristocrats with a history of piracy, gambling, founding the Theatre Royal Drury Lane, and having appallingly disreputable wives. Lady Mary Killigrew, wife of the Commissioner for Piracy in 1574, was actually tried for looting a Spanish ship in Falmouth harbour; Lady Jane Killigrew, wife of the builder of the Lizard Lighthouse (himself a comparatively respectable Killigrew), not only organized the plundering of an innocent Dutch vessel in 1617, but conducted torrid affairs with several officers of the Pendennis Castle garrison. Martin Lister was not a born Killigrew, but only took the famous name; hence perhaps his milder and more thoughtful nature. All he did was to erect this peculiar granite spike on the hills over the harbour. He did it, gloriously, for no particular reason at all. In 1937 some busybody borough council had put a label on the monument claiming it was a memorial to the 'last of the Killigrew family', thus putting a tidy full stop on an episode of history and a motive on its builder. But more recently the new council cleared his name of vainglory, putting an explanatory plaque alongside it which quotes Martin himself. He was not commemorating himself.

He asked: 'That there be no inscription in or about the pyramid or the whole grave – no, not so much as the date of the Year; Hoping that it may remain a beautiful embellishment to the Harbour, Long, Long after my desireing to be forgott, as if I had never been.'

It stands still, forty feet high: not exactly beautiful; but I cannot help liking Martin Lister Killigrew for the thought.

6

By noon the next day we were off the Lizard rolling gently on a long
Atlantic swell and watching a pair of circling sharks. The permanent
electric log read one thousand miles since *Grace*'s launching the year
before; we thought fondly, as we very often do, of her builders at
Robertson's yard in Woodbridge, and of the winter days when we
would drive over there just to look at her, a mess of wood-shavings
and epoxy resin drips, plumbing and wiring, and wonder uneasily
whether this chaotic object would ever get to sea. She came together
all in a rush, during the last fortnight; on the day of her launching we
had a party in the boat-shed, and a vicar to bless her and the Leiston
British Legion Band to play 'Heart of Oak' as she slid into the water in
the lashing rain. I seem to remember dancing a hornpipe with
someone, and Rose hating the band.

Back up on deck, a shout of 'Submarine!', and there was a big
sub cruising close to us, turret and periscope up, its black back
awash. A rare sight; clearly something to do with the naval
helicopter overhead, the plume of sooty black smoke rising from
the Lizard cliffs, and a distant hazy grey battleship south of us. We
had been lucky so far with the various firing-ranges and naval
exercises of the Channel; it is a fortunate yacht which gets all the
way from Dover to West Cornwall without being chased out of
some military exercise or other by a snotty young officer in a fast
guard-boat. On *Sheltie* we were once forced to motor an extra fifteen
miles to keep clear of the Lulworth firing-range, and the overheated
engine melted the butter: Richard sent the army a bill for it (the
butter, that is, although the engine never quite recovered either).

Our goal was St Michael's Mount, a towering rock island linked
by a half-tide causeway to the mainland town of Marazion. Primitive
men thought it holy, a freakish rock outcrop in the heart of a forest;
when the sea made it an island, it was venerated as a remnant of
the lost land of Lyonesse; Benedictine monks spent four hundred
holy years here, and built the causeway. They knew what they
were doing, for the modern causeway follows exactly the same

curve, calculated to throw off the tide earlier and more consistently along its length, as theirs did: it still works better than a straight road would have. Henry VIII sacked the Mount; York and Lancaster, Roundhead and Cavalier, fought over it and used it as an arms stockpile; eventually it fell into private hands, sold to the Roundhead officer who captured it. The National Trust runs it now, but the St Aubyn family live there still. They have been visited, with that royal taste for the spectacular and the symbolic, by Queen Victoria, Edward VII, and the Queen Mother. Victoria's wee footprint is delicately inlaid with brass on the steps of the tiny harbour. We thought it would be a curiosity to land here with our bigger feet, and were quite prepared to pay the price of drying out by the old stone wall.

Rounding the towering rock, it became obvious why this minute harbour used to be the most important haven in Mount's Bay. A bay facing south-west in South-West England has no need more desperate than guaranteed solid shelter close to land. When early villagers built a harbour wall to compound the snugness of their haven, St Michael's Mount became inevitably a centre of trade as well as a spoil of war: tin ore was brought overland from the north coast of Cornwall to be shipped from here; cargoes down the centuries have been landed on this little rock and drawn by horse and cart across the monks' causeway to the mainland. One guidebook describes this as a quaintly topsy-turvy arrangement, with the implication that it was somehow typically Celtic and contrarily cute: but to a boat coming in from the ruffling sea of Mount's Bay with an uncertain weather forecast, it is very obvious indeed why the harbour ruled the waves until Penzance was built. It is just safe, that is all; never mind quaint. The old harbours are still the best ones.

We tied up to a neatly-kept wall, near the cluster of tidy little open ferryboats, under the immaculate row of cottages and the clean, smart, granite castle, feeling a little as if we had landed in Toytown. We tidied our coils of rope up with more care than usual. We had come to National Trustland: the Trust specializes in an atmosphere neat and discreet, firm and nannyish, deeply responsible and severely well-run. One feels, at times, that only with great difficulty do the Trust's officials restrain themselves from putting signs in all their carefully-landscaped lavatories saying NOW WASH YOUR HANDS. We wandered around the harbour area, desperate to climb to the summit: everywhere we found clean, dark green doors barred to us until 10.30 a.m. – opening time – and admonitory notices warning that persons with heart conditions should not attempt the climb anyway. Obediently we refrained from climbing or invading – Lord St Levan does, after all, still live there – and returned a little crossly to play board games and give the children tea on the boat. The local sailing-club skimmed around in red-sailed Mirror dinghies; the low evening light was still around the bay, and we were desperate to climb before the tourists came, and give the Mount some chance of communicating to us privately its story of trade and prayer, timber and tin, war and lookout. We wanted to hear the roars of Giant Terrible, trapped in a pit underneath us by brave Cornish Jack.

Luck was with us. As I was passing the evening by marking up lengths of our anchor-chain with the aid of one measured metre of spare knicker elastic from my chaotic sewing-drawer, a cheerful harbourmaster appeared suddenly, like a grin without a cat, not to warn us of some fearful sill or chasm upon which we were about to descend, but with the cheering message that – the castle being empty of its master and mistress – we were 'welcome to scramble about the Mount, see it in the quiet, like'. Delighted, I rushed towards the green doors – my guide having dematerialized with startling suddenness while I was down putting my knicker elastic away – but they were all still locked. Our kindly guide was clearly a hallucination brought on by too much bending over smelly galvanized anchor-chain. But as I turned back from the closed doors, he reappeared. 'Low door. Over there. The only door that's unlocked, see, is the only one that says No Admission.' It was like being in a Carroll syllogism . . . all doors are locked except the one which says No Admission, one door is not locked but there is no admission . . . I pushed it open.

In dreams and legends, a low door opens in a high wall, and there is a forbidden garden. Here I was inside it. The stony soil was a mass of bluebells and white campanulas, the pale path wound decorously up the hill; but alone in command of the great mound I could scramble freely on beds of pine-needles, between boulders, through groves of umbrella pines. At last, from vertiginous cliffs below the castle gate, I could see across Mount's Bay in the fresh north-easterly blow, make out the Lizard and the points east of Land's End, and look westwards towards our next gateway before the passage northward to Wales. I stood for a long time there, but

Paul deserved a climb too in this matchless golden light; I came back through the hidden door and took my turn at guarding the children in their sleep and tending the cat's-cradle of rope and wire that sees a boat down safely when it leans against a wall. We twanged, and groaned, and settled; the tide ebbed with the light, and we all slept quiet under the shadow of the holy Mount.

The morning brought boatsful of tourists back, with buggies and boob-tubes, denims and shopping trollies and guidebooks, to drink wholesome National Trust tea and admire an extraordinary model of the castle made out of old corks by a former St Levan butler. Modern pilgrims, the video commentary called them, but they didn't seem to be concentrating the way pilgrims should. We avoided them by nipping across the cobbled causeway to Marazion to dig for lugworms on the beach. There was a fresh outburst of temperament from the children when we got back to the boat, and Nicholas wrote his first independent sentence. 'How do you spell Nasty?' he asked severely. I sounded it out in the school-approved phonic alphabet. Shortly afterwards he presented me, triumphantly, with a drawing captioned 'Mummy is Nasty'. I was so charmed by this that I grabbed it for my personal archive, but he screamed and asked for it back. Nicholas is a remorseful, conscientious child: I was afraid he was going to tear it up, and said so. 'I am NOT going to tear it' he gritted. 'I am going to HOLD IT UP for the PUBLIC to see.' And so he did, and the public going home with its buggies and guidebooks craned up from the evening ferryboats to see what the dear little boy on that pretty black-and-white boat was trying to show them. I wished he had not found so very thick, and bold, and black a felt marker to write it with.

We were now in a mood to victual up and organize the ship for her longest passage since the Forelands: a hundred and ten miles round Land's End and northward to Milford Haven in South Wales. The North Cornish coast is no place for cruising yachts in this unsettled climate; nor did we want to get too far up the Bristol Channel, which boasts the second fastest tides in the world after the Straits of Magellan. A south-westerly blow here can be disastrous, with few harbours of refuge and only the uninviting prospect of hiding behind Lundy Island with all your anchor-chain stretched out and the boat jerking and plunging for her life. So we decided to make for Penzance, last town in England, to top up the fuel, water, gas, and stores; and, following my scientific measurement with my knicker-elastic metre, to buy an extra length of anchor chain. Fifteen fathoms, we thought, would be enough (if they would only sell elastic by the fathom, how much simpler seafaring life would be).

After a rolling half-hour motoring across the bay, we attempted to put into Newlyn, the busy fishing-harbour that is the heart of the Cornish fisheries; but it was so clearly unwilling to take us in and so packed with fishing and building activities that we chugged rather ignominiously out again and made for Penzance, a mile up the coast. Yachts are now beginning to use this commercial harbour in earnest – two or three hundred a week in the summer – and rather than meeting the newcomers with a surly reluctance and wishing they were proper ships, the harbourmaster Martin Tregoning and his men adopt an extraordinary policy of welcome. We entered the lock-gates to the wet dock to be met by a beaming lock-keeper who took our ropes, assured us that we could have diesel brought down in cans within the half-hour if we wanted to leave on the dawn tide, lent us a funnel for it, offered us a hosepipe for water and made us free of the town with a sweeping gesture and the words – unglamorous but sublimely useful – 'You'll find Tesco's is just next to the gasometer.'

I found myself liking Penzance a lot. The *Scillonian* ferry was in that night, the Inter-City express from London snorting and humming to itself on the foreshore; it is an energetic, shippy, docky sort of place still, with plenty of evidence of commercial activity. We shared the wet-dock with three other yachts, a little freighter from Greenock loading building-blocks for Scilly, a few fishing boats registered in Fowey, Falmouth, and Penzance, and one of those scruffy, rusty ships which abound in small ports and which it is almost impossible to identify for sure as either wrecks waiting for the breaker's hammer or working coasters merely waiting for the skipper to get back from the Seamen's Mission with a pair of dry socks. I later found out that she was a temporary patient in the Penzance ship-repair yard. Further up the dock, the Trinity House depot stood next to the Custom House, surrounded with the big steel shapes of buoys: the old Watch buoy, the West Constable – a giant black-and-white humbug – the Wreck, the Hats – towering and black – and the cheerful red-and-white chequered shape of the Low Lee. Redundant, these particular ones were; but all Trinity House depots stand thus ringed with buoys, while out in the waves their exact twins dance and curvet in the swell, day and night, until they begin to rust and earn a spell of relief from their earthbound doppelgängers. Penzance had hand-made candles, a shop called Bosun's Locker, and a huge shell parlour called Home of a Million Seashells; but beneath the prettification it is prosaic enough, and keeps busy with its job of being the last town in England. I walked around it in the evening on the usual yachtsman's pilgrimage: trying to take a respectful interest in the statue of Sir Humphry Davy, who invented the miner's lamp, and in the elegant Ionian columns and wrought-iron balustrades of the main street, but ending up with my nose pressed with longing to the window of a service laundry (OPEN 0900, NO OILY CLOTHES). This was a perfectly traditional thing to do: the mate of a small coaster once told me that every port town was nothing to him but a pub, launderette and telephone box. 'Even on my holidays in Spain, I don't feel happy till I've spotted all three,' he said stoutly.

We spent a busy Thursday, Paul and Nicholas taking the taxi to Newlyn for chain and heavy shackles, Rose and I trundling the streets with a borrowed Tesco trolley, organizing gas and food and laundry. The Tesco staff, unlike their colleagues further up-Channel, were delightfully willing to lend their trolley for a trip to the dock; not for the first time, it occurred to me that one of the reasons for the terrifying success of the Cornish tourist industry is that – of all denizens of remote and beautiful places I have ever met – the Cornish locals appear remarkably kind to visitors. Admittedly, this was the early season, before the mass of their 'grockles' had descended; but every passer-by, every ice-cream lady, every harbour official or customs officer or supermarket cashier we met presented a relaxed and affable, chatty and child-loving aspect to us. They share news, too: the harbourmaster's assistant told us with relish of the night the Penlee lifeboat was lost in the great storm and coping-stones blew from the very harbour wall; and of the recent minor disaster when the dredger at the harbour mouth lost its propeller and charged through the moored dinghies in the drying harbour, sinking six. The entire newsagent's shop where I bought a paper had drawn to a halt too, all craning over today's *Cornishman* at a picture of a fifty-pound cod just landed by a tourist on a Penzance fishing-boat. 'My son's boat,' said a lady complacently. 'We'll put that on the advertisement board this summer, that'll do some good.'

I needed some blocks and lines for adjustments to the rigging and mooring arrangements as they were developing on board *Grace O'Malley*, and after some detective work was told that 'there used to be a very old man called Albert, down New Street, who did chandlery'. Armed with rather Irish instructions involving going 'just past the saddler's that shut down five years ago' and turning up an alley, I dived down a narrow side street of some antiquity, and found nothing but a chic little shop selling speedboat accessories and sweatbands. Still, there was a cottage in a narrow alley called Saddler's Cottage, which was evidence of some sort; so I asked the multicoloured-sweatband-boutique assistant. 'Yes,' she said surprisingly. 'He's just behind me.' I went back up the alley. A door, grudgingly, revealed the presence of A. MATHEWS, SAILMAKER. A for Albert, perhaps. I knocked timidly, and entered a bright enough sail-loft, with various items of chandlery hanging from the ceiling. A young girl was serving, but my eye travelled more immediately to a very old, very arthritic man with a choleric gleam in his eye, sitting on a bench. 'What you want in here I cannot think,' he said. 'If ever a man suffered – ' Some things for a yacht, I murmured. 'Speak up! Oh, my bones!' The girl moved forward complaisantly, as the old man's fire was drawn by a fresh customer wanting a fitting for a spinnaker-pole. 'Spinnakers. One born every minute!' observed our host. 'My bones, my bones!' I asked the girl for ten metres of line, reasonable enough since the drum was marked in metres, but she shot a terrified apprehensive glance behind me to see if the old man had heard. 'Yards!' she hissed. All right, I said, eleven yards. Then I wanted a snatch-block; not a normal item of everyday chandlery, but a useful kind of pulley-block that opens on one side and so can 'snatch' round a line or a shroud without either end being undone. The old man came forward with a challenging gleam in his eye, abandoning his spinnaker customer to wander hopelessly around by himself, pretending to study a display of shackles. 'Snatchblock!' said the old chandler. 'You want a snatchblock? Well, I don't know what you'd want that for.' With a crow of triumph, he hobbled over to a hanging bundle and found one: only one. 'That's the size you'll want,' he stated firmly, then returned to his virtuoso grumbling. 'Fools and bones and spinnakers. No time for any of them. Oh, my bones.' He left me to the girl, and I paid my bill (the VAT, of course, being calculated separately and rather surreptitiously by her) and bolted back up the unmarked alley, rather pleased to have found one chandlery in all England which will clearly never take to selling designer dove-grey and pink sailing anoraks or signal-flag jewellery for groupies to wear at Cowes. We left Penzance on the evening tide, and drifted down to Mousehole, a few miles on; our last English harbour, as it turned out, for a thousand and twelve miles.

7

Mount's Bay – that odd, lost fairyland corner tucked under the claw of Land's End – was having a cumulative effect upon us, dazing us under the hot, unseasonal sun. Even Penzance, with its Tesco and gasometer and Inter-City terminus, was full of odd resonances like Trevor Rogers the lock-keeper talking about his wife: 'A Mousehole girl, she was, mind, she's grey now, but she had dark, dark hair. A lot of 'em do. The Spanish, mind, they came and invaded Mousehole, four hundred years ago.' Swarthy descendants of the Armada are still there: grey respectable Penzance wives, with dark eyes full of history.

The bay in the low, golden light was the stuff of dreams: distant gleams of green light and pale sand, sea a deep translucent blue, and gulls wheeling and whirling overhead. When the *Scillonian*, white and graceful, appeared around Land's End on her way home for the night, the gold light caught her pale sides and made her for the moment into a ship of dreams, a creature of romance rather than a workaday mailboat. Astern of us, the Mount rose impossibly from the waters to the glow of its castle. When we turned into the narrow opening of Mousehole harbour and slid alongside its lichened and massive wall, I found myself briefly the victim of a hallucination: this western kingdom was taking me back to Ireland, to extreme youth, the sound of plaintive penny-whistles and the pangs of early love. This could easily be an Irish harbour, somewhere lost in the far West, a Celtic kingdom. When we had tied up, Frank Wallis the harbourmaster appeared above our heads, at the top of the iron ladder. 'Staying the night? Two pounds fifty, my queen. There you are, my robin.' I returned dazed with appreciation to our cabin and to the smell of pressure-cooker stew hissing to its fulfilment. Paul tapped the barometer and peered at it. 'When the glass it rising be, diesel fuel get used at sea,' he observed. 'I know why you've got that silly look on your face. "My robin," indeed. You and harbourmasters. I'm going to lose you to some harbourmaster.' 'It's the uniform,' I agreed dreamily, although if truth be

61

told Mr Wallis's uniform consisted of a cotton check shirt and a blue hat marked HARBOURMASTER, neither of them exactly brushed to a pitch of naval smartness.

But I could resist nothing about Mousehole, from the harbourmaster to the skyline. For some reason – local cussedness perhaps, strong community spirit, Spanish blood, whatever – the surface gloss of Annie's Antiques and Pam's Pantry and double yellow lines and a flashy little hotel called the Lobster Pot utterly fail to obscure the real, essential, Mousehole. Every guidebook tells the tale of Tom Bawcock who went to sea despite the gales and came home to the starving village with Seven Sorts of Fish, which were put in a fearful pie with all their heads sticking out. I had told the story to the children in turn. But if they still eat Starry-Gazy pie on Tom Bawcock's Eve every year in Mousehole, then they do it because they feel like it, and not to please anyone from America or Wolverhampton. If the harbour is pretty, it is because it is practical, a good spot for small fishing-boats, cannily built with its entrance sheltered by the rocky islet of St Clement's. Mousehole, first of all the famous honeypot villages we had seen, remained quite real and definite. Polperro might as well have been shipped stone by stone to Florida and put in Disney World. 'Ah, we do have the advantage, my robin, that we doan't have no car park,' chortled Mr Wallis. 'They'd be like ants if you did. You see, my queen, they can't park, so they goes straight through towards Land's End.' As for yachts, so few these days are willing to dry alongside a wall in a tidal harbour that, 'I'd be surprised if I get more'n seventy in a year. Hired, some of them be. Don't know how to lean on a wall anyway. Chap over there, he did fall over the other night, a fine do that was.' He told me the name of the elderly chandler in Penzance. 'Ah, Mister Willoughby. Fine old chandelier, he be. One of the old sort.'

Paul and I longed, more than anything, to walk together for miles along the coastal path, towards Lamorna and Land's End. The National Trust, showing its more rugged face, owns the path; mock as one might at the scented tea-shoppes and deadly tasteful stately homes, one can only fall into a posture of devout admiration when contemplating Enterprise Neptune, the Trust's far-sighted campaign to buy up as much coast as possible and save it from big business, nuclear power stations, and private caprice. Land's End may belong to Peter de Savary today, another rich entrepreneur tomorrow; but you can, now and forever, skirt it triumphantly on a National Trust pathway and thumb your nose at the lot of them. This face of the National Trust, its ownership of coasts and creeks, small farms and harbours, always strikes me as uniquely splendid and British: it is as if some dear old lady, whose life seems utterly devoted to doilies and lavender-bags and gossiping about what the Dear Duchess said to Lady X, suddenly upped and struck a property developer over his bowler hat with her umbrella.

But we could not walk the path together: Rose would not be able to get far. We compromised, counting our blessings *sotto voce* to dissipate the irritation, and agreed that I should walk through the morning and Paul the afternoon. The children built sandpies with their father while their mother, off the leash, sped up the cliffs and through the forest, over the grey stones and waist-deep through cowparsley and bluebells, looking out to sea.

After lunch, Paul in turn set off and the children and I embarked on our regular search for baths. There is a knack in finding baths in strange places: normally I am rather good at it, homing in unerringly on a small hotel or boarding-house of just sufficient gentility but no foolish pretensions. This time I had more trouble. There were two bed-and-breakfast houses which didn't even answer the bell, and a mimsy little hotel on the waterfront whose receptionist looked at us with rising horror and said she would 'Have to Ask the Manageress' . . . tomorrow afternoon! Eventually we ended up exactly where we should have started in the first place, the Ship Inn, home of starry-gazy pie and convivial local of all Mousehole folk. 'No problem,' said the young landlord. 'First left up the stairs, but finish by two thirty when we close.' For their huge bath and clean towels, the host was unwilling to take a penny; I made the children put a couple of pounds in the lifeboat box. Payment was also voluntary up at the Mousehole wild bird hospital, where oiled and dilapidated seabirds are rescued by the thousand. Here the children were allowed to spend ten minutes gently stroking a real live baby owl, all fluff and blinks, and were thoroughly alarmed by a cageful of malevolent crows. Once again they put money in the box, and asked wonderingly, 'Do you always choose whether you pay in Mousehole?' After much silent thought, Rose announced that the baby owl was far better than the Smuggling Museum in Polperro. I thought so too.

One more call, not something to be dodged. We went to the quiet

63

church: Methodist, spotless, and discreet. John Wesley had found Mousehole in 1785 'one of the liveliest societies in Cornwall'. There in the corner, roped off, lay the memorials to the eight lifeboatmen who died in the great Penlee disaster of 19 December 1981: too new and raw a horror for folksong, too desperate in its local ramifications for light discussion. In Penzance they talked about it casually on the harbour edge, in Marazion the guide book had mentioned it: in Mousehole nobody did. Only in the church and in the hearts of friends is the event engraved. There is a ship's bell, a piano, a carpet, a beaten copper replica of the lifeboat *Solomon Browne*. Above all, there is an octagonal table made by the Church Steward Tom Waters out of the old free seats beside the pulpit. Each panel bears a name. Ordinary names: Trevelyan, Stephen, Nigel, John, Barry, Charles, Kevin, Gary. I read each one to the children, and we stood for a moment; then out we went into the fresh, mild, early-summer sunshine to see the blue innocent sea at our feet.

8

Another evening of watching the changing light on the lichen of the harbour wall, another drink in the Ship, and it was time to go. High time: the weather forecast suggested that the light variable winds were going to shift and coalesce into a reliable south-easterly by Saturday night. If we left on Saturday morning, we could get around Land's End under engine if necessary, and make good progress through the night with a fair wind for Milford Haven on the southern tip of Dyfed. A conversation with the London Weather Centre had ended, too, with the note of warning: 'If you are going, don't leave it too long.' Although at that point the Marinecall five-day recorded forecast (not one to rely on unless checked daily) was predicting nothing more than moderate south-easterlies, the nose of this individual duty forecaster was telling him unequivocally that there might be more in store. There was a 'slow-moving' depression over Biscay, but depressions can speed up rather suddenly. A twenty-four-hour passage with no easy havens to run for is not something to undertake lightly.

And there were no havens. Frank Cowper says sternly, 'The Bristol Channel is not, in my opinion, a suitable place wherein amateur sailors may practise cruising. The tides are far too strong, the harbours but poor ones, and the traffic too busy. The prevailing winds also blow up and down, and the seas are choppy and heavy.' Apart from the heavy traffic, these drawbacks are enduring ones. It must be admitted that Bristol Channel yachtsmen do exist, and indeed the grandly named Bristol Channel Yachting Conference produces terrifying local pilotage notes about their monstrous thirty- or forty-foot tides, their intricate havens and amusing rock islets slapped bang in the middle of approaches. In fact, Paul and I have both sailed in the upper Bristol Channel with Christopher Thornhill, and had piquant experiences like the time *Kathleen* was tearing downstream towards Barry Dock, wind astern and tide doubling our speed, and the topsail refused to come down. With the topsail up, the mainsail will not come down, and with the main

65

up a big gaffer most definitely will not stop. We saw Barry slipping away from us, and almost gave it up for lost, thinking we would have to come back up with the next tide; but someone's last despairing yank did the trick, and we sheltered gratefully among Barry's dank and dripping dock walls for the night. On another occasion, just as we were being swept sideways in a harbour entrance (you do a lot of sideways travelling in the Bristol Channel) the engine covered Christopher in a jet of scalding water, and simultaneously Paul discovered the cabin floorboards floating around. So it can be done. But on balance, with the children aboard and the promise of Welsh islands ahead, we reckoned we would skim across the rocky jaws of the Bristol Channel rather than go up it.

For additional insurance, Mark Fishwick himself came with us as crew. The ease and gaiety of spirits we gained from his company was immeasurable: he is twice as much of a seaman as either of us, has sailed old *Temptress* across the Atlantic singlehanded, rounded Britain, and fished professionally. After a spell at the Exeter Maritime Museum he has a fund of bizarre and fascinating marine lore; and in addition, holds a strange fascination for small children. 'I had much younger siblings,' he explained, trying to account for this. Certainly, he is one of nature's uncles: Rose and Nicholas attached themselves to him like limpets. Rose, normally haughty and reserved with strange men, was overheard in their first few moments of acquaintanceship to say, 'Ho! you've got short arms, haven't you?', and Nicholas drew endless complicated pictures for his approval. We could not, in our wildest dreams, have imagined such a perfect crewman. He even refrained from comparing any of our systems and practices aboard with those on his own boat, an almost unheard-of quality of heroism in a fellow-owner.

Rather to our surprise, we headed out of Mousehole harbour into a large, aggressive sea. The forecast hours of calm had obviously spent themselves in the night. The wind picked up smartly from the south, and whistled us past the headlands at a steady six knots: we raised Tater Du, the newest-born lighthouse in Britain, Penwith Point, and Gwennap Head; then low Land's End itself and towering Cape Cornwall. We tormented ourselves with the question of when a headland becomes technically a cape: all the books sententiously said that Cape Cornwall was the only cape in England (Cape Wrath being in Scotland), but we found it hard to decide why Portland Bill was not a cape, if having water on three sides was the deciding factor; or if it was a question of height, why the Lizard could not be one? Cape Wrath and Cape Cornwall, we would say, stick out no more proudly than – say – Duncansby Head at the north-eastern end of Scotland, so why are they singled out to join Canaveral and Horn and Farewell in the exclusive Cape Club? The sea gradually flattened as we got some shelter from the south-east, and by one o'clock we were eating chicken sandwiches and looking back over the stern, with quiet satisfaction, at the retreating form of Land's End and the Brisons. We told the children the story of the Longships lighthouse, where the keeper was kidnapped by wreckers to sabotage incoming ships. His heroic little daughter kept the light burning by standing tiptoe on the family Bible. We found ourselves surfing along, sometimes making up to eight knots: for a spell the children teased Mark in the cockpit while Paul and I lay below decks reading and revelling in the glorious acquisition of a crew who could steer the boat and keep the children amused all at once. Scraps of conversation drifted down. 'Short arms . . . *very* short arms . . . Mark, do you catch fish? are you bad? do you like my drawing . . .' I drifted happily off to sleep, wondering whether Vicki and *Temptress* would mind much if we kidnapped Mark for the whole voyage.

At five, the wind died away totally for half an hour, so we motored; but it returned with violent suddenness at suppertime, just as I was passing chilli con carne and baked potatoes up through the hatch. Once again we began to roar along with a foaming white bone in our teeth. Fifty-eight miles to Milford Haven, and all was well. The children went to bed uproariously, with a promise that Mark would still be there in the morning.

I slept from eight to midnight while the two men took watches in turn. It was one of those deep, deep sleeps which neither dream nor reality can penetrate: rare for me on passage, and probably due to the extra security of having a third competent adult on board. When I woke to hear a commotion on deck, I looked out and saw a single star dancing wildly in the black opening of the companionway. Sleepily I thought, 'Oh, Paul must have gybed the boat to avoid hitting that star.' More commotion, and the sound of Mark padding up on deck in his socks roused me properly: the self-steering gear had failed and locked rigid, bleeping pathetically; it was probably the strain of steering an overcanvassed boat on a wild, rolling broad reach. A strengthening wind can creep up on you if it comes from behind; we should have reefed down hours ago, for it was now a solid Force Five or Six. Paul reefed the sail hastily while Mark shivered at the helm, fresh from his sleeping-bag, and I pulled on warm clothes and oilskins for my watch. Then Mark, who had not spoken, tumbled back below and fell instantly into a deep solid sleep: no fuss, no thinking, just a dedicated recharging of batteries as soon as the chance arose. It is a single-hander's tactic, and a highly enviable gift.

Up on deck alone, I spent a wild, wonderful two hours. The sky was clear and starry, and a crescent moon was turning from gold to deep red as it set over to the west of us where Ireland lay. The boat drove ahead at six or seven knots, powerful, determined, sovereign of the seas. There is a stage in a rising gale when the boat does not seem small and frail and humble, as she will later on; but bigger than her size, and brave, and strong: as if the power were coming from her and not from the wind behind her. We were in that state of hubris during all my watch: *Grace O'Malley* was hard to hold steady in the broaching seas, her mast and reefed sails described wild curves, swaying shapes against the bright stars and the white horses of the sea; but she felt entirely splendid to me, a seafaring Irish O'Malley, her own land to port of her, Cornwall astern, Wales ahead: carving her way through the Celtic sea. My only regret was that I could not let go the helm for one moment to check the children; but they were quiet behind their curtains, and I had padded them well against the increasingly lively motion.

At two o'clock I handed over to Mark: Paul was deeply asleep, and I entered our position and gave Mark details of lights he might – should – raise on the Welsh side before long: especially the white light, flashing once every five seconds from St Ann's Head outside Milford Haven. Half an hour into my light, chilly sleep, the Decca receiver bleeped aggressively. POSITION SUSPECT, said its lights. Devoutly grateful that I had been keeping up the reckoning of our position by conventional means on the chart, I warned Mark and went back to my bunk to indulge in a sleepy, angry reverie against modern technological arrogance about lighthouses and lightships. Big-ship owners, by unique British tradition, have to pay for all the lights around the coast out of Light Dues (most countries use general taxation, on the principle that if ships get wrecked and pollute the shoreline it is a matter of general concern). Lately a strong body of opinion among shipowners has been saying that most lighthouses and lightships are unnecessary, because of the modern marvels of Decca and Loran and satellite-based electronic position-fixing navigation. Lights have already begun to be 'rationalized' – which means put out – and I had been researching the debate that winter. I remembered being told by shipowning interests that lighthouses were 'archaic', and even by a yachting organization spokesman that: 'It's only the older generation who have an irrational fear of the dark coastline and the electronic bleep in the cabin. Younger people who work with computers all day have learned to trust them. I shouldn't think we'll have a lit coastline for that many more decades.' I thought he was mad at the time, and I thought him even madder now, as we bore down on a strange rocky coastline in a rising gale in the darkness, with a silly little green crystal light in the cabin saying POSITION SUSPECT. It is not only pleasure-seeking little yachts who are subject to these bleeping, glowing apologies, either; a Trinity House captain had told me the astonishing story of a Danish-run bulk chemical carrier flying the Singapore flag, which early in 1988 called up the coast-guard to report the Greenwich Lanby buoy one-and-a-half miles out of its proper position near the Sussex coast. The Trinity ship steamed round at full speed to remedy this dangerous and unprecedented drifting buoy; and found it to be bobbing tranquilly in exactly the right place. The only conclusion was that a bulk chemical carrier was heading blithely for the narrow shipping lanes of the Dover Strait, under the impression that it was one-and-a-half miles south of its actual position. 'Of course it would be impractical,' my Government Spokesman had told me, sounding rather bored, 'to charge yachtsmen Light Dues. So if they are the only real users of most of these lights, that is a problem.' Speaking personally, from fifteen miles south of the reefs of Skomer, I would give them fifty quid a year gladly (the calculation is that five pounds per yacht over twenty-foot would raise half the total lights bill). Even if I gave up yachting, I would put a pound in the kitty occasionally just to stop chemical-carriers and oil tankers from crashing into sandbanks and poisoning the sea. There is nothing quite like a lighthouse when you need one.

It was another hour before Mark saw St Ann's Head, and not a nice hour: no more deep sleep was possible. I had got my trousers soaked by a rogue wave, and was rather stupidly trying to sleep in them under a single blanket. I felt chilled, and cross, and nervous. At the change of watch, I overheard a fretful conversation between Paul and Mark about a strangely bright pair of lights close ahead, which could have been a ship; then Mark came down and fell into another of his comas on the bunk.

At five fifteen I gave up pretending to sleep and came on deck. In breaking seas, with white salt patches on his face, Paul was using a rope around the tiller to take the weight off his arms, and staring grimly through the misty dawn light at the shape of St Ann's Head. He was cold and depressed. 'I've been thinking,' he said morosely. 'Look, really, is it fair to bring the children on something like this?' I peered below, lifting a corner of each bunk-curtain to check. Both baby faces were rosy and peaceful, hard asleep on their clean sheets beneath their fluffy Thomas the Tank Engine duvets. They were utterly oblivious of the leaping and rolling of the boat, of the spray, the useless Decca and the clattering wind. 'Is it fair to bring ourselves, more like?' I asked back. 'They're all right, Jack.' Looking ahead, I saw that the mysterious huge ship-lights were still there: two tall, flaring, refinery chimneys, cunningly placed in the same perspective as a big vessel's masthead lights; a little joke to welcome us to Wales.

The wind had a good deal of east in it by now, and our first attempt at bringing ourselves to a halt inside the great harbour of Milford was not entirely successful. We picked up a mooring in Dale Bay, and put some toast and a kettle on; the mooring turned out not to have been attached to the ground beneath. Discarding it (the call to action came just as I was turning the toast over) we anchored further out; but as it was clearly going to be impossible to land, let alone row back to the boat, we opted to take the flood tide ten miles upstream to the quieter creek of Lawrenny.

Paul rolled into his bunk at this point and became insensible: Mark and I motored up the Haven, amusing ourselves by reading severe passages out of the harbour bye-laws from the local pilot-book:

The Master of a vessel wishing to enter the Haven which is in danger of foundering, or sinking, or is leaking, or which, during the voyage in question has been in collision, has stranded, or has been on fire, or has suffered damage to her hull, machinery or equipment which might make the vessel a

70

danger or a nuisance to other users of the Haven, must report to the Signal Station and obtain the specific permission of the Harbourmaster before entering. Such permission may be granted subject to conditions.

We translated this as, 'Please go and founder quietly somewhere else. We've got oil to load here.' But with the ill-found, illegal, and unsound ships which today lurch around the globe with poisonous and polluting cargoes, it is perhaps just as well that Milford authorities are stern. We passed miles of oil-refinery staging: Gulf, Esso, Texaco; monstrous creations that would have wrecked a gentler coastline, but which looked oddly insignificant next to the rugged, wooded, ancient glories of the Haven itself.

This vast natural harbour must have been from earliest days the jewel of Wales: Dale and Pembroke, Landshipping Quay and Lawrenny were busy ports five hundred years ago, and the river Cleddau was crammed with coal boats for two centuries; corn and limestone were loaded from a dozen village creeks here until the ports of Milford and Pembroke were built in the late eighteenth century. Great ships were built here, Brunel's *Great Britain* among them; and great ships came to rest here, too. HMS *Warrior* spent her inglorious years as a fuel-barge in the top of the river; local legend has it that Prince Philip was the moving spirit in her restoration, since, 'Whenever the Queen came here to visit a refinery or whatever, he'd insist on being taken upriver by launch for one more look at *Warrior*.' Dodging the buoys, searching for clear channels, we progressed upriver and slid beneath the Cleddau bridge, arguing how to pronounce it; Paul woke up in time to see the quiet stretch of river up to Lawrenny creek, where we moored in relative peace and flat water, and where the children at last crawled blinking from their bunks at nine thirty. They had crossed a hundred miles of open water, been through wild seas and high winds, and escaped the open jaws of the Bristol Channel. They had made harbour in a new land and missed seeing several miles of iron oil-jetties. 'Is it Wales?' they enquired. 'Are there dragons?' And, most importantly, 'Is Mark still here?'

Mark stayed with us that day, a quietly enchanted day of distant wind and dappled sunshine. We walked through the silent woodlands of Lawrenny in green tunnels of oak and beech and birch, with the hawthorn just flowering and the drowsy smell of gorse

71

emerging into the May warmth. At the Lawrenny Arms, Mark's magnetic appeal was observed to extend to old ladies as well as small children: a very old lady next to him tipped her whisky into her lager, gulped it down, and told him to 'Enjoy yourself while you can, dear. It isn't always (hic) the old that go first.' Extricating himself from this philosophy tutorial with some difficulty, he came back to the table where we discussed other great drink-mixers we had known. Island communities, cut off from the mainland pubs all winter, are in my experience the worst. I used to work in a pub in West Cork, and when the Long Islanders came to town in the early summer, on Saturday nights, they always ordered things like 'Lager and Raspberry, with a dash of bitters' or 'Whiskey and Lucozade with a Black-and-Tan chaser'. It wasn't that they liked the taste, it was just the result, I theorized, of sitting on a windswept island all winter dreaming of what you would drink when you got ashore: in much the same way as sex-starved men devise unlikely and uncomfortable erotic fantasies, involuntary teetotallers let their imagination run riot over whisky and Lucozade. Mark topped this with hideous tales of people he had known to put Ribena in their beer and do appalling things with tonic water, and the children listened wide-eyed over their chips.

Actually, Mark was realizing the innate incorruptible coarseness of Heiney children by now. That night, as we ate stew and dumpling around the warm lamplight in the cabin, Nicholas retired grandly for a wee in the fo'c'sle. Rose, choking hysterically on her carrots, pointed at his retiring back and announced to Mark, 'He's gone to POINT PERCY AT THE PORCELAIN.' Whereon she collapsed in guffaws. This particular vulgarism was taught to Nicholas by his Uncle Mike, and he taught it in turn to Rose. Our crew sighed, and put down his dumpling. 'For two days,' said Mark sadly, 'I have been moderating my language so as not to shock these children. What a waste of effort.'

The weatherman had been right to send us North without delay. Next morning dawned grim. The wind still howled evilly out of the east, but now icy rain swept across us too, finding its way down the main hatch. After some argument, we agreed that we should all go in a taxi to Haverfordwest: there we would see Mark off, get the laundry done, visit the historic castle and have lunch. It would be better than sitting on the mooring in the rain. After about half an hour of dragging children into inner and outer waterproof layers and lifejackets, we got ashore and piled into the taxi, which got lost and made a three-mile detour, far too fast, down the wet lanes. In Haverfordwest, Paul realized he had come out without a jumper and was going to freeze; short-temperedly, missing Mark's calming presence, not pleased to be a grumpy little nuclear family again, we all stamped into a charity secondhand clothes shop to see if they could sell us some woolly rag in his size for twenty pence.

Here, a small miracle occurred. For the first of many times in the voyage, we saw the children's ability to take control and lift our grimmest moods. From being whining, fretful, boring millstones, they would suddenly turn into leaders and inspirers. Up the staircase of the stuffy little shop, they spotted a huge cardboard box full of hats and a mirror. Instantly, they were in there trying them on, metamorphosing themselves three times a minute. Small, fresh grinning faces appeared under fur hats, felt hats, top-hats; posh hats, battered hats, crushed velvet creations worn to church for years by old ladies; moth-eaten hats, straw hats, and frothy net creations worn once only for showy society weddings in the steep streets of some Welsh town way out west. For half an hour they revelled in hats, then I let them buy one each. Twenty pence, said the lady; I gave fifty for the pleasure of it. Rose marched out extinguished by a dome of grey fur, while Nicholas opted for a dashing brown felt derby with a two-tone ribbon.

Up at the castle, these striking figures wandered desultorily around, admiring the snails on the wall, the armour within, and a curious set of exhibits apparently relating to the Sealyham Terrier Club. My favourite object was a model of Penrhos Cottage. Penrhos Cottage is one of the last surviving examples of a peculiar eighteenth-century rural practice in these parts, the *Ty un nos* – or one-night-house. If you could build a house between sunset and sunrise on common land, furnish it and have smoke curling out of the chimney by dawn, that was your house for good and you could claim all the land within a stone's throw. People used to lay their plans, detail their friends and relatives to stand by for sunset on a good long night; they threw up turf walls at speed, jammed on a roof prepared elsewhere and dragged out by donkeys, thatched it in the dark and got the furniture in and fire lit by dawn. An energetic form of squatting, refreshingly free of planning constraints; but one can see why, as the guidebook sadly put it, 'These houses rarely lasted long and few examples remain.'

We remained stuck all the next day: we moved down to the new marina at Neyland, where the wind grew to a fresh gale until we could hardly stand up on the pontoons. We used the time to muck out the children's bunks and toy-bags, wash their sheets, shower, do schoolwork, and mend the Decca aerial. Eventually Paul took the children to the amusements at Tenby and returned in roaring spirits. 'I'm fine,' he said, 'when I get them to myself. Everything was shut, but we jumped in puddles.' In a good mood, Daddy undoubtedly provides the best outings going in all weathers. The amusements had been closed, the rain had fallen ceaselessly – if you can call it falling when the needles of icy water fly parallel to the ground – but the town of islands and sea-caves and shingle and ancient walls had charmed them. While they were away I idly discovered in the AA guide that a little-known Tudor mathematician called Robert Recorde lived in Tenby and invented the equals sign, a symbol I had taught to Nicholas only the day before. I imparted this thrilling information.

But wet gales are boring and disheartening: it was a hard time for all of us. We had a guest, too, which was unfortunate for her: Janet worked silently in the corner of a bunk through the dull day, and we felt particularly sorry that in her few days off, she was not likely to get any sailing. It brought home the particular charm of our own four months' grace: that whatever good weather did come and whenever the sun showed its face, all we had to do was put our heads out of the main hatch, and we would be in it. Normally a summer is judged, as patient weathermen often explain, not by how much fine weather there is, but by how much of it happens to fall at the weekends; we had, for once, freedom to judge the summer on its own primitive terms.

I rang the weather centre in the evening, where a cheerful forecaster said, 'Ooh, your rain does look lovely on my rain radar,' but promised little respite. The next morning was less wild and drier; we dressed up in oilskins and got the boat ready. Then we sat around irritably as the wind rose again. Finally we accepted Lord Nelson's dictum that harbour rots ships and men alike, and set off downriver to see what would happen.

Fortune favours the brave (or brave-ish, anyway). The sun came out, we sweltered in our oilskins, and although we encountered big seas off St Ann's Head they were not breaking, and *Grace O'Malley* rode them disdainfully with a fair south wind on her port beam.

After a couple of hours we had confidently identified the Blackstone, first marker rock for threading through the Jack Sound. We had been advised against the Jack Sound, a dog-legged passage through the rocks inside Skomer, by the harbourmaster in Lawrenny. 'Don't do the Jack!' he had said doomily. 'No, no, go right round outside Skokholm!' Paul and I had then huddled over several pilot-books and decided that the Jack was perfectly all right, given a slackish tide and a fair wind. The trouble with local advice is that all locals in rockbound, fast tidal areas tend to assume that visitors have never clapped eyes on a rock before and are navigating with an out-of-date AA book. You have to listen, and then try to sort out the dark bombast – 'That's where the lifeboat was lost with all hands . . . I've seen bowsprits snap off in those seas . . .' – from the genuinely useful unpublished snippets of local knowledge: 'You'll get an inshore eddy half an hour before the book says, by going north-east of Devil Rock.'

Complacency, however, is a mistake: after making our course for the Blackstone, we got close and suddenly found it was the Mewstone all the time. We had to retrace our course rather hurriedly. I do not know why British pilot-books cannot do what Irish ones always do, which is to describe the actual rocks: a tall grey pinnacle is quite different from a low grassy lump, but they look much the same as symbols on a chart. Janet had a worried air. Luckily the wind was benevolent and moderate; before long we came level with the northern edge of Skomer island, and Rose revived from her queasy position prone on the side-deck and enquired, 'Is it Coconut Island?'

We anchored under sail with only the minimum of marital sniping over the anchoring routine: a few remarks like, 'I can't get it over the bow unless you slow down' and, 'I said FIFTEEN METRES!' Judging from the similar cries we have heard echoing from many a boat in many an anchorage, these disputes between bow and helm seem to be an inescapable part of family cruising. They are all very well unless something else begins to underlie the merely technical discussion: 'Port, I said, Port!' can easily come to mean, 'I had the children all yesterday and cooked all the meals, what did you do?' Similarly, 'Where IS the anchor-buoy, anyway?' can translate as, 'I'm not happy about your asking that appalling man to sail with us, even if he is an old flame of yours.' Half the screaming matches between husbands and wives that you hear on the Broads or on a

South Coast weekend are not about mudweights or mooring-ropes at all: they are about the fact that she wanted to go to Greece, and that he can't stand her mother.

We anchored. When we looked up from our small preoccupations, Skomer North Haven lay around us, and silenced us all.

9

How can one describe such islands as Skomer? Rocky peaks of underwater mountains, rising from who knows what ancient submerged kingdoms: blessed places, haunts of saints and madmen. These are the holy islands of the West, isolated by fast rocky tides and winter storms: I have loved them since my first sight in childhood of Western Ireland, and find echoes of the old love on Skomer, on Skokholm, Lundy, Bardsey, Ramsey, even placid Anglesey. We had anchored in a cloud of puffins, who swam and dived and made absurd splash-landings around the boat. The late afternoon light was glorifying the cliffs beneath which we rolled gently in the swell; gannets and shearwaters and gulls wheeled and cried around us.

We rowed ashore and climbed and made our peace with the stern Warden's Assistant, promising not to leave the paths or speak unkindly to the birds. Eventually we stood on the high point of the island. Acres of bluebells stretched down to the bluer sea; in this primitive glory, we seemed a hundred miles, not ten, from the refinery chimneys of Milford. Rabbits ran everywhere, gaily cropping in fields whose shapes were determined by prehistoric farms. From the cliffs at the western end, we looked down on the seals at the Garland Stone. And from this new eminence too we were able to see for the first time the beauty of St Bride's bay to the north of us.

We had not known what to expect of this Pembrokeshire coast. We knew that the high mountains lay well north of us, and that South Wales is scarred by industry and depressed by economics; we had not known of this perfect bay lying between Skomer and St David's Head, a gentle mountain landscape sweeping round with a hundred colours in its rocks. Entranced, we looked at St Bride's Bay as at an unexpected present, trying to distinguish on its far edge our next harbour of Solva. This is impossible. It lies behind an island called Greenscar, indistinguishable until you get close up. It must have been a wonderful surprise for the Vikings, hunting for shelter among the Welsh rocks; no wonder they gave it the approving name of Sunny Harbour – Solva derives from the same root as Sullom Voe.

It was an oddity of this voyage – of all voyages, I suppose – that wherever we went, almost our first action was to unroll the next chart, climb the local hill and look towards the next harbour. It sounds like impatience, but did not feel so: it was more as if every stage of the coast had to be considered from ahead, abeam, then astern in order to add something to the mother-of-pearl layers of the voyage. The voyage itself was becoming a possession: a single, increasingly precious object. I was making the children keep scrapbooks; they resented the effort of writing, and thinking what to write, but gradually were saying more interesting things. What began as bald infant statements like I WENT ON A LITTLE TRAIN WITH MY DADDY were beginning to flower into more thoughtful remarks: YOU GET SAD WHEN YOU LEAVE HARBOURS BUT WHEN YOU GET TO HARBOURS YOU FEEL HAPPY, wrote Nicholas; and Rose I STROKED A BABY OWL, VERY FURRY TOO. The poems continued. Rose composed a song:

> In the bluebell rushes
> There is no birdies
> And only bluebells grow everywhere around
> Any trees you can see and pears fallen
> And you eat coconuts.

Pandering to this obsession with coconut islands, we thoughtfully buried a couple on the shingle beach at Skomer and let them be discovered, cracked open, and shared around: mainly with the seagulls, because it must be said that any coconut which has found its way to Tesco's of Penzance, and then lived in the bottom of a boat for a fortnight, tends to be a little dry in texture.

That night the Manx shearwaters kept us awake with their rowdy shift-change routine. One parent keeps watch over the eggs in the burrows by night and the other by day; at dusk they march in and out with great commotion. Like the puffins, they wander far and wide all winter before converging on a few rock islands like this for the breeding season: one quarter of all the world's Manx shearwaters breed on Skomer or its neighbour Skokholm. When I looked out of our rolling boat across the anchorage, under the coin-bright moon, the racket made this astonishing statistic seem perfectly likely. Most of the shearwaters opt for Skomer, because of the rats left over on Skokholm from wrecked ships. In the morning we woke to find the jolly puffins diving and swimming around the boat again, catching their morning feed before going back to their land burrows. If there is one nail still to be hammered in the coffin of E. E. Middleton's reputation, it is for me the fact that this dreary man hated puffins:

These pugnacious, pompous, stupid, selfish, brutally-quarrelsome, dirty little birds command the whole cliff above the North and South Havens.

He wasn't much of a conservationist either. About seabirds in general, he wrote:

It is argued that the birds are being exterminated, because fewer than usual flock to our shores. This argument is not sound without its complement, namely, that the total number of sea-birds is lessened throughout the world. It is possible that, like human beings, they may relish new habitations.

I like the idea of restless dilettante guillemots and puffins, forever seeking out fashionable new rocks to nest upon; but I cannot swallow his insult to puffins.

Janet left us that day, hitching a ride on the tripper-boat to the mainland, and we hauled up the sails for the ten miles to Solva. Oddly enough, now that we were no longer beleaguered on every side by Heritage Exhibitions and Smuggling Museums, a real sense of history pressed in hard upon us on every side: the Viking names of the islands and of Solva, the prehistoric farm borders still visible on Skomer, the holy places of St David's lying ahead of us in the morning sunlight, all became as significant as wind and tide. Belloc sailed these waters, and made them known in the classic *Cruise of the Nona*; I read him again in St Bride's Bay with the usual mixture of exasperation and worship, and read, too, Jonathan Raban, his perceptive critic and modern-day counterweight on the left. Reading both, while crossing the same waters, I realized I would never make a political philosopher. Try as I will, I have never been able to draw any political or moral message from sailing the coast other than a sense that mankind is a very small thing and his spirit illimitably great – a vague enough philosophy, of no harm to anyone, and suitable for putting in pokerwork or on a sampler in the most timid of drawing-rooms.

It is nothing to do with the female sex. Paul will never make a seagoing political philosopher either: his current reading was a perfectly dreadful little book he found in a shop in Tenby called *Comfort in Small Crafts*, published in 1925 by a Norfolk Broads' yachtsman called S. J. Housley. He is full of pompous phrases – 'The rivers of Norfolk are a judicious schoolmaster'; 'Rome was not built in a day, nor is seamanship to be learned in a month'. Most of the book deals with furling, lacing, parcelling, and doing seaman-like things in manly inverted-commas up on the deck, and maintaining cleanliness below:

'Wood-work and brass-work' being finished, you may call 'spell-oh', rig up a pipe and remark that 'this is a long ship'. The satisfaction of having your ship really clean, like the satisfaction of being well dressed, confers a spiritual calm beyond the power even of religion to bestow.

Hilaire Belloc kept a very untidy ship, on his own admission; perhaps that is why he had so much time to inveigh against parliamentarians. Certainly Housley has no time for gloomy Bellocian political philosophy because he is too anxiously concerned with doing the correct thing and imparting good domestic practice to his presumably helpless bachelor readership. Half a page is devoted to the art of tucking in one's blankets correctly; a full page to frying an egg:

Break the eggs. Take a teacup, crack the shell boldly but neatly on the edge of the cup, open the two halves of the shell, and let the contents drop into the cup without breaking the yolk . . .

Under the page-heading DILUTING MILK he deals with how to dilute milk for coffee; after various digressions (quite interesting, today) on how to devil eels correctly he delivers a brief, stern sermon on how to wash up:

The 'crew' should 'stand by' with the drying and polishing cloths to complete your work. If after a day or two you find your drying cloth becomes greasy, the washing has not been done thoroughly and the washer requires to be severely reprimanded. Wash the plates, knives, forks etc. *one by one*. Never put them into the wash-bowl all together as is the custom of shore folk . . .

And so on, to the final instruction as to how to hang out the teacloths to dry.

Paul was quite spellbound by this book. I think it brought on a wistful sense of how much better things used to be in the days when a gentleman was not expected, in the ordinary course of things, to know how to make his own coffee, let alone his children's supper. He had been doing marvels in his role as chief cook, but the shine was wearing off it by now.

We had a good reason for going to Solva rather than pressing on round to Fishguard and dismissing St Bride's Bay as just so much pretty coastal scenery: two years before, on a flotilla holiday in Greece, we had frequently found ourselves rafted up next to an amiable party of retired people from Wales. Paul had taken a particular shine to one Richmond, an ex-RAF pilot complete with bristling moustache, who had a fine line in descriptive melodrama. 'Well, I hauled on that anchor, boy,' he would say in his drawling Oxfordshire accent, 'and damme, the sun went black, the sky went purple, I could hear bells ringing, the whole of my life flashed by . . .' All we knew about Richmond was that he sailed his small boat out of Solva in Wales. We made an exploratory phone call to the harbourmaster there, and found ourselves rerouted to the club secretary (we discovered later that the harbourmaster's dog had just been squashed by a JCB and he had been sent on a fortnight's sabbatical to get over it). The secretary revealed that 'Yes, indeed, my goodness, we all know Richmond,' and we promptly rang him and revealed ourselves, unexpected invaders from the sea.

Solva creek is a small narrow fjord, thoughtfully blocked by nature with a black rock called Black Rock, making it safer against swell. We crept in slowly, the echo-sounder bleeping in alarm although it was barely an hour to high water. A man in an angling boat looked at us curiously as we crept up the right-hand side, then shouted: 'The river is actually over here!' We moved sheepishly off the sandbank we had been scraping over (there is no chart of Solva harbour) and made towards the high stone quay. Willing, inquisitive hands took our ropes: heads peered down at us from stony heights overhead. Within ten minutes we had learned that the Solva Boatowners run the harbour co-operatively, hiring their own harbourmaster, Sharkey Phillips, but that he was away because his dog . . . (we knew that bit); that constant improvements are being planned, but that there is currently no perch or marker on the confusing outer rocks because Sharkey's son (or it could have been someone else's son) had 'gone off to the Cayman Islands with the cement-mixer'. We also learned that the cascading torrent of water which flowed from an outfall pipe just astern of us was not, as one might fear, sewage; but a mountain stream so pure that 'the home-brew boys come especially to collect it'. Then Richmond appeared, with the other couple from their flotilla boat, Ray and Rose; without their Greek suntans, but full of the vigour of the healthy retired British middle-classes, that energy which makes their languid children feel so tired. They gave us baths and came aboard for a drink. Certain quantities of whisky later, we had learned much of Solva: of the beauties of St Bride's and the fearful treachery of the currents in Ramsey Sound to the north of us, of the lost trading history of the place, which used to be the sole source of many commodities ('Even Marmite, damme') for the roadless St David's peninsula; of the convenient system by which small yachts are laid up for the winter by the resourceful Solva Boatowners Association ('We pick them up in the bucket of the JCB at low tide, and dump them in the car park'). So determinedly does the tide go out of Solva harbour, indeed, that children can stroll across the river ankle deep, under the keels of biggish boats, catching crablings and shrimps in mid-channel. We learned about the Solva dolphin, recently dead, which for two-and-a-half years lived in the great sea caves at the entrance and allowed swimmers to ride on his back; and of the ships which used to dock here in their dozens, bringing limestone to be burned in the village's kilns for fertilizer, and taking granite for building the Smalls lighthouse. We heard of various denizens of the place, of Sharkey himself and his late dog, and of St David's mother whose ruined house is preserved on a field to the west. Above all we heard tales of Richmond's great exploits out lobster-potting in the dangerous Ramsey Sound. 'Last year I caught . . . one . . . lobster. A good one.' Stress was laid repeatedly on the hazards of the rocky narrow passage between Ramsey Island and the mainland, and once or twice Richmond nobly swore that 'I'd take you through myself and be happier about it.' We exchanged glances, and took the hint. Solemnly, away from the womenfolk, Richmond and Paul walked off down the quay. When they returned I was told that we would depart as soon as we got afloat the next day, Richmond shipping with us as pilot; and that Richmond should bring his own personal chart, dividers, and pencil. 'I am prepared,' he said with dignity, 'to Sign the Log.' While they were away I heard how Peggy, his wife, Solva born and bred, had captured this wonderful man during the war. He was sent to rest from active RAF flying service; he came to Wales expecting slagheaps and grey-faced, grim-hearted Nonconformist mining folk; he found the gay blue waters of St Bride's Bay, Solva, and Peggy. He stayed.

The children and I spent the morning catching tiny fish and crabs in the streamlet which yesterday had floated the majestic form of *Grace O'Malley*; Rose having wet her bed in the night, I amused the locals by availing myself of the sluicing harbour stream to rinse it out, and hung duvet cover and sheet defiantly along our mooring-lines. I have developed a duvet-cover-corner-laundry-hitch which would have delighted Mr Housley in its unnecessary complexity. Richmond and Paul, lost in their formal naval dreams of pilotage and flat hats, looked faintly disapproving on returning to find the boat looking like a giant maritime Scotch Airer, so I took it all down again.

With a scrape and a heave the boat lifted herself from the sand at two thrity, and Richmond took the helm as we chugged out to face the dreaded Sound. I had enjoyed Solva, although it had not felt very Welsh to me; it suffers from the phenomenon – only too familiar from Ireland and Cornwall – that all the best and most lucrative shops and businesses are now run by somewhat hard-faced English people with accents no farther west than the Fulham Road. But the natives like Peggy and the long-term incomers like Richmond seemed in perfectly affable harmony with the regular weekenders and immigrants from England. 'Ah yes,' they said of one man. 'That'd be Dai Photograph. Down from London already, is he? Dai Photograph, we call him, yes, he works for Reuters . . .' I hoped that not too many Dai Property-Developers and Dai Estate-Agents got their claws into the St David's peninsula too soon. It has the advantage of being too remote to be any big city's playground; farther north, we were to find the Lleyn peninsula crammed with Mancunian caravanners and the sort of men who smoke cigars in speedboats.

The sun shone on our passage. Ramsey Sound produced a few little whirlpools to justify Richmond's status as pilot, and he took us through it with an expert caution – 'It might just be that I am a fusspot' – and a wealth of esoteric local information – about farms, chapels, rocks, and precisely where some famous local yacht had been lost with all hands (there was a slight touch of the *Cold Comfort Farm* brand of local knowledge here). But Richmond had, we found, certain set-piece tales which remained with us. The best was the one about the lifeboat wreck: 'And one of the crew turned to the coxswain and said – and this was told by a survivor – he said, "You've turned too soon, skipper. You've put us on the Bitches! You'll find our bodies washed up on such-and-such a beach, at nine o'clock tomorrow morning." That was how well he knew the way of the tide. And sure enough, the boat was wrecked, and the man's body came up at nine the next morning on the very beach . . .'

For the rest of the trip, every tricky bit of pilotage was accompanied by one or other of us crying, 'You've turned too soon, skipper. You've put us on the Bitches!' Richmond had never sailed with a topsail up before, so with repeated cursing (something was going very wrong with our tangle of lines around this troublesome white triangle) we got it set for him. Happy as a grig, his moustache bristling with satisfaction, our pilot steered us on fast and lively around St David's lofty cliffs, and east for Fishguard harbour.

Here we met a man in the yacht club bar who had just come through the Ramsey Sound using nothing but an Ordnance Survey map. We left Richmond at his side, trying to convert him to a proper sense of danger.

10

In Fishguard the weather closed down on us. All night the wind rose from the south-east, howling in the rigging, groaning and rattling every loose object, and slapping the sides of the boat with angry wavelets. Caught by the wind, the boat's bow would sail off first to one side, then the other, being brought up with a metallic jerk by the anchor-chain. When we woke up, the rain was lashing down without a pause, so thick in the air that we could barely see the pierhead a few hundred yards away; it never stopped raining for one minute until after dark. It was too rough and windy to risk taking the children ashore in the rubber dinghy, so in the morning, Paul went alone to shop and to see whether some radio parts had arrived poste-restante. (Objects were still following us hopefully around the country. The only eventual failure was my replacement spare left contact lens, which travelled to Falmouth, on to Solva, and eventually got back to Suffolk in August.) The children did a session of schoolwork with me. This was meeting with some resistance by now, especially from Nicholas. Eventually I found that his trouble was a sad and simple one: the sight of his familiar Infant Mathematics workbooks reminded him too much of his friends at school and the life he was missing. We did some adding-up on plain paper instead, and hurried over the ritual reading about Jennifer Yellow-Hat, Ramu and Sita, and the other multicultural figures of the reading scheme. It all seemed rather pointless, even to me, here in the middle of bleak Fishguard harbour in the wind and rain.

Paul returned, wetter than I would have dreamed it possible for one man to be. We whiled away the time trying to phrase a social worker's report on our circumstances. 'Family of four . . . living space no more than twelve feet by eight . . . no opportunity to go outside, no garden . . . primitive sanitation appears to open on to eating area . . . family sleeps, cooks and eats in one small space . . . only flimsy curtains between children's and parents' sleeping-quarters . . . inevitable tensions within the family unit and clear signs of aggression . . .' Rose was weeping silently into a cushion because Daddy had, quite rightly, shouted at her for drawing on the walls; Nicholas was hitting his toy otter in equal rage because he dared not hit me again. We wondered whether we should give ourselves up to the authorities and hope to be rehoused. The temptation to pile into the dinghy and make for shore was great, but more yachtsmen drown from their dinghies than at sea, and conditions in the open stretch of water between us and the inner pier were very wild by now. At teatime Paul urged that we should get the anchor up and go in close alongside to dry out against the quay; I was lethargic, nervous, and opposed the idea on the grounds that we were at least safe on our anchor, although thoroughly fed-up and rather too close to the sewer outfall. But Paul was right: in the end I agreed, and we nosed in alongside the little boat belonging to Tony the singlehander, the very man who had so shocked Richmond by coming through the Ramsey Sound with an Ordnance Survey map.

'Fishguard Bay,' said Frank Cowper a century ago, before the Irish ferry service, 'is one of the prettiest nooks I know.' Looking around the Cwm, or Lower Fishguard village, even through the curtain of rain we could see why: guarded by green and graceful hills, the little houses run casually up from the stone harbour in unforcedly picturesque style. Nobody has 'discovered' it too enthusiastically yet, except for the damp stalwarts of the Fishguard Bay Sailing Club. This institution was in the middle of a big dinghy racing weekend, and we hoped for little from it. Dinghy racing clubs on the South Coast are often bored and contemptuous of cruising yachtsmen. But up here, a yacht was an interesting event, a yacht with tiny, soaking children on board even more so; the club made us warmingly welcome. Hardly had we squelched inside its slightly dilapidated building on the quay to make a telephone call than we were led to the bar and offered baths in a private house for the children. We had actually been offered the baths the night before when we brought Richmond ashore, by a lady with upswept grey hair called Mrs Chapman: 'Drop in any time, we're just up the hill,' she said largely, waving a glass. We have learned not to take too seriously any offers made in a yacht club bar after 9 p.m., but we misjudged her: she reiterated the offer now, with the information that clean towels were laid out waiting, and that her husband would give us some bubble-bath. We squelched up the street, speechless with gratitude, and I gave the children a hot, wonderful bath and had one myself. Mr Chapman – in the middle of decorating his front room – paused to bring tea and orange-squash to us and leave it by the door. Nicholas and Rose repeated wonderingly, 'Isn't that kind . . . aren't they kind to let us have a bath, Mummy . . . I was so wet and sad and they let us have a hot bath. And orange squash. Isn't Mr and Mrs Chapman *kind*?' I reflected that if they were learning nothing else from this attempt to sail round Britain, they were learning one useful lesson for privileged middle-class brats. They were discovering what it was to be a vagrant, an immigrant, a petitioner at the mercy of charitable impulses. A few days earlier we had actually had to knock on a cottage door in Lawrenny asking for a glass of water for Rose. Nicholas was asking a lot of questions about beggar children, little matchgirls, and wandering minstrels; I made the connection, all right, and did not regret the lessons that were subliminally sinking in.

Tony the singlehander was bound round Britain as well, from Rochester. We lured him aboard for supper and compared harbours visited so far. Only two out of our twenty ports and anchorages were the same as his. Clearly it would be quite possible to do the trip round again and never repeat a thing. He had been reading E. E. Middleton and McMullen and Belloc and Jonathan Raban too, and we discussed the problem of lone sailors tending to come back from the tempests and the tides as prophets of the extreme Right. 'I can see why,' said Tony, blinking nervously (he was a diffident man). 'You sort of think, Well, if I can face those conditions out there, then everyone else ought to pull themselves together too and not need propping up with welfare. But then . . .' He looked even more worried. 'I suppose I don't actually want everyone going out to sea, because it'd be chaos.' We decided that there, indeed, were all the ingredients of a Fascist philosophy: pride in the elite, impatience with the weak, conviction that the weak are always with us and need keeping in their place.

We drank a lot of wine in the attempt to solve this problem, which made us rather less fit to solve a more practical one at 1.30 a.m. when our port leg began to creak horribly. In Charlestown, where the tide had gone down smoothly, the frightful noises of the leg in the night had been brief. Here, with a considerable swell from the wind outside, and almost enough water to float us during the lowest two hours of the tide, the dreadful creaking and tearing sounds through the hull never stopped at all and began to drive us out of our minds. Rose wept as she slept, hands pressed to her ears; Nicholas moaned; I comforted each in turn, and Paul set out into the falling rain, spanner in hand, to try and take the blasted thing right off. The mud was soft enough to sink into, and anyway after half an hour of creaking we had decided we would rather fall over sideways than put up with any more of it. After much clanging and grunting, blessed silence fell. 'Daddy made it better,' said Rose with serene faith. 'I love Daddy' – and she was asleep.

Half a wine-box and a bad night are not the best foundation for a seventy-mile passage across exposed water. But a south wind was what we needed to cross Cardigan Bay, that wide shallow divide between North and South Wales, and if we were to make it through the critical tidal 'gate' of Bardsey Island, we had to leave not long after ten. The children went on strike: they wanted to see nice Mrs Chapman again. They had fallen in love with Fishguard; the post office had made a fuss of them, the yacht club had pinned their drawings up on the board and let them run to and from the kitchen to the bar even in the midst of its preparations for a holiday weekend dinner. Rose, days later, made me write in her scrapbook the legend, MRS CHAPMAN LET US WATCH HER COUNT POTATOES. It was as much of a highlight as any outing or castle we had produced for them so far. Despite the lashing rain and the lack of a beach, they loved Fishguard dearly. And now we were taking them away at ten in the morning, before the club even opened. Like two sad little barflies, they gazed back at it and moaned.

We had to go, though: we were driven. This southerly weather would most likely be replaced by equally unsettled westerly, then northerly winds as the depression which had been plaguing us for a week moved across the Irish Sea. We could not stay in Fishguard in a strong northerly anyway, without great discomfort and some danger. If we were caught out in Cardigan Bay in a gale from the north, we might even be forced back round St David's Head and into Milford Haven, losing fifty miles' northward progress. But if we went now, out into the horrid rainy morning and the uneasy, sickening swell left by yesterday's wind, we could be in Caernarfon within twenty-four hours, and set for some gentle cruising inside the Menai Strait. We had to go.

A wet day and a following sea are bad conditions for seasick children. Below decks it was dry but nauseating; in the cockpit, fresh air abounded but they got soaked. Both children, with pills inside them, sat up on deck in their diminutive yellow oilskins and reached that terrible state in which one longs to be sick but can't. So did I. Paul stayed at the helm, fiddling with the autopilot, under an unwritten family law which says that since he is the most prone to seasickness of us all he is excused babycare in rough weather at sea. So, pea-green, I read my way solidly through the adventures of Peter Rabbit, the Flopsy Bunnies, and the Tailor of Gloucester, while the children concentrated with that terrible, grim, unfocused stare of people who are trying not to vomit. Still fell the rain. The wind fluked up and down, so my reading was periodically interrupted by visits to the mast to take reefs in and out: we dared not slow down too much in case we missed the fair tide round Bardsey and hung there for four or five hours in awful seas.

When the rain stopped, Paul slept for an hour while I steered and told the children all the Welsh stories I could remember, in order to avoid reading any more about the Flopsy Bunnies. They were much struck by the gallant Minstrel Boy who took his harp to the wars to cheer up the soldiers, and made me sing the song eight or nine times, not an easy feat when I was still queasy (high C is no joke in a high sea). Then I slept in turn, and woke to find everything much better. The sea had flattened, the sun was out, and Paul and Nicholas had baked a fruit loaf. We ended up motoring for five hours, around Bardsey and along the northern shore of the Lleyn peninsula, in high family spirits. Paul and I sat together at the helm with a poetry book singing 'The Road to Mandalay', then I read the whole of *The Inchcape Rock*, and most of Jean Ingelow's *High Tide on the Coast of Lincolnshire, 1571* ('Cusha, cusha, cusha calling / Ere the early dews were falling') to a wary but interested small audience. The light along these western mountain shores is stunning: one island, one holy peak, one shaft of cliff-face, will suddenly be gilded while the rest lie shadowed in cloud: green and black, grey and blue, pale mountain-top and speckle of white cottages are picked out in turn; distant crosses, castles, lighthouses rise against the troubled sky. Too late, I remembered that I had forgotten to salute Sarn Padraig to the east of us, St Patrick's causeway, whose tolling bell-buoy set Belloc off on a magnificent train of thought about the mysterious reef that bisects Cardigan Bay; the lost path, to him, of religious unity:

The bell thus swinging on its buoy far out to sea, swings on the western edge of that strange, long undersea road which they call the 'Sarn Badrig', which means the Causeway of St Patrick, and cannot but awake the great story of the coming of Europe to Ireland.

How right they were to call that sunken ridge pointing straight to Ireland 'the Roman Road of Patrick!' And how its sudden cessation symbolizes the break, the wound, the rupture, by which this island was cut off from that: more than two hundred years ago. The ridge ends suddenly in deep water and continues no more. But the bell tolls on, appealing.

But on reflection, with the last of my queasiness leaving me, I came to the ungraceful conclusion that all these Bellocs and Middletons and Rabans who wove political philosophies from their cruising might not have done so if they had had to sing 'The Minstrel Boy' twenty-two times in one afternoon, wrestle children into pyjamas, find teddies, and clean small sharp white teeth in a rolling sea. I had had to do all this against the clock in order to get the family settled before we hit the Bardsey overfalls. Let these philosophers and heroes, let Ridgway and Knox-Johnston, Clare Francis and Moitessier, do their voyages again, I muttered, only this time with two toddlers! Let Belloc toll his great prose bell after a hard morning of Peter Rabbit! We rounded Bardsey Island at the last lonely tip of North Wales, near enough to see the birds in the bracken; and turned north-eastward.

We dropped our anchor by moonlight under the headland of Trwyn Porth Dinllaen, a freak headland on the smooth northern face of the Lleyn peninsula. We thought we would go to Caernarfon in the morning, but saw such a nice-looking sandy beach that we decided to give the children the day off to compensate for leaving Fishguard. While they dug and threw balls and revelled in the childish world of sand, I walked along the beach: minute by minute, curious figures advanced towards me, like pilgrims of old bound for Bardsey, with votive offerings burdening them down as they struggled over the rocky beach: surfboards, windsurfers, folding catamarans, wet-suits, kayaks. Of course: Spring Bank Holiday Monday. North Wales, unlike peaceful St Bride's Bay, is the playground of Liverpool and Manchester. By noon the beach was convivially packed, despite the half-mile walk from the nearest public car park, and in the pub men in dark, dark glasses (despite the gloom) were talking loudly about being 'Off to Dallas and NY next week – away two weeks in four last year – export really booming . . . fifty-K contract . . .' Outside in the watery sunshine anoraks and Barbours, beach stripes and trainers and tattered jeans milled around, and the usual extraordinary spectacle was to be seen as it is everywhere north of Bristol: of little girls coming down to the beach in white socks and white sandals, not taking off either but sitting primly, pale-footed on the sand. Why white socks? What is this fetish about clean feet for females? What awful damage are they doing their psyches by not running and feeling the sand between their toes like their brothers do? Will they grow up into those women – also rather in evidence at Porth Dinllaen – who tittup across rocky sands in high-heeled strappy sandals? My own filthy little mudlarks stripped down to their multicoloured knickers and waded around, only sometimes needing to be scooped from under the wheels of four-wheel-drive fun jeeps and Range Rovers which criss-crossed the firm sands hauling speedboats to the water for privileged beach-front houseowners. 'Got the Jag up at the car park,' said the driver of one. 'Sandra ran me round in her Suzuki.'

I wandered up the beach. Morfa Nefyn and Nefyn itself, praised in our 1970s guidebook as typical Welsh villages, had grown and conglomerated together. There was some evidence of workshops aided by development grants, but rather more invasive evidence of chalets and holiday bungalows. I suppose there is no democratic reason why such seaside paradises should not be aspired to; but the heart still sinks at the heartless, centreless, half-year-empty villages they create. Maybe Nefynians have some reasonable life of their own – sheep grazed there, a school window showed the silhouettes of cutout lambs – but it cannot be the same as if the visitors did not own locked, dead houses on their green land. But holidays rule: I discovered, back on the beach, precisely the meteorological reason why Nefyn and Porth Dinllaen were crowded today. 'If it's raining in Abersoch,' (the other side of the peninsula) said a man, 'it generally isn't here. And vice versa.' 'My auntie in Abersoch,' volunteered a Mancunian, 'usually rings me to say which, early on a Bank Holiday morning.' 'If you want to get away from this lot,' said a more thoughtful type from Chester, 'climb up a couple of thousand feet to the Iron Age fortifications.' Still, a more dramatic fate could have befallen Porth Dinllaen: it could have become Holyhead. In 1804 a company was formed, and in 1806 a Parliamentary Bill brought forward, which would have made it the packet port for Ireland. Holyhead won the battle, and in 1837 it won the railway, too; the herring-fleet left when the herring vanished, and Porth Dinllaen was left to dwindle slowly into a row of holiday cottages and a golf club. We had seen the golf course from the sea, high on the headland; the sea-bed hereabouts must be paved with lost golfballs.

The afternoon turned dramatic on us. Paul rowed back to the boat, and just as I was beginning to feel like another hot, lazy beach Mummy with my legs turning brown, we noticed *Grace O'Malley* moving from her anchorage. Odd: I could see no reason. The water was a bit ruffled out there, but so still and hot was the beach that it was impossible to believe in any wind. Shortly he re-anchored closer to the shore and rowed to the beach wearing a life-jacket. 'Quick! Get those children!' Paul was shaking, with sheer reaction to effort and apprehension. I dragged the dinghy as far upwind along the beach as possible while he explained that the wind was getting up rapidly, the forecast was strong, the new anchorage not very secure, and that he had nearly been flipped over in the dinghy while trying to restart the outboard engine. Certainly, once we were out of the immediate shelter of the beach, dinghy conditions were not pleasant; we rowed out with some difficulty, and got the family together again on board. The wind by now was howling nastily. The forecast was for south-westerlies, up to Force Seven: too strong for a stranger to risk an approach at dusk to the narrow winding channel which leads over the shallows of the Caernarfon Bar. We would have to stay the night, at least. At one stage I went on deck to let out more anchor chain, when a gust caught the boat with its full weight on the bow: the chain flowed suddenly through my scorched fingers like a hot metal river, and I could barely get a turn of it around the windlass. 'See what it was like?' said Paul. 'Getting it out alone? Do you wonder why I wanted everyone on board?' The problems of being short-handed in a heavy boat were borne in upon us: there was no need for the children to have been whisked off the beach, except that both their parents, their sole minders, were necessary to control the boat even at anchor. We set them to doing jigsaws, and made a call to the London Weather Centre who faithfully promised no northerlies yet. (They did not really believe that our southerly wind had got up so strong, so fast, either; saying rather crossly that it must be associated with a rain-squall. When we said that the sun was shining, a perceptible sniff came over the line.)

Paul invented a sausage casserole to keep his spirits up, and made the children a disgusting packet mousse. 'Poor little things,' he said. 'They've been so good lately, I think they deserve some E433 and anodized aluminium glutamate, or whatever.' He ate some too, and I could not go downwind of any of them for hours: they smelt of school dinners. Eventually, with the wind tugging us against our anchor, we settled for the night under the great Lleyn peninsula, its Iron Age ghosts returning in the mist. The holiday shore lost its colours in the dusk, and became a mere beach under an ancient cliff; I shivered a little, and hoped fervently for a dawn lull in the wind to see us safely into Caernarfon. I did not want to be in this open anchorage any longer: I wanted a town, the shelter of castle walls, and the motherly bulk of Anglesey to keep the coming west winds out.

11

It was a pitch-black, moonless night. A single beach-house light twinkled through the drifting rain, and the wind rose. It whistled through the hills, rattled round the mast and made the boat snatch and rear viciously as she fought the short, rippling waves; loud clunks came from the anchor-chain at every snub. Worse, the wind veered: the southerly wind which had made the whole of Caernarfon Bay into a flat, sheltered lee was now a south-westerly, ripping along the coast and blowing – a glance at the chart concluded – straight on to the Caernarfon Bar.

We sail the east coast of England; we are used to tidal bars. There is nothing essentially alarming about a wall of sand over which you must wait for sufficient water to cross. But Caernarfon Bar is the only southern entrance to twenty miles of narrow, churning strait between Anglesey and the mainland. Its narrows are not fixed by rocks, but defined by mobile sandbanks; Frank Cowper had gone aground there and observed that the sands moved so often that 'buoyage could be of no earthly use in such a place'. Every pilot-book aboard warned graphically and specifically of the perils of the entrance, the gloomy Mr Kemp saying, 'It is important not to be trapped into this NE angle of Caernarfon Bay only to be faced with an impassable bar.' The topography of the area is that of a delta, set up by the harsh scour of the ebb-tide coming out of the straits into St George's Channel: in other words, we were about to sail up an ever-narrowing funnel, towards a crooked shallow passage, with a very fresh south-westerly wind behind us. We were going to thread a needle, at speed, and without much option of changing our mind. The chain clanked on, and Paul and I lay sleepless in our bunks, trying to reason ourselves out of our nervous fears.

At 1.30 a.m. the anchor made that peculiar, whisperingly metallic sound, a grinding and muttering, which means only one thing. I had sunk into half-sleep, and said, 'What does that sound like to you?' Paul was already in his boots and trousers. 'Dragging,' he said. 'Of course.' I admitted it, and together we groped on to the deck and felt the tension of the chain over the bows. It was leaping and loosening: our anchor must be moving stealthily across the sea-bed with every gust, leaving us bound sternways towards heaven knew where. Cursing, we winched the cold chain up and eventually got our anchor in view: it was draped in four times its own volume of green slimy kelp. It was a wonder it had lasted so long in that wind. Paul motored the boat around the anchorage in gusty rain, while I lunged furiously with the boathook to knock off the bundles of weed from the anchor; five minutes later we dropped it again much further from the shore, and were rewarded by a sickening rolling swell which poured around the headland and rocked and rattled us into fitful sleep again.

I am not abnormally nervous and not particularly brave. Once during every cruise that I can remember I have had a night of real, hopeless, despicable funk. I have trembled and sweated in mid-Atlantic, simply because there seemed more miles of emptiness below, behind, and ahead of me than I could emotionally accept. I have lain rigid in an icy sleeping-bag listening to the wind keening across a deserted Irish anchorage, and wished that the boat would be driven ashore and wrecked, and us saved, so that I could go home on a nice big ferry. These fears generally evaporate with morning, activity, and the need to do prosaic and familiar jobs like raising the sails; but while they last they are a torment of hell. All that night I drifted in and out of nightmare, thinking of Caernarfon Bar. I saw great surf waves, buoys vanishing, buoys mistaken, ourselves pounding to pieces on banks far out from shore. Once I fell asleep and blissfully dreamed that I had gone in across the Bar to do some shopping, with the boat in my handbag, and was about to take it out and wake Paul to tell him all was well. Then I woke, and we were still in Porth Dinllaen, still rolling, the wind still shaking our mast mockingly as it tore on its way to push more walls of white water up against the sands of the Menai Strait. Again and again the poem 'Crossing the Bar' unrolled itself in my head like a song-sheet:

> May there be no moaning of the bar
> When I put out to sea

I moaned, and tried to settle in my narrow bunk, on my hard mouldy-smelling pillow.

> Twilight and evening bell
> And after that the dark!

I wondered whether I had put the Kendal Mint Cake into the liferaft survival canister, for the children. I wondered what happened when a liferaft was thrown by a white wave on to a hard shore. The poem came back, infuriating me as usual with its conclusion:

> . . . I hope to see my Pilot face to face
> When I have crost the Bar.

Mercifully, irritation at a poor metaphor jolted me out of my terror: because surely you *drop* your pilot, not see him face to face, when you have crossed the bar going outwards? And the speaker must be going outwards, because he says 'when I embark', to rhyme with 'dark'? I tossed, turned, rolled uncomfortably against the taut canvas lee-cloth, longing for a real bed.

That night I was sick of the wind, sick of the voyage, sick of the boat and the whole damned idea of sailing round this treacherous, unforgiving, inconvenient coast which traps you up bays and then shrieks at you. I awoke weary and unrefreshed. The children slept on while Paul and I clumsily made sail and crept out of the dubious shelter of Porth Dinllaen towards God knew what fate.

Funk, funk, melodramatic funk. For one thing, we could perfectly well have hauled the sails in and got round to perfect safety in Holyhead, almost up to the last minute; for another, Dinllaen turned out to have been one of those curious wind-holes, harbours in which the distant wind sounds far worse than it actually is. Outside, things were not too bad. With our craven double-reef in the mainsail we slipped along in moderate, gently rolling seas at five knots with no cause for panic whatever. The children woke up feeling cross and a little queasy, and were pacified; we saw a gleam of sun, and cheered up. Eventually, after some miles of heading towards an apparently solid coastline, we found the first Bar buoy and made for it.

Caernarfon, however, did not get its reputation lightly. The No. 1 and 2 buoys gave no trouble, nor 3, 4, and 5; but when we turned down towards the Mussel Bank buoy the seas rose sharply astern of us. And ahead of us. We lost sight of the vital buoy, while all around us, on South Sands and the Mussel Bank, we saw breaking white water and – disconcertingly – the mast of a wrecked fishing-boat rising from the spume. Mercifully, the buoy reappeared behind a wave-crest ahead. Faster and faster we surfed towards Abermenai Point; the tide was about to turn against us, so we used the engine and blessed once again the day at the London Boat Show when I had accosted the designer, Roger Dongray, and asked him precisely how much speed under sail we might lose if we replaced the two-bladed propeller with a three-bladed version. Roger, a racing type himself, sucked air through his teeth and said portentously that we might lose an eighth, even a quarter, of a knot because of the extra drag; thanking him effusively, I rushed up the stairs and entered into negotiations with propeller manufacturers without delay. The loss of a fraction of sailing speed, as against double efficiency of the engine, was not a difficult decision to make with small children in the crew. As the new propeller pushed us efficiently towards the point, the last night's horrors suddenly seemed less irrational: one false move here and we really would be rolled and bounced among these whitecaps and on to the hard, ribbed, sandbanks around.

Suddenly, with one last wild roll and a loud complaint from Rose who was clutching round my neck like the old man of the sea, we slid into flat poppling water; we were still gripped by the curious swirling tides, but upright again and breathing freely. Paul, who had been on the helm for the last part of the bar, wiped his brow rather shakily. Beautiful Anglesey dunes lay on our left, high Wales on our right, and we had crost the Bar. Half an hour later we turned towards Caernarfon's castle: it was a strange medieval moment, with the grey walls rising triumphantly ahead, and Paul poised with the brass trumpet at his lips like Triton about to blow his wreathéd horn. One blast on the foghorn is the signal for the swing-bridge to be opened, but we had been watched; the bridgemaster opened it before we could blow, and with a seductive smell of chips floating across the deck, the castle flags fluttering overhead and the gulls shrieking our arrival to the skies, we tied up alongside the town quay. There were one or two fences to mend, small apologies to make for any harsh words which might have been exchanged during the period when the sail got stuck aloft just off buoy No. 10 and abreast of the sandbanks. 'My fault . . . should have reminded you about the topsail-sheet being jammed under the liferaft to stop it flapping . . . no, no, I should have checked . . .' The children saw little point in any of this, rightly, so we dressed them up tidy and went ashore for fish and chips.

Frank Cowper put his finger on the oddity of Caernarfon Castle:

Somehow, to me, the castle was disappointing. I now know why. The grouping and proportions of its three towers have been copied in all the modern stucco castles which are to be found in the suburbs of almost every large town. I even seemed to recollect Jack Straw's Castle. Instead of living up to the age of the great Edward, I meandered down to the level of the successful shopkeeper who is determined to live in baronial 'alls, and have two lodges one hundred yards from his feudal fortress, defended by towers à la Carnarvon.

Gazing up at the grey walls above our mast, I shared his faint sense of let-down. It is a huge, seven hundred-year-old cardboard fort; a great big cliché. The disappointment is compounded by the fact that it lies entirely in the blasé, ungrateful, spoiled eye of the modern beholder. As with oaken beams, diamond windowpanes and gothic lettering, we have ruined castles for ourselves. The only comfort was that even in the 1880s the process had begun; and the only counterweight was to share the children's vision of it. They did not care a fig about Jack Straw or architectural snobberies; they thought it the finest thing on earth to be tied up next to a great castle, and crept persistently from their bunks in the evening to gaze at it under the floodlights.

After ten minutes, I was hopelessly in love with the town of Caernarfon itself. For despite the castle, despite the hordes of coaches marked SUNSHINE DAYS and PLEASURAMA LTD, Caernarfon is no one's playground. Its roofscapes are dignified in blue slate; its streets have never been wrecked by town planners. Its harbour office, 1840, and its slate-merchants' offices are harbour offices and slate merchants still. Along Stryd yr Eglwys, rows of neat Bed and Breakfasts vied with one another in the freshness of their laundered tablecloths, the even stuffing of their chintz armchairs, the correctness of their VACANCIES signs. ('Competition is hot, down Church Street,' observed a drinker at the Royal Welsh Yacht Club, mildly. 'Caernarfon is the end of the line, see. We don't get so many visitors, not so as they stay all night.') The houses – Victorian, Edwardian, Georgian, modern, all blending beneath their slates, cluster amiably together around the castle. So uncorrupted by estate agents, shopping malls and 'prestige' development is Caernarfon that, at the very heart of the city and under the castle's shadow, humble washing still flaps in covered alleyways; and the young men unloading computer-paper for the bank were singing softly together in Welsh for their own enjoyment.

We were to hear many sneering remarks about Caernarfon over the next few days, from the English-bred entrepreneurs and incomers – 'End of the line . . . dirtiest town in Wales . . . bone idle, no idea of development'; but of all the places we had seen, this was a town to live in. If chance brought me to live in Caernarfon, I would not complain. The crass planners of the 1960s, the enterprise culture of the 1980s, have not been able to reach it: dignified and distinctive, Caernarfon stands at the end of its non-existent line – for British Rail closed the station decades ago – and we were the richer for seeing it.

Everywhere I walked, Welsh was spoken routinely, casually, predominantly: in the post office queues, in the cafés, among the youths and girls who loafed by the waterfront. In Pembrokeshire only Peggy Bobart had spoken Welsh, and among her imported or Anglicized neighbours was thought a bit eccentric for doing it. Caernarfon felt like a foreign city, and we were the odd ones for not speaking its language.

In love, enchanted with the dignity of the place, I wandered off in the dusk towards the Conservative Club. Here, according to a worn notice outside the post office, the Caernarfon Male Voice Choir rehearses on Tuesday nights and admits observers. Climbing the three flights of stairs I found an ugly room marked 'Churchill Hall', with an orange matchboard bar, tangerine and pallid green walls, a horrible carpet of floral squares; from here floated the sound of angels warming up. I crept cautiously in. Fifty-odd men sat in a semicircle: old men with white hair, stern middle-aged men, dry-looking men in the cast of Norman Tebbitt; young muscular louts in Lacoste sweatshirts, tweedy men with legal briefcases. They were an ill-assorted lot. But the young men were taming their macho to the softest of Alleluias, the old and weak striking in suddenly with firm basses. Overcome by female shyness, I slid behind a screen and watched covertly from an abandoned barstool. Attentive, concentrated, tender, the men sang on, pausing for brief, rapid instructions in Welsh from their conductor: they transcended maleness, transcended humanity, rocked the hideous hall with celestial harmonies.

Then came a pause for club announcements and the result of the weekly Tote Draw, and the angels began to cough, fidget, wink at me, and generally act like men at a meeting anywhere. I slipped off before the magic could fade and went back to where *Grace O'Malley* floated quietly in the floodlit castle's reflection. The tide fled silently away, downstream and down-Strait, to smash itself against the wind still blowing on the Caernarfon Bar. Safe in the twisting Seiont river, no rattle or creak disturbed our long, refreshing sleep.

12

We declared a holiday from progress. The weather was still dominated by a complex depression which had been bothering us since Fishguard: the wind rarely blew more than Force Five, but would suddenly gust up to something close to a south-westerly gale with very little warning, and might veer to the north-west at any time. There did not seem much point in setting off for the Isle of Man in such unsettled weather. Besides, some helpful people had come down and given us the key to the Royal Welsh Yacht Club, whose pleasantly run-down premises and showers were inside one of the remoter turrets of the very castle itself. Since the children's nanny Virginia had joined us for a couple of days to keep her memory green with them, Paul and I were able to haunt the club bar. Here we fell in with the young Emrys Jones, the pilot for the Straits. 'My father was fifty years a pilot, but I do it mainly now; you should have seen him, chatting away, never even looking hardly while he steered a ship under the bridges. I haven't got that calm about it yet.' Emrys and old Mr Jones ran the tripper-boat between them, supplementing a living which had become suddenly more precarious when the Shell tankers stopped berthing at Caernarfon. Slowly but surely, commercial traffic in the Menai Strait is dying away, and with it their art. Emrys, however, had a little two hundred-and-ten-foot Esso tanker in that week, and offered us a ride through the dangerous Swellies passage and under the two bridges on Friday when it left; so we had yet another incentive to stay.

The Swellies is a remarkable mile of water. The rising tide from Bangor at the Northern end of the straits comes sweeping in, and meets the incoming tide from the other end, pushed across the bar more often than not by a south-west wind. At the point where they meet, the channel narrows and is obstructed by numerous half-tide rocks; to add to the entertainment there are the narrow arches of the two great Menai bridges – Telford's and the Britannia. 'In the season,' said Emrys Jones earnestly, without relish, 'I reckon sometimes we've had one yacht a week wrecked on the Swellies.

They keep trying to go through with the full tide. You don't want to do that. It's too fast to steer. High water slack is what you want. Then you can go over most of the rocks anyway. The tide table says you'll get slack at fifteen minutes before High-Water Caernarfon, but my Dad and I, we say twenty.' He was full of such small, precious, idiosyncratic pilot's details: which eddy swirls back here, which rock covers deceptively soon, which of the guiding buoys may disconcertingly vanish at spring tides, dragged right under-water by the force of the current. We accepted with alacrity the chance he was offering us of a ride on the coaster: how better to see all these horrifying things happening for the first time than from the Olympian height of a coaster's bridge, with someone else taking all the responsibility?

Staying within the Strait, we moved *Grace O'Malley* to an old slate dock which serves as Port Dinorwic Yacht Haven. Its proprietor, Ivor Jones, bore a startling resemblance of manner to Leonard Rossiter playing Rigsby the landlord, and seemed intent on stopping any yacht from ever leaving. 'Caernarfon? Ugh, no, terrible place, you come up here to a bit of civilization. Where are you going next? Beaumaris? No, terrible anchoring, stay here and go by taxi . . .' Paul, still addicted to shopping, which he admitted was a source of emotional security, went to wander around supermarkets in Bangor, and Virginia and I took the children across to Benllech on Anglesey for some bucket-and-spading. Paul, in fact, had a curious aversion to going to any seaside resort in Wales. It sprang, he explained, from his Sheffield upbringing. 'People who had caravans in Wales,' he said, ancient class-resentments springing up, 'really reckoned they were summat. Ooh, we'd say, she's going to Rhyl. Get *her*.'

What he missed by traipsing around Bangor with his cheque-book was a piece of quintessential all-British seaside. Benllech has sand, it has rockpools, it has trampolines, ice-cream, chips, and a bouncy castle. Better still, it has donkeys: six mild-mannered, rather dopey-looking grey beasts with shining coats, owned by a wiry chap who doubles up as the Auxiliary Coastguard; every few minutes his eyes would swivel away from the ambling procession of overawed toddlers perching aboard Coco and John and Edward and the rest, to take note of some fool on a Li-lo drifting hopelessly out beyond Trwyn Du. 'Have a leaflet, boys,' he said magnani-mously to our children. Rose was generally taken for a boy in

Wales, owing to the lack of white socks and sandals. I read them the safety leaflets he gave us; Nicholas was enthralled and spent the next few days threatening everyone who crossed him: 'I'll make you swim off a headland! I'll push you into the Dangerously Strong Undertow!' In fits of five-year-old frustration, every safety warning becomes a potential new murder weapon.

While the children paddled, I walked along the wet sand and springy turf, picking my way over outcrops of sharp rocks to discover a classic patch of Hut-Land: seaside shanties, haphazardly placed on the foreshore but surrounded by intensely British pseudo-suburban landscapes. Every hut owner had built a little wall out of beach stones, created a private patio, and shielded his family with unofficial borders. Further up on the fields, nylon settlements had sprung up, this time with windbreaks and toilet-tents erected to mark the owner's boundary. I attempted the guidebook's vaunted walk across the sands to Red Scar Bay, but the tide was in, and I got my trousers very wet; then I sat on a rock and read a very funny article in the *Listener* about audience participation in TV shows and ate a bar of chocolate. I was enjoying myself exactly as I used to thirty years before, setting out with a comic and a Crunchie to sit under the old wartime pillboxes on a Suffolk beach. Sometimes, the whole point about escaping your children for a while is to be a child yourself. I jumped over one or two of the hut boundary walls feeling like Just William.

On Friday morning, the cheerful Emrys met us on the oil jetty at Caernarfon and took us aboard the *Oilman*, a 997-ton tanker on charter to Esso, fresh from discharging her smelly cargo into the storage tanks. Ships no longer come in over Caernarfon Bar, as it is too shallow: they come in from the north and go back the same way. Emrys's task was to guide Captain Mahoney through the Swellies, beneath the two bridges, and safely towards Beaumaris. Paul, whose last journalistic sortie had been the paying-off trip of HMS *Ark Royal*, was vaguely expecting a captain and mate in gold braid with highly polished shoes. He manfully disguised his shock at the appearance of Mahoney, bearing two steaming mugs and wearing a fawn anorak and grey slacks with trainers. ''Allo, Em,' he said in the unmistakable tones of Humberside. 'Tea?' The mate, Howard, appeared in baggy orange overalls, yawning. Having sailed on such a ship before, I knew that the actual seamanship of these scruffy individuals would probably outweigh that of most modern naval officers. Naturally so: the ships they serve are less well-powered, less well-equipped with instruments, and expected to run to a ruthless budget.

'There's not much work for small ships in summer. In winter, people use more oil, so we flog up and down the West Coast in all the bad weather,' said Howard. He revealed that the secret of his personal prosperity was certain undisclosed oyster-beds in the Solent region. The bridge was the usual friendly jumble of copper speaking-tubes, instruments, controls, empty mugs, dog-eared tide-tables and mildly naughty pin-ups in silk knickers; moving up the Strait towards the bridges, Emrys and the crew chattered easily of winds, buoys dragged off station, money and trade. Howard asked me to give his regards to the harbourmaster at Scrabster, but didn't know his name. 'Well, he doesn't know mine. Just say the mate of the *Oilman* sends his good wishes. We spent Christmas in the Orkneys one year, then went into Scrabster for New Year. Pheew.' Going under the Britannia Bridge, Emrys lined up the ship on a pyramid on the shore and slid through, improbably close to the bank; then he altered his course, unaccountably, to avoid some rocks lurking deep – but not deep enough – beneath the flat whirlpools of the surface. He made for Telford's bridge, a beautiful thing of brick and wire slung from one deep, wooded bank to another, and passed it without incident. The pilot boat swung alongside the coaster with a lad at the helm, we jumped down; wild tidal water churned between ship and boat, and we were clear. The *Oilman* steered off alone up the Strait towards a weekend's anchorage off Puffin Island. 'Waiting for orders. Not many jobs around in summer for them. They'll do a lot of fishing,' said Emrys. 'Don't know if we'll ever see them back, the way things are going.'

Port Dinorwic, sheltered and convenient as it was, began to oppress us. Not only does it feel odd to be in a seagoing boat locked up in a deep-sided canal-like ravine; but the whole existence of the place made it impossible to ignore the real significance of the castles on the skyline: Edward I's annexation of Wales six hundred years before. Caernarfon's pride had informed us that we were in the heart of Welsh Wales; Port Dinorwic represented something different. The marina was planned as Phase I of a £25 million development of new houses, hotels, 'prestige apartments and smart offices for solicitors, architects and insurance brokers' – all the things the area is blessedly light in – and it had run into stormy local opposition. The creeping 'yuppification', familiar to the rest of rural Britain meant here a worse thing: Anglicization. These estate agents and bistro-barmen would be, feared the locals, English speakers. This would dilute the ancient, secretive, song-filled culture of Wales, which nationalists cherish. Worse, the incomers would be richer than the natives. Reading the controversy in the local paper, seeing the MARINA NA! placards in severe little slate-roofed houses, and listening to Ivor Jones's rather impatient diatribes on the 'extremism' of certain Welsh politicians, we tried for a while to remain impartial. Passing visitors from the sea ought to be impartial, when faced with another land's political problems. But it was no good. I fell rapidly into the MARINA NA! camp.

For the Welsh battle to preserve a language is only a dramatization of the far wider, and now largely lost, battle fought in every remote proud corner of rural Britain. East Anglia's 'culture', for instance, may not have included a language; but it was a real thing, and it is dying now as the electrified railway line comes deeper and faster into the remote places, bringing people with city money – people like us, I suppose – to live there. Cornwall, the Lakes, Gloucestershire are all disfigured by the quasi-derelict, richly appointed but usually empty cottages of the Londoner; but more insidiously, they feel the slow change brought about by the incoming full-time resident. He may use the shops, even the schools; but he still has city values and a loud wife who apes the old county set and dominates the parish council within weeks. In Wales, he speaks the conquerors' language, and not the natives'; but he has more money.

And why, in common justice, should the elders of this odd, cross, withdrawn little community at Port Dinorwic become reduced to the status of some brassy matron's 'marvellous little cleaning lady' or 'super little man who does our garden'? The odds are that, by the time you read this, Caernarfon and Port Dinorwic and a dozen other settlements will have bowed to the financial odds stacked against them, and to the preferences of their own impatient teenagers; but I see no reason to abet the process. I was glad to have the luck to be only a passing sailor: yachtsmen are in a curious position, part tourist, part vagrant. No hotels shelter and protect us; no prestige developments are any use to us. Like local residents, we need proper food shops, ironmongers, tradesmen with spanners, life on the streets; we appreciate everything to an extravagant degree, because nothing adds more charm to a humdrum little market-town than having rowed in from a stormy anchorage.

One haven of national – if not international – feeling we found by accident, at Plas Menai, the national watersports centre. Waiting in Mr Jones's cavernous lock-chamber, we had suddenly seen arising from the boat next to us the tanned, fit, bright-eyed figure of one Bob Bond, an old acquaintance of Paul's, former RYA national sailing coach and now Principal of Plas Menai. He took us up to his immaculate, slate-roofed palace of physical fitness for a swim. We found ourselves a bit awed by its atmosphere, and Bob kept calling it 'a centre of excellence' as he showed off the mountaineering practice wall, the racks of neat canoes, and the vast pool. Paul and I are not good at 'excellence'. We do not have a yachtmasters' certificate or a swimming medal between us: we just sail. When I helped the children into the pool, I was fiercely lectured by a charismatic German instructor called Hans on the evils of inflatable armbands. To demonstrate his thesis, he snatched little Rose out of my arms and took her off, bandless, ordering her to kick. She did. Then he ordered her to dip her face in the water – normally abhorrent to her – and after one startled, horrified glance back at me, she did so. What is more, once I had recovered her from the hands of Hans, she continued to do it, overcome by his charisma. 'Ah yes,' said Bob happily. 'I've had letters from people saying they've been afraid of water for thirty years, until the day came they found they were more afraid of Hans.'

We took Bob back for a drink on *Grace O'Malley*. He envied the voyage, having done a round-Britain himself in 1964. Being excellent, he did it in a third of our time, five weeks, and he did it in a racing open catamaran. 'We once did one hundred-and-seventy miles in daylight. We had to go through the Caledonian Canal because the coastguards were getting sort of threatening.' We drank to our differing philosophies and left him to pursue excellence while we bumbled off to Beaumaris in the hope of catching some of the festival events there. Any pursuit of athletic fine-tuning would have fallen to pieces, anyway, at the point when I dropped the boathook in a fast tide while trying to pick up a mooring.

I cannot claim to have witnessed our triumphant safe passage through the Swellies: Rose, having put up with a lot of tedious shopping and fuelling-up in the morning, announced ominously that today was Jingle's birthday. Jingle is her white teddybear. 'And he needs a party.' I took on the role of Renaissance Woman, encompassing all duties, as I flashed between the heavy and intricate job of getting the bowsprit back in place and visits to the cabin to pop little cheesy puffs and dolly-mixtures on to plates for various teddies, otters, and monkeys. As I passed the chart each time I ticked off the various beacons and buoys in the Swellies. It was a stretching intellectual exercise. The children steadfastly refused to leave the party and come on deck for this historic moment, even when I told them the story of William Williams the cobbler, who when the first chains were suspended for the building of the Menai Bridge, sat on the top one with his feet on the lower, and made a pair of shoes in a day which sold at a premium price.

Beaumaris was in a festival frenzy. Entering the intricate and beautiful castle, we saw real knights on the battlements and found a Plantagenet Society re-enactment about to flare up. There was first an unconscionably long display of medieval ladies dancing. 'Well,' said my neighbour, a fringe member of the Society, 'they have to let them do all that because the men won't let the women be knights, but if the women won't knit the chain-mail they can't get their battles together.' A Rotarian type in a splendid jerkin got a grip on the microphone and began an equally interminable pre-amble about how these chaps in tin suits were all really Knights of Virtue and Hubert de Montfort and Humphrey de Bohun and Rupert the Red; then with fearful bangings and gruntings, the spectacle of hand-to-hand combat with axe and sword and knobbly flail began at last. During the preamble, a huge knight with a fibreglass gold lion on his helmet ('I'm a Bohun') came up to us and, in rather muffled tones, introduced himself. 'We met before,' he said tinnily. 'At the husky dog sledge racing in Scotland.' I was charmed to think that there must be a salty stream of eccentrics running through Britain's bloodstream: stout hearts who emerge from insurance offices to race husky dogs in winter, dress as knights in summer, and practise heaven knows what excesses at the equinoxes.

Outside the castle, a group of men waited in clown face-paint, ragged costumes apparently made out of old ties, odd rugby socks, bowlers and clogs. Nicholas, experienced beyond his years in such things, asked with great politeness: 'Are you Morris men or Mummers?' The ringleader gazed benevolently down at him. 'We are a development of contemporary street theatre.' Then they got out their accordions and revealed themselves as an extremely noisy breed of Border clog-dancers. A member in civvies stood next to me, off sick, as he explained, with a dancing injury; he explained that they were iconoclasts who shock Morris and clog purists by using women as well as men. I was glad to see that the female presence had no refining influence whatsoever. Staves clashed, whistles blew, and the troupe yelled and stamped in an authentically unruly manner. 'This 'ere's an old plumbing dance from Manchester,' they would shout, embarking on another ferocious ronde. We applauded loudly and asked if we could put money into the hat; it was evidence of the sweet unworldliness of the group that they had temporarily lost the hat.

The whole rackety event was being watched by a group of silent figures on high stilts, draped in purple and white robes like very tall ghosts. I asked my companion whether they belonged in some fringe manner to the ragged clog troupe. 'No, no,' he said. 'They're nowt to do with us. They're the Blaenau Ffestiniog Stilt Dancers.' The what? 'Well, they move in formation to music. It's difficult to put in words what it's loike, really.' I imagined it would be, but when Paul and the children drifted off to the delights of the Beaumaris Victorian Gaolhouse with its real working treadmill, I stayed to see the tall, mournful figures going through their routine. The Blaenau Ffestiniog Stilt Dancers jerked and swayed and stamped and waved their arms, in close formation, to a disco beat; looking closely under the drapes, I noticed that few of them could be over fourteen. 'We're called Wotan,' they said. 'We're all from Blaenau. We want to be on "Opportunity Knocks", ackshully.' They had, as far as they knew, invented their art form themselves. 'We're all under eighteen. Geraint is only twelve.' Their odd robes flapped in the breeze, and their black stilts clumped under their bound feet; they shifted constantly as they spoke, partly out of shyness and partly to avoid falling over.

Behind them lay the golden castle, beyond them Snowdonia's peaks in the warm, faded light. I thought of Emrys and the coaster, of the angel voices of Caernarfon, the restless Rossiter of Port Dinorwic, of Benllech donkeys and the burning eyes of Hans at Plas Menai, and marvelled how little one can tell from charts. In that harsh south-westerly two days before, with Caernarfon Bar ahead of us, we had very nearly decided to go round by way of Holyhead.

We would have missed all of it. What else were we losing as we carelessly crossed bays and skipped islands? How many times would we have to sail round Britain before we got any real grip on it? Tomorrow we would spread our brown wings and fly away northwards towards the Isle of Man, pulling down the Welsh dragon flag. But we would not forget Menai.

The children were exhausted by their adventures, and fussed horribly at having to row back to our borrowed mooring in the dinghy. Nicholas had developed one of his secret fears about the dinghy ever since the rough row out to the boat at Porth Dinllaen. But as usual, he had his own odd solution to family tension. 'Please may we have a dinner with speeches and proper grown-up behaviour?' he asked. So Paul was toastmaster, banging a wooden spoon; I made a short speech, to the effect that I was honoured to be there; then Nicholas arose with nervous dignity to propose a Vote of Thanks. 'Thank you for the honoured speech, Mrs Heiney, and we hope you like your dinner.' We said grace, and made adult conversation with each other like, 'Where do you live?' and 'What do you do?' and 'Would you care for some ketchup?' Heaven knows where the idea, or the method, came from: scattered remarks about our public lives, perhaps. But familiarity had probably been breeding a bit too much family contempt; and Nicholas's formal cure for it worked on all our spirits like a charm.

13

During all this time, the children's moods swung wildly, their anxieties waxing and waning. We had passed beyond the length of any normal family holiday or school break, yet they could clearly see from the plastic relief-map of Britain on which we marked our progress that we were far from being halfway round. Virginia had been impressed by their independence and cheerfulness, and especially the physical prowess they had gained in a month's intensive cruising. This had happened so slowly that we had hardly noticed, but after four weeks it did suddenly occur to us that to expect a three-year-old at the end of a long day to face twenty wet iron rungs of a harbour ladder with a strange, fishy-smelling trawler at the bottom was perhaps unreasonable, and that Rose's sangfroid in these circumstances did her great credit. But after Virginia left us at Port Dinorwic, a few shadows had fallen. Nicholas wept desperately one evening and at last admitted that he missed Nelson, the cat; Rose, who has a morbid taste for gravestones and tales of terminal illness, began with a certain conscious pathos to announce that she thought various friends, grannies, etc., 'might be dead when we get home'; and both of them were subject to sudden untypical rages. We tried, with all the patience at our command, to convey to them the nature of time: how short the next ten weeks really were, how long the routine days at home had lasted, and would last. But as we set off northward from Puffin Island Sound, crew morale was low, pulled down by this insistent infant undercurrent of discontent.

It was not only the infants, either. Paul, suffering from a strained neck and shoulder after his anchoring feats in Porth Dinllaen, had been complaining of a certain sense of dissatisfaction. He said that this cruise did not seem to have the old, wild magic of our first journeys together to Ireland, and that the small punctilious pleasures of seamanship – whipping loose ropes' ends, sailing slowly instead of motoring impatiently into harbour, getting the flags up and down at the right times – were being overlaid with the

110

relentless domesticity imposed by the children. Since I was in charge of toys, clean clothes, and education, he had volunteered to be in charge of food. The cruise had begun with wonderful casseroles and pressure-cooker vegetables and stews; lately, as his morale dropped, we had eaten ashore too much, and on the boat every lunch or light supper for days seemed to have consisted of ham-and-piccalilli sandwiches. Moreover, since his stiff neck, they were tending to be ham-and-piccalilli-and-a-light-tinge-of-embrocation sandwiches. Alone of the crew, I was relishing the whole adventure. I felt rather guilty about this because I had originated the whole thing, set the dates, organized the finance and the empty house for it, and effectively dragged my whole family off to sea.

The wind was against us, too. Forecast to turn westerly, it remained implacably in the north-west, blowing directly from Port St Mary, our destination fifty miles away at the southern end of the Isle of Man. Heavy-heartedly, we hauled in the sheets and prepared to beat to windward all the way. Rose threatened sickness. Nicholas kept trying to crayon in the cabin and emerging to gulp fresh air on deck. The peculiar pitching motion of a boat hard on the wind affects Paul badly, and Nicholas seemed to have inherited the weakness. When the wind freed us a little, the sea stayed rough; we could point only thirty degrees off our destination. There was a sideways tide obligingly pushing us the right way, so the sailing was not entirely frustrating. Morale, however, stayed resolutely low.

I realized that, as the only happy human being on board, I had a duty to improve our lot. There was only one way to do it. 'If we put the topsail up,' I said carefully, 'we would go faster and point up better.' 'Can't face it,' said Paul, briefly. The topsail – the white triangle which, carefully hoisted, fills in the gap between the slanting gaff at the top of the mainsail and the mast itself – is our main light-weather sail, but it has always been troublesome. Paul had got it up half-a-dozen times, but always with a great deal of cursing, sweating, overbalancing and miscalculation. Intricate patterns of rope are not his forte, especially when he feels sick. Gradually the topsail had grown into a bogey: something not to be mentioned. The last time it had been up was for Richmond's benefit, and we had had a particularly bad tangle both on the way up and on the way down. I had never put it up myself. Yet there it lay, on deck in its long blue bag, its two spars attached to it; there was its rigging draped infuriatingly around the mast, getting in the way; and if we would not use our topsail in this quintessentially topsail weather, I felt that we might as well turn on the engine, and give up all pretensions to being gaff sailors. In short, we might as well admit to ourselves that we have a gaffer for ornamental reasons only, and can't be bothered to sail it properly. It was part and parcel of the frustration Paul had expressed that we were not yet sailing *Grace O'Malley*, or maintaining her, to the degree she deserved, because of our shorthandedness and our small children.

All these things were quite clearly going through Paul's mind as well as mine, when he said, 'Can't face it,' and they left me no option. 'Please ignore me,' I said, 'but I am going to play topsails. It's time I had a go.'

Up on the foredeck, which rolled and pitched irritatingly in the sloppy sea, I pulled the bag off the tangle of spars and rope, and looked at it. Slowly, over fifteen minutes, I worked out what went where, and fixed various shackles on to its three corners. I hoisted it: it jammed, as it had so often jammed for Paul. I felt my teeth setting into a rictus of hate, my back tensing, my hands jerking furiously against the invisible obstruction above. I could see why Paul's language was so immoderate when he did it. I counted to ten. I told myself it was only a bit of Terylene cloth, obeying the obvious laws of physics: if it stuck, it was stuck against something. It was not a demon. It was not an enemy. It was not (I was growing demented) a punishment sent by God to people idle and arrogant enough to abandon their proper calling for a whole summer to sail round Britain admiring bits of rock. The white shape lurched and flapped above my head like a Blaenau Ffestiniog Stilt Dancer. Eventually I pulled it down and looked at it, much as Eeyore looked at his bits of burst balloon; and shackled it on a different way. Up it went, like a glorious white bird; stuck again, came down again, and at last after a lot of heaving and lashing and making fast, we were bouncing along faster through the sunshine, pointing a degree or two more convincingly towards the Isle of Man, and feeling – on my part – better. Paul refused to applaud my achievement, seeming oddly unimpressed. 'Yes, fine, very good.' I consoled myself with the belief that in getting the topsail up alone I had somehow wounded the dark flame of his male pride.

The sea flattened, the day wore on; both of us managed a nap in preparation for the night, or half-night, passage. The children gradually revived. Nicholas had been whining, 'Why do we have to go to sea today, I hate this boat,' but seemed to pick up as evening approached: suddenly, while I was washing up supper, he said, 'I love kettles that whistle, on a boat. It is friendly. It makes me wake up feeling happy in the morning.' 'Do you like being on a boat?' I asked. This was normally a taboo question, as we could not risk the answer 'No. Take me home.' He looked me straight in the eye and said, 'Yes. And I like the voyage. I think it's worth it, isn't it?' Later, he sat in the cockpit with Paul eating crisps, while Rose and I dozed, and I heard him say: 'Let's do this again some time Daddy, just you and me in the evening, chugging along on the very gentle waves.' We were chugging, by then; the wind was almost gone. At 2.30 a.m., tired but satisfied, we slipped into the fishing harbour at Port St Mary to the pleasant sound of an Irish Yacht Club having a serious sort of hooley aboard their various boats. 'Holy Ground once more, FOINE GIRL YOU ARE!' they sang. 'Fine girl you are,' said Paul, generously, at last. 'Well done with the topsail.'

All the revellers had sailed away by the time we woke up, and we walked through Port St Mary with an open mind, wondering what the Isle of Man was like. 'Old-fashioned,' they had said in Caernarfon, that home of bed-and-breakfast hotels and community singing; a place that Caernarfon thinks old-fashioned must be quite especially so.

And so it was. A dignified Monday morning silence reigned. Beyond the Mariners' and Fishermen's Shelter, beyond the deserted harbour office and the quietly busy rows of trawlers fitting out for the season, lay neat, drab pastel houses and small, faded shops. There were window displays years old, with sun-bleached boxes of Afrika Korps models and ancient sets of Airfix; groceries lay in unassuming, unflamboyant heaps, speaking for themselves. There were no special offers, no Dayglo labelling, no neon signs. The most go-ahead shop in town still bore the label MANX CO-OPERATIVE SOCIETY in old-fashioned lettering; estate agents' very placards (for there were many vacant possessions, many blank-eyed properties, in Port St Mary) were set in typefaces straight from our 1950s childhoods. I had a sudden urge for a bottle of Vimto. We peered into a wood-turning shop, a closed charity shop, and at terraces full of net curtaining. There was an old-fashioned tin sign saying BUS STOP, but it was difficult to believe that Port St Mary was ever visited by anything so disruptive and controversial as a bus.

When I asked at the hotel whether we might have a bath, I got a polite but regretful refusal: 'We're full up,' said the manageress, indicating her silent, ghost-haunted Edwardian premises. 'It's the first day of the TT races. That's why the town is so full.' Since I had passed a total of three fellow human beings on this fine morning, one of whom was pushing another in a wheelchair, I wondered what Port St Mary was like when it was empty. But the Manx voices – faintly Irish, conceivably Welsh, a shade Scottish – were polite and friendly enough in a quiet, distant way. A fifties British way, I suppose, untouched by brash American glad-to-see-you. The Isle of Man was altogether the least American place I had ever been to on the surface of the earth, except perhaps one small village in Communist China.

As we travelled on the little gleaming steam railway in the bumpy Victorian carriages, we saw village after village cast in more or less the same mould: ancient typography, cluttered little village shops, neat red phone boxes, little boys in grey shorts – divided by fields of small size worked by small tractors with hedgerows and silent lanes of cow parsley and lush green grass. It was England, England of pre-war memoirs, England before (some say) the Fall; it was an illusion, surely, a Theme Park? Yet nobody seemed to care enough to make it a Theme Park; they just lived there. Even the railway, designed to draw tourists, had taken on a look of inevitability: the old chocolate-coloured carriages were exactly the sort of transport you would expect the inhabitants of these villages to prefer travelling in.

We found a curious playground, with roundabout horses powered at slow and dreamlike speed by a waterwheel operating off the overflow of a murky boating lake. On the lake itself, antique paddlewheelers lurched and leaked from bank to bank with equal sloth. Here the children made two friends, Ben and Laura. Swinging on the climbing frame and giggling on the swings, they cast off thoughts of their voyage and their parents for an hour, while I talked to Jane, the children's mother. 'It's half-term this week because of the TT. Most of the children can't get to school because the roads are closed.' Leathery figures had shot past us in the lanes, dreaming their alarming macho dreams, but we had kept easily away from the routes so far. 'Real nuisance, the TT. But it's been going since 1918, or something.' Her husband was a deep-sea sailor and now worked the Douglas ferry, having lost months of pay in the seamen's strike. 'I'm from Prestatyn, really. North Wales. But the Isle of Man's a good place to live. I wouldn't go back across, not now.' She confirmed what I had suspected: that the trains, the horse-drawn trams, the general dilapidated gentility of the place were not entirely a tourist ploy, but a real expression of the views of a community which simply cannot see the point in change for change's sake. Proclaiming its own laws on Tynwald Hill, licensing its own cars, nipping over to Holyhead for the cheaper shopping but returning thankfully to its sturdy old buses, neat fields, and net curtains, the Isle of Man remains a thousand miles further from America than mainland Britain can ever be again. 'We never had the sixties here,' said Jane. 'Not sure we've had the fifties yet, really.'

It began to rain dismally. I felt we should have had a little house to go back to, to eat steak-and-kidney pie and cabbage and blancmange, and watch Cliff Michelmore beaming at us in black-and-white and saying 'The Next Tonight will be Tomorrow Night.' We climbed down to *Grace O'Malley* instead, and found that Paul had cooked a fine dinner of bacon and potatoes. Then he lay beatifically on his bunk, by lamplight, listening to the rain. 'I'm enjoying my cruise again now,' he said. 'I do like a nice wet evening in a dull place, with trawlers. Lovely.' What had been wrong with him, clearly, was a surfeit of sunshine, scenery, and holidaymaking. I remembered that he once went very gloomy on an idyllic Brittany cruise, and had been doubtful about both his flotilla holidays in the blue Mediterranean: if you want to make a Yorkshireman happy, you have to give him a dollop of rain, a grey mizzling sky, and a row of houses full of folk who mind their own business and don't say owt much. Nicholas felt it too. 'Cosy,' he muttered, settling far earlier than usual to sleep. 'Cosy on the Isle of Man.'

14

I awoke to see a brilliant Mediterranean-blue sky through the cabin porthole. It turned out, on inspection, to have streaks of rust running down it, and to be the flank of the big motherly trawler under whose wing we were tucked. The real sky was implacably grey. But at ten o'clock my new friend Jane turned up, puffing slightly, with Ben and Laura in tow. 'Sorry – nearly didn't get here – I'm a caterer, got a sudden order for lunch today – been buttering sandwiches since late last night.' We took the four children, scampering and playing at trains, up the road for an ice-cream while we drank coffee, and Jane looked affectionately round her at the clean café, the quiet street, the distant green fields full of aimless sheep. 'They've been quite good about stopping people buying holiday cottages and leaving them empty,' she said. 'And about letting people in to work who aren't Manx. It's still very Manx, you know, in spite of all the businessmen and accountants. Everyone says hello to the fairies when they cross the Fairy Bridge.' I expressed disbelief.

'Oh, yes they do. Even businessmen. If they drive over it and forget to say hello to the fairies, awful things happen. One man got a flat tyre, and missed his plane. Another one got the time of a meeting wrong.' The Manx fairies would appear to go in for malice rather than major tragedy and *crimes passionels*. She wiped Ben's mouth. 'I wouldn't want to come to the Isle of Man on holiday, because there's nothing much to do. But I love living here.' Ben and Laura climbed down the iron ladder to the boat – quailing at the height – and played games with Nicholas and Rose while I sat unobtrusively on the cabin roof. The relief and pleasure the children got in being back in a friendly, squabbling, unsupervised playroom world was almost palpable.

But we took them from it as usual, and by two o'clock we were tacking along the misty cliffscape of Man's western edge. We were going northward towards Peel. Rose and Nicholas fished, with spectacular lack of success. Rose groaned, unable to persevere with anything, three years old and impatient for world domination: 'Oh, I give up, oh, I'll never catch a fish, I'll never be a real trawlerman, I hate you, I'm going to break the whole universe, you pigs.' Nicholas doggedly hauled and re-cast his hookful of bacon-rind, still getting nothing. At seven that evening, with sudden unexpected joy, we turned around St Patrick's Isle and found ourselves in Peel.

The surprise was complete. Having seen the dull prettiness, the maidenly retirement of Port Erin and Port St Mary and the near-miss handsomeness of Castletown, we did not expect a place so salty and forceful as Peel upon this dreaming island. But Peel, in the first few moments, proved remarkable: on the one hand a classic miniature of an English seaside landscape of the 1930s – sweeping beach, green headland scattered with villas, Edwardian and Victorian hotel buildings, and a prom of peeling stucco and cramped, half-hearted sweetshops – on the other hand, a working harbour, herring-rich, busy, purposeful, set beneath the extraordinary island fortress of St Patrick's Isle. Delight piled on delight: this place was not genteelly moribund like Port St Mary, it was vital and scruffy: narrow, rough backstreets huddled behind the promenade, an estate agent's dream of decayed quaintness but as yet unsold and unchanged; these were houses inhabited by decent people who drink cocoa and peg out washing. Beyond the town, men went through their silent rituals on a velvety bowling green, and girls with sturdy white legs played tennis on a green court. Bikers in black leather roamed everywhere, as mild as milk despite their fearful appearance; they picked up Rose when she stumbled with a fatherly 'Whoops!' and posed for self-conscious group photographs around famous TT bikes. Mistaking my attention for envy, a group of middle-aged leather wearers tried to show me the best place on the map from which to watch tomorrow's races: 'They do thirty-seven-and-a-half miles in nineteen minutes, the best ones. You mustn't miss it.' I have hated motorsport for years with an instinctive, entirely unreasoning hatred of noise and smell and death; four men had died already in this very season, and it was only on its second day. But I found myself warming to the bikers. 'See that boot? That's worn down at the side by tight cornering. He's nearly professional, aren't you Dave?' 'Mummy,' said Nicholas primly, returning from the beach, 'why were you talking to those space-men?' Paul's expression said much the same.

117

Rackety though they might be, TT supporters are as much a legitimate part of the Isle of Man as the chaps in Viking helmets who throw 'banquets' in the Long House near the kipper smokery on Peel Quay, and sail around in plastic replicas of longships with horns on their hats. TT has been on the island for eighty-one years, since the 1907 Nortons and Matchlesses raced here. And at least the bikers go away at the end of the racing. There are more insidious enemies at large: Colin Clague, the harbourmaster, inveighed against them.

'Peel has been the way it is for fifty years, and I like it. But it's all changing. Property prices are up fifty per cent in ten months. The government's giving the place away. It's too easy to get in here if you've got money. Places like Peel don't have a chance.' The coming cataclysm, it seemed, was due to Jersey. 'They've virtually closed the place down to outsiders now. So they're coming here in their tax exile. And the government does nothing.' With a gesture of despair, he indicated his green hills, his prosaic port where the trawlermen and their small sons painted and sanded away the rust for the coming season; it took in his neat white pierheads and silvered bollards, the well-cared-for harbour and the seedy, decaying promenade. He liked it all, and so did I. A memorial tablet, very Manx in its bare understatement, said:

IN MEMORY OF
THE SEAMEN OF THIS ISLAND
LOST AT SEA
IN WAR AND PEACE

A scruffy child walked past it with a packet of sandwiches, and threw them down to his father who was painting a trawler's beams down on the mud-berth; the child walked back, whistling, the few paces up the hill to his mother's cottage. If you inject money from London and Manchester, from European capitals and the books of sharp accountants, into this fragile homeliness, then within a generation the crooked streets of cottages will be prettified, yuppified, suburbanized; pine-kitchened, microwaved, and Laura Ashleyed out of all recognition. And where, then, will that boy's future son have to carry sandwiches from? Some hideous council estate a mile away? Yes, there were, on the whole, more fearsome enemies of Peel's domestic peace than the bikers who roared their engines excitedly on the seafront.

We walked across St Patrick's Island in the morning, and found a lump of rock, not particularly high or wild, but with a thousand years of buildings crumbling together on it. The tourist leaflets were making much of its alleged position as Arthur's Isle of Avalon, but heaven knows it has enough authenticated history to manage without such picture-book ravings. The Celts had a small Christian community of monks and children living humbly here in wattle-and-daub; the Norse kings built a fortress, the medieval church a cathedral to St German; and the medieval state more fortifications; the inescapable Edward I threw up more ramparts, and later struggles even more. On the hummocky green grass strange, irrelevant pieces of wall still rise, labelled ARMOURY 16th CENTURY or SUNKEN PATH 17th CENTURY; stony holes for arrows, for cannon, for muskets pierce through every shape of loophole. We looked through them at *Grace O'Malley*, standing placidly below us on her low-tide wooden legs among the trawlers. But at the heart of St Patrick's fortress isle lay a little square block, the sort a weary tourist will use to tie a shoelace. Its old plate read:

IN HAC DOMO QUAM A, VERMICULIS ACCEPI
CONFRATRIBUS MEIS SPE RESURRECTIONIS AD
VITAM IACEO SAM: PERMISSIONE DIVINA
EPISCOPUS HUIUS INSULAE SISTE LECTOR:
VIDE: AC RIDE PALATIUM EPISCOPI
Obiit xxo die Mensis Mai

It is the tomb of Samuel Rutter, Lord Bishop of Sodor and Man from 1661 until his untimely death in 1662. It was the word 'Sodor' which, as we spelt it out on the label, made Nicholas and I suddenly realize together that the Rev. W. Awdry's Island of Sodor, home of Thomas the Tank Engine, must have been the Isle of Man all the time. Everything fitted: the neat little steam railway lines, the Toytown countryside (and even, I thought privately, the somewhat self-righteous society: when the big engines go on strike, the little engines do their work gladly because they are glad the strikers are being 'taught a lesson'). Awdry, as befits a clergyman, took the name 'Sodor' from the Bishop's ancient title.

The translation of good old Bishop Sam's epitaph was far from self-righteous. It pleased us:

IN THIS HOUSE WHICH I SHARE WITH MY BROTHERS THE WORMS,

IN THE HOPE OF RESURRECTION TO LIFE LIE I, SAM, BY DIVINE GRACE BISHOP OF THIS ISLAND. STAY, READER: BEHOLD, AND LAUGH AT THE BISHOP'S PALACE.

Back on the boat, we read Ladybird books about Vikings, with the usual fusillade of moral questions from the children about the Vikings' behaviour, then Paul took them off to see the replica Viking ship and paraphernalia lovingly maintained by the replica Vikings of Peel in memory of their bloodthirsty forefathers.

I had planned a quiet afternoon's writing, followed by a saunter around Peel; but one of those interludes occurred which distinguish a sailing voyage from a normal holiday. The tide came in. All day the wind had been freshening from the north-west, and blowing straight on to the beach and up the harbour. All day, unworried, we yachtsmen alongside the quay had watched the waves on the beach and thought how pleasant a harbour we were in. Colin Clague, the harbourmaster, had looked worried at forecast-time, and muttered about this being a bad place in northerly swell; we had all looked complacently at his nice high stone piers and thought little of it. But it is fatal to assume – as outsiders normally do when thinking of yachting – that once you are 'in a harbour' you are safe and secure: that somehow the proximity of chip-shops and estate agents' windows conveys the blessings of static civilization upon you. It does not. There are huge numbers of harbours which become virtually untenable in certain winds; everyone who sails has probably had the unwelcome experience of having to put out to sea at bedtime, or at suppertime, or in mid-shower at the yacht club, merely because the wind has changed and the swell is threatening to drag the boat off its anchor or pound it to pieces alongside a harbour wall. The worst position to be in when the wind changes in a dubious harbour is to be aground at low water, waiting for the returning tide to lift. You may have gone down with whispering gentleness, but you will come up again with a bang, or a series of bangs. The worst thing of all is to be dried out on legs in such a situation.

Which, of course, we were. Our sturdy wooden pillars, requiring an effort for one person to lift, suddenly seemed as frail as matchsticks. I was roused from my book by a crash, and came on deck to the terrifying sight of great breaking rollers whipping around the corner of the pierhead and surging, like the mighty

Rose on deck

Matthew and Nicholas,
sailing home around
Norfolk

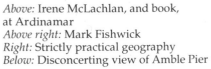

Above: Irene McLachlan, and book,
at Ardinamar
Above right: Mark Fishwick
Right: Strictly practical geography
Below: Disconcerting view of Amble Pier

Above: Charlestown
Below: Steering lesson
Right: Richmond Bobart negotiating
a tricky bend in Ramsey Sound

Above: Nicholas's
personal flag
Right: Using the pelorus
to take bearings
Below: Evening at sea

Left: Paul at Bridlington
Above: Granny Purves in the role of
Queen Christina
Below: Armada lessons in the
Devon seas

Charlestown: on legs

Eyemouth

Summit Reach, Crinan Canal

Above: Crinan Canal
Left: An exercise in trust,
Bridlington Harbour
Below: Storing up

eygre of Severn, up along the line of boats. The trawler ahead of us merely moaned and shifted slightly in her sleep; the yacht between her and us was banging its rudder angrily on the ground, and *Grace O'Malley*, caught by the flood, shifted suddenly from leg to leg as she attempted to float. On each wave she rose, in each trough she dropped back violently, jarring on the hard sand. Astern of us, a little white eggshell of an Irish racing boat was pounding on her rudder, and the two men in charge of her were both sitting right out at the bow to protect it. Minute by minute, the banging and pounding became worse; our bow slewed violently round so that the bowsprit struck sparks with its iron collar on the stone wall; a mooring-cleat and brass fairlead pulled themselves off the deck with one yank of the taut mooring-line, and the legs began to groan ominously at every blow. I raced around, adjusting lines to make us lie straight to the wall, then lay on my stomach with the big spanner and struggled to pull off one of our legs. The one between boat and wall could not be touched for fear of losing my hand in the process; so with the outward leg off, I put out more fenders and took myself and the heavy anchor to the outer side to heel the boat over and save our remaining leg from being broken or wrenched out of its housing. Eventually, the water rose enough to cushion us, and rather shaken I returned to the pierhead. It was clear that we could not afford to risk another low tide in that berth; and since there was nowhere else to go, we might well have to make a night passage to Portpatrick. Paul, returning, looked extremely glum at the thought and went off to negotiate with the trawler skippers further up the creek; at last he found one who had not actually put a new coat of wet paint on that day – no easy task – and whose crew were sympathetic, if mildly amused, by our predicament. 'You lean on us,' they said generously. 'We're not out tonight. We're between seasons – scallops finished, herring just starting.' We were, as so often, amazed and grateful for the fatherly tolerance most trawlermen show towards yachts: they have a hard, precarious and dangerous living to earn on big steel boats with endless work to be done; we swan around in our pretty little cockleshells and take up valuable space in their harbours. Yet most trawlermen will come to their berth inside a yacht with delicacy and infinite care, rearranging the little boat's ropes kindly; will give advice, suggest themselves as windward shelter in nasty weather, and put up with parties of aged relatives and fractious children being chivvied across their rusty, fishy decks towards the harbour ladder. I once asked a French fisherman whether he didn't get irritated by yachts. 'Ah, pouf!' he cried. 'What do they take from us? *Le vent, c'est tout*! and the wind is free, *non*?' He actually gave us a lobster, out of the kindness of his heart, and we had to force beer on him in return for it. There are many darker tales told by other yachtsmen, but in ten years' sailing I have rarely had so much as a harsh word from a trawlerman. These Manxmen on board *Don Pasco* smiled at the children, reassured us about the swell, and tied our ropes to their cleats with punctilious care.

15

Putting out to sea is always an act of faith: in yourself, your boat, the Meteorological Office, and God. Sunny days turn vile, fair winds back round and shriek defiance at you, reliable navigators run you on to rocks. Perhaps a light aircraft might fall on you, as it did on some poor devils in the Solent a while ago, out of a blue untroubled sky; more often, you merely get wet and terrified on a passage which you began in shorts and vest, playing the concertina at the helm without a care. All you can do is cultivate an unusual mixture of constant wariness and devil-may-care insouciance, and take life as it comes. Our passage out of Peel was a case in point. We were bound northwards for the tip of Scotland where the Rhins of Galloway stretch southward towards the sea-border. We were promised a north-easterly, not more than Force Five, and good visibility: since that wind would enable us to sail the forty miles directly without tacking – albeit in some discomfort and leaning over on our ear – it seemed that we must go. On the other hand, the wind howled all night, pounding swell continued to plague the little harbour, and the only way to catch the fair tide through the narrow North Channel between Ulster and Galloway was to leave by 6 a.m. Few ideas have ever appealed to me less. Only the rousing composition favoured by Radio 4 as a prelude to the dawn shipping forecast served to raise my morale: 'Men of Harlech', 'Rule Britannia', 'Heart of Oak', 'Danny Boy', a brazen medley of sentiment helped a little as I drearily drew on my clothes and shivered into the cockpit. We could not dodge the passage; we had friends to meet, and there was always the shelter of Belfast Lough to run for if we could not lay a safe course to Portpatrick. The children's reaction to a really stiff trip worried us, but Rose had woken in the night and been slipped a pink pill, so we merely tucked them more firmly in their bunks and reflected that their last really bad experience had been a month ago, and they had got over that quite quickly. Above all, we had to go because if this wind were to grow to a real gale, we would have to clear out of Peel anyway and go back to Port St Mary. Paul remained calm and determined; I fluttered, but agreed we must go.

The breakers in the harbour mouth were so big that it took all our twenty-seven horsepower to push us out through them: Paul, at the helm, needed every ounce of power and of nerve to hold us off the shore. Waves broke over me on the foredeck as I struggled to rig the bowsprit and get the fenders and ropes stowed; it is the first time I have ever wished I was wearing a life-harness while still inside a harbour. We had bought a half-stone box of Manx kippers, which was frequently and heavily re-salted as it lay ripening beneath the liferaft. I struggled back to the cockpit eventually, and we set the sails for our course: it was possible to steer directly for the Rhins, even to go reasonably fast, but the boat was heeling to her maximum, groaning and creaking under a heavily reefed mainsail and jib, and smashing her bowsprit into waves rather larger than we had expected. So there we both clung, drenched, dispirited, and eventually very seasick, watching the Isle of Man disappearing astern and longing wistfully for a sight of Scotland. The children slept on. After a while, I saw a baleful little face looking up from Nicholas's bunk; eventually he admitted he felt sick. Coming on deck was still almost out of the question for a child: it was bad enough out there for an adult, soaked to the skin once a minute by cold solid lumps of water, so down in the lurching cabin I held out the pot for him. He cheered up enough to admire the retreating Isle of Man through the hatch, then fell asleep. Paul and I continued queasy and cold, lethargic and shuddery, steering in turns as the sun gradually warmed the morning and the mountains of Scotland appeared grey ahead of us; then Rose awoke, threw up neatly, and sank back to sleep.

Fortune favours the brave, I muttered as usual. It has to. And indeed this miserable morning suddenly improved. The sea flattened a little, the wind eased enough to let us sail upright, and magically we began to smell the grass of Scotland, green and fresh on the northerly breeze. We have smelt distant land before and it is unforgettable; usually it is grass that sends its soft message over the water, or the dung of farmland. It cheered us immeasurably. Soon it was apparent that the tide was pushing us onward for a late lunchtime arrival. We tangled with two nasty tide-races in succession, with a flat patch between, just off the Mull of Galloway; but the irritation of having the boom flung to and fro and the crockery leaping out of its shelves was offset by the very interesting and satisfying discovery that these tidal overfalls were both very precisely marked on the Admiralty chart, and that a nearby trawler was describing a prudent curve around them. We resolved to pay more attention to the wavy symbols on the chart in future. By this time we were moving along the majestic coast of the Rhins, a peninsula of clifftops running north and south, with the cleft of Portpatrick fifteen miles up its bleak western side. Nicholas and Rose had got up, and were dancing in the cabin to 'Nellie the Elephant', still in their pyjamas, Paul and I were singing along in the cockpit, and the kettle was on. From being at the limit of survival, or at least feeling that way, we were transformed into a pleasure-boat you could have taken your old granny out on.

Entering Portpatrick for the first time at dead low water is a sporting enterprise. Having cruised along the coast with no sign of a pierhead, you aim finally between two largely demolished piers of rubble and make as if to run straight up a small sandy beach. Just as seagulls are walking around nonchalantly beneath your bowsprit with the water barely up to their yellow knees, you swing sharp left into a deep little dock. It contained an army boat and a lifeboat and a couple of Northern Irish yachts. One of these yachtsmen, on a regular weekend milk-run from Belfast, explained to us that Portpatrick harbour is a relic. Although remarkably handy for yachts going northward into the Clyde, and for weekend parties out of Bangor or Belfast, it is no longer officially maintained, charges no dues, and is actually owned by a firm of seedsmen from Cambridge. Still, official or not, we were inside and fairly comfortable.

We lay alongside a medium-sized flashy motorboat; the owner, a loutish business type, had the sort of aggressive Ulster accent which leads the most moderate Englishman to mutter 'Cut 'em adrift! Mad, the lot of them!' when it is heard on a news programme spouting one or other side's bigotries. He not only spilled diesel fuel on our deck without a word of apology or a swipe of a mop, but barked peremptory orders at us when he decided to go out; nor did he remove his black cigar while doing so. We had been lucky to have got this far without meeting a disagreeable yachtsman: we shook our fists at his vulgar showy wake and muttered imprecations about him to the amiable boatload of old boys from Bangor on our other side. 'Ah, he'll be in a hurry, I'd say.' His cigar-chewing presence did at least explain something which had mystified us.

My new cellular telephone had been working intermittently all the
way round: fine along the South Coast, it had lost any signal once
we were round the Lizard, and managed a faint one in Pembrokeshire; nothing in Caernarfon, but a wonderful strong signal all
around the Isle of Man. We had decided that it was an abnormally
sensitive indicator of the moneyed areas of the United Kingdom:
reacting, via the placing of aerials, to the presence of a high
concentration of accountants. Why on earth, then, did it work so
perfectly in Portpatrick, here at the back of nowhere in the mountainous Rhins of Galloway? The answer was provided by the
motorboat-man's cigar: of course, Belfast lay only twenty-five miles
over the water. And 'Dere's plenty of money in Belfast, if you know
where to look for it,' said our new neighbours sagely.

We let the children loose on the curving little beach, where a
clean stream runs down across the hard sand, waiting to be dug
and rechannelled into lagoons and islands and deltas and fast-
eroding cliffs. We all needed a therapeutic dig after the rigours of
the morning. I built a tidal model of the Rhins of Galloway and
Rose stepped on it; Paul and Nicholas worked tirelessly to deflect
the Mississippi. An odd day for a child, I thought: in bed until
midmorning, waking up sick, recovering and spending a morning
without discipline or proper occupation in a pitching little world,
while spray drips incessantly off your parents' hoods as they hand
you sweet biscuits for your breakfast; then an afternoon on an
idyllic beach, ice-creams and teashops all around. It must be like
coming out of a sickroom into a summer holiday.

Portpatrick was not always a sleepy, easy-going minor seaside
resort and yachtsmen's stopover. It is, by geographical accident,
the only port accessible at all tides between North Wales and the
Clyde. It also overlooks the shortest possible crossing between
mainland Britain and Northern Ireland: twenty-one miles separate
it from Donaghadee, the same width as the Straits of Dover. (The
same breed of adventurers, in fact, keep crossing and re-crossing it
by swimming, waterskiing, and driving amphibious cars and rafts.)
Its town history boasts the usual guff about St Patrick's footprints
and ghostly pipers under the castle rocks, and tells a rather good
tale of a fisherman who once had a giant cod washed down his
chimney by a freak wave (I have met that cod, in various guises, all
over the British Isles; and in Brittany they tell tourists about a giant
tuna thrown down a chimney by a freak storm). But the history also

tells a true tale of the rise and fall of a key port. In 1634 flat-bottomed boats were already plying regularly to Ireland, with the important cargo of bloodstock horses; one account, by Sir William Brereton, tells of seventeen horses and eight men in a squall, driven off course to Carrickfergus after a grim crossing. Hunting men and military riders might reflect how many of the ancestors of their Irish-bred horses made their lurching journey into, or out of, Portpatrick. The Elizabethans made military use of the harbour for communications; by the late eighteenth century a mailcoach and mailboat were well established, and Smeaton, the great lighthouse engineer, built a pier and lighthouse. The landing of cattle on the Sabbath became a great local issue, and embarkation of celebrities a local pleasure: Sarah Siddons arrived one day at dawn on the mailcoach to fulfil an engagement in Belfast, and stood rapt on the beach in her best stage pose to recite:

> Methinks I stand upon some rugged beach
> Sighing to the winds, and the waves complaining
> While afar off the vessel sails away
> On which my fortune and my hopes embarked . . .

The crowds cheered her on, but her husband, clearly well used to these displays, gripped her by the arm and remarked, 'Egad my dear, if we don't hurry the vessel will be gone absolutely,' before bundling her into the packet-boat's tender. Even more romantic traffic came the other way: runaway lovers from Ireland used Portpatrick as their Gretna Green until 1826. Colourful imported fights, too, entertained the locals: there is an Irish saying still: 'I can't get at you here, Paddy, but Divil help you when I meet you at Portpatrick.'

The harbour grew even more in the nineteenth century. Thomas Telford himself came in 1802 and criticized its utter invisibility from the sea and the heavy tidal swell: precisely the things we had been plagued by when we came in. A new harbour was built, with two splendid piers and a lighthouse to seawards and provision for pulling sailing ships in and out with cables. Eventually, the railway came, cut through the rocks; but no sooner had the new steamship dock been finished than Stranraer, a few miles north, replaced it as the port for Ireland. Portpatrick declined; in 1869 the final indignity was the removal of the lighthouse, which was sold to Colombo in Ceylon (no wonder we couldn't find it from the sea that morning).

Five years later, public maintenance of the harbour was ended, and the piers fell into ruin. Fishermen stayed at Portpatrick, and smugglers found it handy; a lifeboat was established. But on the whole, the town turned placidly inwards to become a resort of golf courses and tennis courts and bowling greens.

But in the end, geography triumphs over social movements. Three times in the last twenty years, Portpatrick has been a key port again: it has a new, if intermittent, career as the major strikebreaking port for Ireland. In the seamen's strikes in 1966 and 1970 fishing boats broke the embargo successfully with a wide range of goods and illegal passengers. And a few weeks before our own arrival, the 1988 strike had brought extraordinary days to sleeping Portpatrick. One waitress at the café – stout, motherly, law-abiding – spoke of it with an authentic piratical gleam in her eye: 'It was like bedlam down here. Trawlers in all day and night with every sort of stuff, lads from here loading it on the vans – every morning, even at three in the morning, we'd say, "Let's go and see what's in," and my husband and I would come down to the dock and fill up with all sorts of stuff – mushrooms, yoghurt, anything – ye ken, the moment they dropped it off the lorry it was anyone's and the lads who knew us all did a good bit of dropping . . . it was like *Whisky Galore*.'

This good-natured clandestine trade was alarming to the DoT, especially when 'The little local boats, open fishing boats, everything, were coming over crammed with passengers . . . well, they stopped that. There wasn't a single lifejacket on any of those boats, leave alone for the passengers.' Somewhere, the ghosts of those fast-buck sailors who overloaded their flat-bottomed scows with horses must have been watching and approving these disgraceful scenes. Portpatrick was itself again, after a hundred years' decline. Then Stranraer went back to work and 'Overnight,' said the waitress sadly, 'it all stopped.' Now only the military range-boat parked austerely in the corner of the dock knows what unwelcome objects or people come in from the direction of Belfast Lough; and nobody talks about such darker cargoes on the street.

We had one more night in Portpatrick, by which time we had unfortunately found ourselves in the position of yacht-nearest-to-the-wall. This meant not only that we would have to extricate ourselves from the usual tangle of mooring-lines in the morning, but that the denizens of the outside yachts – five of them by now –

had right of way over our decks on their way to the ladder. Next to us was a red yacht, whose skipper after an hour or two modestly admitted to being, 'Er – a service boat, sort of. We're in the um, army, I'm afraid.' Down on the South Coast army boats, whether clubs or adventure-training vessels, whizz around proudly with defaced ensigns and other army marks upon them. Up here, with Belfast frowning twenty miles across the water, their profile is conspicuously lower. I hadn't the heart to tell the officer that we had guessed all along that he was running an army adventure training boat. It was a simple enough deduction: in what other social circumstance would you find a middle-aged, soft-spoken, cultured and civilized type of man voluntarily sailing with a crew of four huge, sullen, thick louts bursting out of their T-shirts with undirected muscle-power?

The army, at least, tried to be quiet. The rowdy Northern Ireland yachts beyond them sent feet stamping to and fro across our deck until midnight – about fifteen men in all passing to and from the pub which played its siren music on the front, wailing out 'Baybee . . . save the larust darnce for me' at the threshold of pain. Then these big lads began to rearrange their mooring-lines so as not to be disturbed by the army boat's early departure at 'Oh-five-hundred, lads'. We lay in our bunks fuming at 1 a.m., thinking of our forty-mile passage early next day, of our friends arriving and needing to be entertained. Paul, one of those Englishmen who will keep silent while muscles jump in their cheeks with rage and they phrase cutting letters to *The Times*, just lay muttering to himself in a half-sleep. I have more volatile Celtic blood in me, so eventually I shot up furiously through the forehatch, under the big sneakered feet of the oafs who were dragging warps noisily over our vibrating lifelines. They looked horrified, as anyone might when confronted in the darkness by a large, furious, dishevelled woman in a candy-striped nightshirt. 'Precisely how long will you be doing that?' I squeaked. Sheepish mutters, 'Um, sorry, er'; then there were fifteen minutes more of (now painfully muffled) male stomping on our little world's roof as they untangled themselves with loud, harsh, Derry-accented whispers. It was almost worse to hear them tiptoeing than clumping. When silence fell, I dozed off musing on the social oddities of yachting. One lot, in one boat, may be macho young men out for 'a bloody good thrash to windward' or 'a hairy weekend's racing'; tied up next to them, with barely an inch of

129

plastic hull between, a family like ours may be leading a decorous suburban existence afloat, with potties and pot plants. But, I muttered, we face the same sea as they do, and I bet we go as fast. To hell with them.

16

The banging and stamping began again at five with the departure of HM Forces for another day's adventure. By seven, our friends had arrived bright and eager off the Stranraer sleeper. We had a convivial breakfast while the children woke up, delighted to see faces from home, and especially these. Richard Woodman is captain of the Trinity House tender ship *Patricia*, and spends alternate fortnights out at sea, mending and laying navigation buoys, serving lighthouses and lightships, and supervising such dangerous maritime activities as Channel cable-laying. When he comes home, he writes the Nathaniel Drinkwater series of rousing eighteenth-century sea stories; he is a thorough salt. Christine, his wife, is a painter and art teacher. We set out for Arran island in splendid style, therefore, our family life enhanced by Christine producing some magically bright, soft crayons and a ball of clay, and Richard shinning persistently up and down the mast to sort out our topsail blocks for us. He was like a monkey; we felt earthbound and incompetent, staring up at his lithe, bearded figure struggling away with our badly-aligned blocks. The topsail has come up and down smoothly ever since: ten minutes of real seamanship is worth months of cursing by the likes of us.

We sailed still northwards along the mountainous line of the Rhins of Galloway. I told the children the bloodcurdling story of Heather Ale, and read them the poem by Robert Louis Stevenson: how the last of the Picts was dragged from his hiding-place by the Gaelic invaders, and tortured for the secret of the wondrous Heather Ale; how he made a bargain with them that they must throw his son over the cliff first, so that he should not hear his father betraying the tribe; how they threw the boy over, and the father crowed triumphantly at his trickery: the secret now was safe in an old man's heart:

> For I feared the sapling courage
> That goes without the beard.

As Frank Cowper neatly puts it, 'There is one prevailing character-istic about Scotch legends as about Scotch weather – they are almost without exception gruesome.'

We sailed towards the Isle of Arran in a light headwind. It was too light, and too much of a headwind. By mid-morning we were motoring into a big and highly unpleasant head sea, unjustified by any wind (big seas drive you crazy in a calm: they seem so desperately unfair). Worse, both Christine and I became very sick indeed. Why seasickness is considered to be connected mainly with the stomach, I do not know: to me, in my rare serious bouts, it is a disease of the dizzy head, of the icy feet and hands, the strangled neck, the heart which plummets into unreasoning depression. The children were fairly quiet, sick too: I fell on to the bunk beside Rose, and we lay there frowsy and comatose and miserable for several hours while Paul – miraculously unscathed – and Richard sailed the boat and motored it, alternately, as sea and wind served them. Seldom have I passed a nastier day. Christine fell into total lethargy. The sea would not flatten. We gave up Arran and aimed for Girvan, ten miles nearer; by three it was clear that Girvan lay beyond monstrous seas and tantalizing, still light headwinds. There must have been a great storm far up to the north of us, with swell sweeping round the Mull of Kintyre; nothing else could explain that sea. Then the wind rose against us more strongly, and Paul and Richard decided jointly to give up. We must have done something to offend the Pictish ghosts. Christine and I were too ill even to vote on what we did; we did not care. The boat sailed south again, towards Lough Ryan. Looking at the chart, it became apparent that the Woodmans' weekend was destined to be a nice little ellipse around Stranraer railway station. Still, downwind we all felt better, and Richard and I began to untangle the whys and wherefores of the old harbour rivalries. Sheltered Stranraer took the trade from exposed Portpatrick, just as further down the coast Porth Dinllaen had been pipped to the post by Holyhead as a steamer terminal. On the face of it, today it seems obvious that the present harbours would win in each case: Holyhead is naturally sheltered by Holy Island, Stranraer has Lough Ryan as a perfect natural harbour hidden from the west by the bulky Rhins. But Richard, as a maritime historian, pointed out the flaw in this. 'To a sailing-ship these natural harbours were a very mixed blessing: you can be stuck up a narrow inlet, as well as protected by it. With the long piers to haul sailing ships out from, Portpatrick could let a vessel safely and directly on to the open sea. It could be stuck for days trying to beat out of this Lough.' Similarly Dinllaen, with its wide tacking space outside, would be far better for a sailing-ship than narrow Holyhead. Steam changed the priorities forever: once the steamers came, the choice was obvious. Using the deep holes in the coast meant cheaper harbours, and less building of piers. 'And think what the coming of engine power meant to people maintaining lighthouses, like us,' said Richard. 'Before that, the trouble was that you couldn't land on them when there was wind, and when there wasn't any you couldn't get out to them.'

The Pictish curse stayed on us. As we ran down into Lough Ryan, Rose used the pot in the cockpit, and I chucked it overboard on its lanyard as usual; the knot came undone, and our faithful yellow potty, which had sailed with us for nearly eight hundred miles and through four kingdoms, floated away. It was still upright, still with its cargo topped with paper. We made several brave passes to get it back, but grappling a potty with a boathook is never easy. Perhaps the army should include it in their adventure and initiative training tests. After a while we gave up and sailed on into Loch Ryan. There is a spit of sand to avoid; we passed the buoy with Richard Woodman on the helm, and pointed the boat at the caravan site on the bank, as the Clyde Cruising Club book instructed. Richard warily kept an eye on the echo-sounder, but at the critical moment the children were engaged in a knightly battle with their wooden swords and shields from Beaumaris Castle, and a bold parry blocked his view. The shallow alarm went off, and at once we ran smartly aground. There was no real danger (unless you count the danger to a master mariner's pride of running someone else's yacht aground in three feet of water) and the tide was rising; but when a local fishing-boat buzzed by we accepted their offer of a pull off. At least, I suspect that Paul and Richard would have refused, grandly, and gone to the trouble of dragging us off with the anchor and dinghy; but I was up there on the foredeck with a rope before they had a chance to open their mouths or formulate a plan. Nobody is as quick with a tow-rope as a mother anxious to get her little ones a run ashore.

In Richard Woodman's defence, let it be admitted that a month and five hundred miles after the grounding incident in Lough Ryan, we finally found a piece of paper with the Corrections to the Clyde

Cruising Club pilot-book, which quite clearly tell you *not* to point at the caravan site after all. Enough said. The fishermen were most affable, and directed us to a mooring-buoy; a passing Scottish yacht called 'Welcome!', and we settled very happily down with a programme of reels on the radio and our evening diversions of supper, fishing for crabs, and hauling the children up the mast. I still felt oddly ill, and wondered whether the seasickness had in fact been crab poisoning from Friday's supper: we all slept heavily in our unplanned anchorage, having sailed twenty-six miles in eight hours to make precisely seven miles of northward progress.

The Picts had had their fun with us. The swell all vanished overnight, and northward we went, sailing at times but mainly motoring monotonously across oily flat water, passing the time with Richard's stories of seafaring literary life. 'There's a hell of a swell builds up off Whitby,' he said seriously. 'I once anchored there in old *Patricia* and we rolled so much the photocopier broke.' Good Lord, we replied, how could a ship live in such straits? By what great feat of seamanship did he bring his vessel safe to port without a photocopier? 'It was tough,' he said modestly, 'but my publisher understood.' We read Cowper's account of the coast we were passing, larded with yet more gruesome legends. There was a chieftain who threw all his wives over Bennane Head, until in the village of Culleyne he found a dainty, sweet damsel, and made her his eighth wife. With her, too,

> He suggested a stroll on the cliffs at sunset. The dutiful wife made ready for the walk. What happened is not exactly known; but that evening the Lady of Carleton returned alone. Her cheeks were flushed and her eyes were bright. It was no doubt the hectic light of mental anguish, caused by the terrible accident of which she had been a powerless witness.

In other words, she pushed the baron off Bennane Head, and good riddance. Cowper revels in irony:

> The grief of Lady Carleton would have been terrible no doubt; but fortunately, the castle bugle sounded for the arrival of a guest, and the strict code of medieval courtesy forbade any undue display of sorrow before a visitor . . . The pilgrim, strange to say, was the lady's former lover . . . The moral is

that however successful a man may be, in the long run a woman will beat him.

'Is there a poem?' asked the children, who had become accustomed, not to say resigned, to my dragging out some long narrative verse to attach to all these Border tales. Yes, there is: at the end of the ballad Sir John demands that his wife undress before he throws her over:

> O, turn ye then aboot, Sir John,
> And look to the leaf o' the tree,
> For it never became a gentlemon
> A naked woman to see.
> He turned hissel' straight roond aboot
> To look to the leaf o' the tree
> She has twined her arms around his waist
> And thrawed him into the sea.

We all stared respectfully at Bennane Head, then outward to the enormous, lonely bulk of Ailsa Craig lying ahead of us. Cowper gets the last word on that, too: he tells how a simple inland farmer was taken to the sea on a hazy day, looked out at it and remarked that never had he seen so large a meadow with such a big hayrick in it. Ailsa Craig does look exactly like an old-fashioned hayrick. It made Paul briefly homesick for his Suffolk farming activities, but on such a day nobody could repine.

Certainly the children did not. A change from their parents' exclusive company was working wonders for their mood: Rose was cuddled up to Christine, exerting all her charm to get stories told to her. Richard was even better for Nicholas: his easy habit of command and his enthusiasm for the seaman's crafts got Nicholas really working and concentrating to learn some knots; with us he had merely refused advice and tangled away on his own. We rigged up two blocks as a purchase, hanging from the boom via the centre hatch, and showed him how with this mechanical advantage he could hoist Rose's three stones almost effortlessly and swing her over the chart table: entranced, the pair of them hoisted and shantied the afternoon away. Then a blessed breeze sprang up, and gave us two hours' fine sailing up to Troon; the sort of sail when everyone's senses are heightened, and you try – beyond the call of mere safe navigation – to identify every rock, every feature on the landscape of the coast with endless compass-bearings and cross-references, just out of a longing to preserve and understand every aspect of the rising, falling, ragged green-and-golden lands around you. We were particularly baffled by the Ailsa boatyard shed, which appeared long before Lady Island lighthouse, the land around Troon or anything else at all. It appeared as a huge shimmering white slab, doubled by refracted light: I said it was a distant cliff, Richard swore it was the upperworks of an anchored ship. Three miles off, we agreed that it was a shed. At last, towards evening, we made Troon marina with its shimmering promise of diesel, water, hot showers, and washing-machines. Shoals of mullet swam tantalizingly around the pontoons: Rose devoted herself to the art of fishing, with the usual lack of success. I bled for her; it was not even as if her intentions were particularly murderous. 'If I caught a fish,' she announced, 'I would not hit it on the head with a winch-handle. I would keep it in a tank, as a pet fish.' We doggedly ate more of the Manx kippers, but relented enough to let the children opt for sausage and chips in the café. Richard and Christine left for their train early next morning; we would gladly have kept them for a month.

North of the Scottish border the coast, having progressed northward hitherto in decorous swoops, suddenly dissolves into a thousand rags and tatters, riven by ancient glacial torment. From being hard-pressed to find one safe harbour in a seventy-mile bay, the small boat is suddenly offered a thousand anchorages in ten miles: there are bewildering options on every side. Lochs and Mulls and Firths and Sounds abound: confused and dazzled, Paul and I tried to make sense of the Clyde Cruising Club pilot-books and of our profusion of borrowed charts.

Anywhere around the coast a pile of Admiralty charts with their titles baldly stamped on the back can bring on giddiness (well, test yourself: where in Britain would you expect to place WORMS HEAD TO WATCHET?). But here we had hours of groaning confusion over such titles as SOUND OF GIGHA AND GUNNA, GULF OF CORRYVRECKAN, COLONSAY AND ORONSAY, LOCHS CRINAN AND GILP, BUIE AND SPELVE, ETIVE AND CRERAN, A'CHOIRE AND ALINE, SCRIDAIRN NA KUEL. It was days before we became comfortable with them, and even so we kept on finding very detailed additional charts of places we had just left; we had usually shoved them back under the bunk-cushions in the mistaken view that Corrywhatsit, or Loch Thing, was still fifty miles north of us. We were still more awed by Scottish waters when – drifting in a light breeze past Arran and towards Loch Fyne the next day – we suddenly saw the depths beneath us, more fathoms deep than anywhere in the English Channel and yet we were barely three miles offshore. It was odd, unnerving sailing: on the calm oily waters, sudden gusts funnelling through a deep glen would mark the water ahead of us with a dark blue thread, then heel the boat over sharply as we crossed the wind-line, only to drop us again as another cliff reared shaggily to windward. The seas were alive, too, more alive than at any time in the journey. Since North Wales we had been able to see clouds of dusty plankton, gleams of fish, and flocks of seabirds. Gannets, cormorants, guillemots, and shags abounded; shearwaters, the odd stray puffin, and handsome black-backed gulls were everywhere. In the harbour wall at Portpatrick, next to our berth, was a long deep hole made by falling stones; cross, busy little guillemots kept flying in and out over our deck, and when we shone a torch into the depths, there was an unhatched egg. Herring-gulls too, those airborne vermin, went about their business with vigour: I left a bag of shopping on Portpatrick harbour wall while I took the children down the ladder, and when I returned after three or four minutes the gulls had not only stolen half a loaf of sliced bread, but punctured a carton of butterscotch pudding and some suet dumpling mix, and were attempting to fly off with Nicholas's discarded white-and-red striped sock.

Among such creatures, and with few other boats for company, we moved northward up the Firth of Clyde, bound for Loch Fyne and the entrance to the Crinan Canal. Like its big sister, the Caledonian Canal, the Crinan was built to save ships the trouble and danger of rapid tidal headlands, in this case the Mull of Kintyre. It makes sense of the journey round high ragged Scotland: at a stroke, the Crinan joins Glasgow and its sheltered waters to the Highlands and Hebrides. We sailed up the precipitous rocky cul-de-sac of Loch Fyne, feeling it odd that we would not have to sail down it again but could escape via this narrow thread of water. Indeed, at one point we wondered nervously if we were, indeed, in Loch Fyne at all: so many peaks, cliffs, islands, and inlets beckoned that a pair of metal-framed binoculars incautiously put down next to the compass for five minutes could easily have diverted us up one of the Kyles of Bute, or somewhere. As my flying brother puts it, 'There's many a plane hasn't made it back from the Algarve owing to the golf-clubs.'

Five miles up the loch, there was still no sign of our destination for the night, Tarbert, where we were to meet my mother on a grandmaternal tour of inspection. We had decided that the Crinan Canal was the only fifteen miles of the journey we could guarantee in advance as taking place on dead flat water, so she was making for it. We edged onwards, and suddenly found a hole in the rocks opening up; within seconds all the landmarks and seamarks promised in the pilot-book appeared together: the fish farm, Eilean a' Choic, Sgeir Bhuidhe, and the delicately-washed simplicity of the town itself. At the heart of the harbour lay a fine man-made stone island, square, bearing a capstan for pulling the old sailing ships in and out of their berths with ropes.

Portpatrick had not felt particularly like a new land, and all we saw of Troon was the bleak fence of the yacht marina; but Tarbert was as Scottish as A. J. Cronin. The crown-and-lantern folly on the parish church hung over grand stone Scottish-Victorian buildings, a solid library and an uncompromisingly respectable atmosphere. An old castle of the Bruce, falling into ruin, adorned the hill; we lent our signatures to a furious petition in the newsagents' to prevent the Secretary of State for Scotland complacently allowing the ivied ruin to disintegrate. 'It's no' decent,' said the shopkeeper. The Bruce hauled his ships over the neck of land between the Atlantic Loch Tarbert and this Clyde inlet of East Loch Tarbert in the fourteenth century; there is a hole in the ground to this day where one of the ships fell over, Ship Hollow. So the woman in the library said. As Lord Cockburn put it in 1837 (there is nothing like a proud municipal library to set you right):

> Tarbert! East Tarbert! – there it lay, calm and silvery – a curve of twenty or thirty small houses drawn around the upper end, all comfortable looking – the ruins of an old castle standing on a rocky knoll at the left side of the entrance – a striking beautiful spot like a scene from a theatre.

So it is: if Tarbert were in Cornwall it would have been made unbearable by now, in Devon or Sussex even worse. But it is in Scotland, and the church bell still rings over the fishing fleet, the Kintyre farmers come to shop at Blair's Provisions, and the castle shall not be allowed to fall down: not because of the tourist trade, but because, as the town newsagent put it – 'We'll not break Tarbert's heart.' The Duke of Argyll, he said, had signed, and all of the Argyll and Sutherland Highlanders. 'It's more than a wee heap of stones.'

The children, alas, chose Tarbert for some frightful behaviour; three long days at sea had unsettled them, and Paul took one of his intolerant moods; he actually set out for a walk with the children and returned on bad terms half an hour later, saying Rose would have to be sent home as she had become impossible. Rose wept in her bunk, Nicholas sulked; all was discord. I persuaded the children to make a WELCOME GRANNY banner; we met the bus, fed my mother a salmon lunch, and gradually returned to family equilibrium in the evening. Paul and Nicholas went off for a long dinghy trip round the point; I stifled my irritation at that law of nature which allows fathers to appropriate the elder and easier child while the mother always has the company – for better or worse – of the little, unreasonable, slow-walking, demanding one. But Rose began to blossom again, no thanks to me: it was the slow, friendly, storytelling attentions of her Granny that improved her mood. A small child needs someone who will sit and chat as if time had no meaning. It has none for the very young and for the old; I felt ashamed at my need to rush and regiment the children, and wished – as often, but always vainly – that I was better at simply sitting and looking at a harbour, without needing to dash around it, climb it, row it, meet half its inhabitants and/or write about it. I am not a good mother to three-year-olds: I am fine with small manic babies and fine with over-fives; the pace of three drives me insane.

Still, my restless habit of poking around bore fruit that evening: with my mother on the boat, Paul and I were free to follow the main road across to West Loch Tarbert, the Atlantic entrance to the town, to find the route by which Robert the Bruce dragged his ships in the absence of a Crinan Canal to go through. On the way back, seeing the minister and couple of helpers tending the church grass, I stopped to admire the rare belfry and the eighteenth-century roof painted with stars and Norse symbols, and was politely offered coffee by Minister Scott McCallum in the vestry. He was a new broom of eleven months' standing. 'The kirk needs brightening up a bit, in all senses.' He fizzed with new enthusiasms; but Tarbert's gaunt old church had seen such new brooms come, grow old, and go. I admired his tower. He laughed. 'Aye, the tower's a great favourite with the local RAF. They use it as a mark in their low-flying practice, come about forty feet over it.' Yet again the armed forces were haunting us, as they had off St Ann's Head and Lulworth firing-ranges, as they had in Portpatrick, and out at sea by submarine and warplane, and by the low-flying grey helicopter that buzzed us alarmingly off the Cock of Arran. I went into the church to forget them, and there made a most happy discovery: a copy of *Sankey's Sacred Songs and Solos*, not a hymn book so easily found in an established church south of the border. It fell open at the very words of a hymn I had been searching out for years. Only the day before, I had been arguing with Richard Woodman about this hymn's existence, since surely if any service used it as an anthem it should be Trinity House. To prove it to myself, and him, I wrote the words down with a leaky biro of Mr McCallum's:

> Brightly beams our Father's mercy
> From his lighthouse evermore
> But to us he gives the keeping
> Of the lights along the shore.
> > Let the lower light be burning
> > Send a gleam across the wave
> > Some poor fainting struggling seaman
> > You may rescue, you may save.
>
> Dark the night of sin has settled
> Loud the angry billows roar
> Eager eyes are watching, longing
> For the lights along the shore.
> > Trim your feeble light, my brother
> > Some poor seaman, tempest-tost
> > Trying now to make the harbour
> > In the darkness may be lost.

17

All the way up the West Coast, Saint Patrick had haunted us: the Sarn Padraig causeway in Cardigan Bay, the little Pembrokeshire beach whence he had sailed for Ireland, St Patrick's Isle at Peel, Portpatrick itself with the Saint's footprint made at the moment he leaped across the twenty-one-mile strait with one step. 'To leave such marks,' observed Cowper, 'a man must be very much loved, or very much feared.' But if the Saint had left marks upon the psyche of the whole long coast, a more solid figure had left physical signs upon it. Thomas Telford died in 1834, but became in 1988 a sort of hero to us on our passage around the coast.

It was not just Portpatrick, St Katharine Docks in London, or his last great work, the Menai Bridge, which spoke to us of Telford. Far earlier in his career this remarkable engineer had built over a thousand miles of roads, the Caledonian Canal, countless harbours; he understood rock and soil and water and the materials he worked with, and had a fervent Victorian belief in improvement not for profit's sake alone, but for the people of the Highland region to which he returned again and again. In 1811 he was called in to improve and repair the Crinan Canal, that troubled little waterway started eighteen years earlier when canal-building fever caught the Duke of Argyll. It was clearly a good idea to link the quiet Clyde with the Hebrides, and they began in good heart. John Rennie, a young consulting engineer from East Lothian and architect of the Kennet and Avon Canal, had begun the work; but unlike Telford (who seems to have been a close supervisor of his projects), Rennie saw no need to spend his time on the spot. His Resident Engineer had never seen a canal in his life before, and the contractors were dubious. The finished canal was the most disaster-prone in Britain: a whole lagoon leaked off into the sea at Bellanoch, Lock Eleven was built on sand and leaked continuously; in 1805 the banks burst and the canal was closed for a year. In 1811 a storm smashed more locks and it closed again. Up came Telford, remodelled the floor of the canal and rebuilt locks: by 1817 it was in fine condition, and years later we were about to take grateful advantage of it in *Grace O'Malley*. No need to put up statues; not of Thomas Telford. *Si monumentum requiris, circumspice.*

The Crinan Canal, and these upper reaches of Loch Fyne which we were passing through with Granny at the helm, crop up now and again in the classic of Clyde puffers, *Para Handy*: a gentle canon of tales which we had been enjoying as we came up the Clyde. I had not read *Para Handy* before, having been erroneously persuaded by the name that it must be about some gung-ho parachutist; I was charmed by Neil Munro's mild, ironic tales about the little *Vital Spark* and her crew, plying and puffing around these islands and peninsulas with their various cargoes, beaching in little harbours to unload, falling foul of stiff-necked 'laandry-maids' in their courtships, and cruising from inn to inn.

'There was never the bate of her,' said Para Handy reverently of his ship. 'I have sailed in her four years over twenty with my hert in my mooth for fear of her boiler. If you never saw the *Vital Spark*, she is aal hold, with the boiler behind, four men and a derrick, and a watter-butt and a pan loaf in the fo'c'sle. Oh man! She was the beauty! She was chust sublime! She should be carryin' nothing but gentry for passengers, or nice genteel luggage for the shooting-lodges, but there they would be spoilin' her and rubbin' all the pent off her with their coals, and sand, and whunstone, and oak bark, and timber, and trash like that . . . I wass ass proud of that boat as the Duke of Argyll, ay, or Lord Breadalbane.'

I am particularly sensitive to the smell of stagy Scottishness; my father was from Cupar, Fife, a quiet and unemphatic man. He used to curl with visible pain at Harry Lauder, at crooked walking-sticks, kilt jokes, and people who said 'Haste ye back' or 'Lang may yer lum reek.' Like him, I would rather Scotland was never mentioned at all than mentioned in these embarrassing terms. But Para Handy tales lack the cuteness of the stage Scotsman; they reek authentically of kippers and coal-dust and gentle bewilderment. My favourite tale of all is set in the Crinan Canal region. The widow MacLachan is to go into the poorhouse, and plans to walk fifteen miles from Crarae to Lochgilphead at the southern end of the Crinan Canal, rather than let anyone know she is bound for the Lochgilphead poorhouse. Para Handy offers her a lift, letting her come aboard after dark because he is 'aawfu' careful o' her feelings'; pretending to remember her late husband (and, indeed, to owe him money, which they press on her), the soft-hearted crew of the puffer cluster round this 'old done woman' as they chug down the loch. They give her boiled eggs. 'Keep on boilin' em. Things never look so black to a woman when she can get a cup o' tea, and an egg or two'll no go wrong wi' her.' Eventually they discover by accident that the widow MacLachan is about to have a seventieth birthday, and will therefore be entitled to the new, wonderful, old age pension brought in by Mr Lloyd George: five shillings a week.

'Did nobody ever tell you that you wass entitled to a pension when they knew you were needin't?' asked the captain, and the widow bridled.

'Nobody knew that I wass needin' anything,' she exclaimed. 'I took good care o' that.'

I could not remember where else I had met Lloyd George recently, until I had a sudden vision of Caernarfon, where his stone effigy forever shakes its fist at invisible opponents hovering over the Seiont.

Anyway, there we were in proper Para Handy style, chugging up Loch Fyne with a pensionable Granny of our own. At seventy-three, she said she had never steered a boat before. It seemed the moment to start: she took the tiller and overhauled a herring-boat like a professional. 'I doubt whether I look like Garbo as Queen Christina, dear. Which way do I push it now?' At Ardrishaig, we stowed away the bowsprit and organized some mooring-lines which could be worked entirely from the cockpit. We were in for some strenuous exercise. There are no manned locks except at either end of the canal, and our pilot-book firmly told us that 'while a family can go through the canal unaided, it is much better to work in a team of boats'. One gloomy yachtsman at Tarbert had told us that 'The Crinan is a swine. No help at all except at the sea-locks, twelve heavy locks to work on your own, midges everywhere so big you could shake hands with them, and they charge you a pound a foot for the privilege.' We had time to prepare, anyway: the keeper was off for lunch and we could not get out of the sea-lock into the canal proper for half an hour. Paul leapt nimbly ashore up the neat, white-painted ladders and covered himself with neat white stripes to match. Some conscientious keeper had been going around with a brush, 'fettling things up' as Nicholas puts it. Eventually the keeper returned, we paid our dues, shuddered in Dad's memory at the injunction on the lock wall to 'Haste ye back', and rose in stately fashion some ten feet above sea level. *Grace O'Malley* was at the highest point she had achieved since her journey as an empty hull two years before, riding a low-loader lorry from Cornwall to Woodbridge. I ran ahead to the first do-it-yourself lock, took the ropes off Paul, made fast, and nipped down the ladder to tend them as the boat rose. He wanted to work the first lock, so he climbed the ladder, then grasping the instruction book, worked out which was the sluice-control, which the handle, and which way the balance-beam must be pushed to close the gate in that snug V-shape which is so satisfying in a canal-lock. We rose another ten or twelve feet, and chugged out feeling pleased with ourselves. Granny sat perched tranquilly on the side-deck with Rose, Nicholas conducting operations from the hatch.

But alas; the Heineys had never been canal-boating before. We were ignorant of the simple facts of life. Having found a ladder in the first lock, we assumed in our innocence that all canal-locks were equipped with ladders. Why should they not be? We chugged into Lock Three, looked ahead of us at the waterfall tumbling over the lock gate, then gazed around with a wild surmise. We realized there was no ladder. Only slimy walls. Nor was there much chance of reversing back to somewhere I could step ashore, not without damage and disgrace. Nobody was in sight above us on the high brim of the lock; a dozy early-afternoon calm lay over the clipped grass and the little white British Waterways cottages. Seeing no alternative open to me, I jumped on to the slippery beams of the open lock-gate itself, and prepared to scale it with a rope in my teeth. Halfway up, panting and wriggling to get under the beam, I met a tourist with a camera, rather puzzled at this interruption to his afternoon's scenic photography, and stuffed my rope into his hand temporarily while I got through to the bank. Then, with puffing uncertainty, I too worked my first sluices and gates, and up again went *Grace O'Malley*: maybe, we thought, she was now at her highest point since the low-loader went over the Orwell Bridge.

Now Paul, back at lock-top height, decided that I should drive the boat up into the next lock. Normally, I shy away from close-quarters manoeuvring. It would, he said, be good for me; besides, he fancied another go with the sluice-handles. My mother and both children scrambled ashore to stroll up the towpath and assist; alone aboard, I edged *Grace* out of the lock and round the gentle bend towards the next one. Then a cry rent the air, in my voice, startling the photographer again just as he lined up a pretty tree with our stately mast for some serene photographic study . . . 'MUM!' I shrieked. 'See that bridge! DOES IT COME BEFORE THE LOCK OR AFTER?' Mum looked vaguely ahead. 'It seems to be sort of, well, sort of over the lock,' she said. And so we met our first Bridge Lock: a harmonious Telfordian arrangement whereby the bridge spans one end of the lock-chamber. Our end, as it happened. The bridge showed no sign of moving, and Paul seemed unconcerned, strolling along the towpath; he had not noticed yet that there was a bridge in my way. I put the boat into reverse, looking nervously at the nearness of the muddy banks. Canal-boats are designed to be bumped into the bank by hopeless charter parties: yachts are not. Then the bridge swung suddenly out of the way, and I got into the lock-chamber and threw Paul a rope. He missed, and dropped it back in the water, and began howling, 'GO INTO REVERSE!' as I scrabbled the rope back and the boat glided unconcernedly towards the torrential waterfall at the top of the lock. 'DON'T BE A FOOL! I'M NOT REVERSING OVER A ROPE IN THE WATER!' I shrieked back, and threw the wet coils with immense force fifteen feet above my head and right into his face. 'JUST BLOODY GRAB IT!' Granny remained silent, reflective, staring into the blue distance. And up we rose, another step, into the relative tranquillity of a three-quarter-mile reach of flat canal.

The sweat and terror of the first locks apart, it is a great treat for a sea-boat to go suddenly into a canal. All is calm, all is flat; you glide past banks of rhododendrons, swathes of honeysuckle, tidy cottages: you blow your brass horn and bridge-keepers swing their bridges away for you; in the distance the green forest rises to the crags, and sometimes there is a heady glimpse of the sea, spread out so astonishingly far below you. Queen Victoria came through the Crinan Canal in her yacht many times, remarking that it was a little 'tedious'. Spoilt woman. What she needed was a good hour's work winding sluices and pushing balance-beams. At the Cairnbaan bridge the keeper kindly gave us two brown trout which he had just caught in his lock-basin; contentedly and far more expertly by now, we pushed and ran our way through a flight of four more locks. It is certainly hard work for a crew of two, and we were grateful to have my mother as a minder for the children as they tore around in their yellow buoyancy-jackets, loving the freedom of the little lock-platforms to cross the canal by, playing Trolls and Billygoats Gruff; but we were thoroughly enjoying ourselves by now, shifting sixty-five thousand gallons of water at a time with these wonderful Victorian handles and bars. Along the half-mile stretch of Summit Reach, flying sixty-eight feet above sea-level, we tried to improvise a tune to the Clyde Cruising Club's song about the Canal. We had the words in their book:

> The Crinan Canal's for me
> I don't like the wild raging sea
> The big foaming breakers would give me the shakes
> The Crinan Canal for me . . .
> It's neither too big nor too wee
> It's lovely and calm when you're frying your ham
> Or taking a nice cup of tea . . .

At last, in the evening sun, we tied up just before Lock Nine, the first descending lock, and while the children took rowing-lessons with me on a trout lake alongside the cut, Paul lit a portable barbecue to feast us on Tarbert butchers' sausages, brown canal trout, and a couple of Manx kippers. *Grace* lay beneath a jagged forest of pines, her tall reflection complete beneath her in the brown water. Later, in an authentically dreary Scottish pub with peeling ceiling, bare walls, and a general air of betting-shop austerity, we drank port and whisky, and nine fluffy ducklings followed us along the towpath. 'Perhaps we'll give up sailing. Do canalling,' said Paul, dreamy with Islay whisky.

The freedom of the seas, however, began to seem more appealing the next day when a cheerful canal employee called Bob appeared and told us that Lock Nine might not actually be working. 'Sluice is leaking the other end.' With much waiting, puffing and grunting, the gate was opened and we began our progress downwards through five locks. Bob kept up a flow of chat as he urged us onwards. 'Ugh – shove – there – this is the bit that ruins your golf swing, lassie – and other things, aye – right, you run on to the next one – hey, no, you wind, I'll get down and kick this sluice clear – brilliant engineering these, they always stick under that ledge – if I get wound down I'd better tell ye this joke first, the one about the skindiver – ugh – did you hear it?' – he kicked the sluice rod clear and emerged, not 'wound down', which I took to be a graceful lock-keeper's euphemism for decease or drowning – 'The canal's nae too full – it's been a dry spring – think she'll be fine though, till Tobermory Week when the racing yachts all come through.'

As we hauled ourselves through the last lock, he glanced drily at my mother who sat admiring the scenery, out of the way on the cabin roof. 'Aye,' he said admiringly. 'Granny's nae bother.' Mum took this as the compliment it clearly was. 'Weel, you wouldn't believe it, but half the trouble we get is no' from incompetent boaters, but from people – well, Granny perhaps, mother-in-law or the wife – doing' – he made expressive quacking gestures with his fingers – 'yakking . . . at the wrong moment, like.' A waterways man's life, in the high canal season, is a hard one. 'Six o'clock in the morning, you say tae yourself, today I'll be nice, I'll tell 'em jokes. Twelve o'clock you're biting your lip. Six o'clock at night, you're fit to tie, violent, the idiots drive ye mad.'

But in that gentle Highland voice I heard no violence: our *Glasgow Herald* from the day before lay on the chart table with tales of thuggery at the UEFA Cup game at Stuttgart, knifings in Glasgow, and an infant thrown into the Crinan Canal itself; but Bob might have belonged to another species. We were finding more and more of a contrast between life and newspapers as we sailed around the coast: every paper reflected hideous violence, aggression, abuse, and the disintegration of society, and everywhere we went seemed almost abnormally placid. Fuelled by a few sensational cases, feature-writers revelled in giving the impression that it was no longer safe in Britain for any woman or child – or, indeed, unarmed man – to step outside their own front door even in the most peaceful of market towns. Meanwhile, in a constant succession of strange new places, we were walking alone at dusk along headlands, chatting to hulking youths in back-street launderettes, and placidly settling off to sleep in an unlocked boat in the middle of town docks.

At Bellanoch lagoon, a wider bay opening just before the canal narrows down to a channel hewn laboriously through solid rock down to Crinan, we stopped for a fried breakfast; then dawdled along the last reach, between high banks studded with periwinkles, honeysuckle, rhododendrons, and poppies, to round the final bend and see Crinan sea-lock ahead. The canal had done us well as an antidote to too much sea; but ahead lay the freedom of the Hebrides. We saw my mother off, and took a last little dose of canalside cosiness among the grass and daisies and buttercups of Crinan locks. I complimented the sealock-keeper on the tidiness of it all. 'We try,' he said Scotchly, 'with the co-operation of the yachts-people, tae keep it that way. But it only takes one or two . . .' We tied up our rubbish-bags tighter than usual, and buried them deep in the bins. An old man hawked kippers and crabs very persuasively around the basin; a postman appeared miraculously with some mail for us. We had rather foolishly had it addressed to POST OFFICE, CRINAN, and discovered too late that there is no post office in Crinan; but he found us none the less. As the sun went down, the Crinan fishing fleet began to come home for the weekend, glisten-ing, shouting, winching, banging, smelling freshly of herring and cod, crab and scallop, as we sat on the manicured grass with our drinks. Discipline, clean white paint, Scottishness, courteous firm-ness, and fresh fish smells acted on us like a balm.

Apart from the midges, which as Para Handy promised were 'that big I was driving them off by throwing stones at them', only two things disturbed my tranquillity. The hotel's pleasant little coffee-shop was one: it held rank upon rank of little souvenirs, gewgaws, fancy soaps and perfumes and toys, and a cupboardful of pretty sweaters. This was fine; the tourist industry is as honour-able in its way as any other, and with fishing on the decline all along the coasts and manufacturing industries so aesthetically unlovely, seaside tourism is probably the only bastion we have against ruin and waste of our rocky edges. But at Crinan the gewgaws and soaps were all from Crabtree and Evelyn (of USA and London, England); the toys were Italian, the sweaters, apart from a couple of Shetlands, were imported from Guernsey. What point is there in a craft shop that does not reflect its hinterland? I asked moodily. Why should remote and dignified places act as nothing more than middlemen for international companies to peddle charac-terless tat? My mother – maker of miniature teddybears in Aran sweaters – looked wistfully at it all, and reckoned she could restock half the shelves from the wares of other old ladies like herself; and I for one would rather keep a Scotswoman in business in her own home with her own mountains around her, than benefit some Italian souvenir factory. Somehow, the sight of that stock crystal-lized an unease I had been feeling about the whole journey: a sense of Disneyland closing in, of harbours as adventure playgrounds and theme parks. The banging of the Scottish fishing fleet at dusk and dawn reassured me only a little.

The other unease was about the children. Their Granny's visit and departure had brought on an unprecedented volume of brattiness; they were getting to sleep later and later, in the almost endless daylight, often playing in their bunks at eleven at night; they woke at nine correspondingly cross and hungry and unpleasant to know. Paul wrote in his journal: 'The children are more cheeky and volatile than ever. I think they are fed up with this voyage.' Repeatedly, Rose asked, 'Why do we always leave harbours as soon as we get there?' and dwelt with her usual morbidity on the possibility that Tibby and Nelson and Virginia and Joyce would be all dead when we got home. Rose is habitually fascinated by death and pathos, and loves to act out tragic little scenarios; but this was too emphatic and frequent to ignore. Nicholas seemed to be impatient with constant voyaging, too: I reflected that perhaps children are never driven to travel and adventure the way adults are, because they are still capable of seeing the endless spaces of their own front lawn and the eternal mysteries of the apple tree outside the window. However it was, they had lost their impetus to travel. It had only been borrowed from us, in the first place. Like orphans attaching themselves to foster-parents, they made each harbour passionately their home, and left it with grief.

18

So vile a temper did Rose awaken with the next morning, so sharp an edge was there on her aggressive reaction to every suggestion – be it getting dressed, putting on socks, or being quiet for a moment so that we could hear the weather forecast – that my maternal irritation and sharp-tonguedness tipped over, with a suddenness I had experienced before, into maternal worry. Taking the screaming, shaking bundle on to my knee I cajoled her into saying what really was the matter. Homesick? Jealous? Feeling ill? 'My neck is stiff,' she said. 'Every day. And my other bits.' Off we went to the telephone box in the Crinan hotel, to try and contact a doctor: you do not ignore stiffness and sadness in a baby of three. Not when you are bound for remote and silent islands where – as the pilot-book warned – VHF coverage may be patchy and coastguards uncontactable.

In a grim surgery in Lochgilphead, reminiscent of the poorhouse from which Para Handy had saved the widow MacLachan, a sandy-haired young doctor assured me that she had nothing but a passing virus. So we set off in the early afternoon sun after a dull grey morning; our hearts rose a little as *Grace O'Malley* sank back to sea level through her last lock-chamber. A westerly breeze sprang up off the sea, and we made for the narrow Dorus Mor Sound, one of the dozen gaps between islands and islets leading out of Crinan Bay. The bay was too beautiful to motor through: we tacked carefully towards the gap, then were taken by surprise by the violent swirling force of the tide moving through it. Only three miles away lay the notorious Corryvreckan, the Witches' Cauldron, worst tide-race of the coast. Its influence was felt even here. It is odd to be in a confused tide-race: the boat seems undecided at any moment whether to obey the tiller or the unseen forces below. You feel you have a casting vote in which way the boat will go, but not much more. We scorned to use the engine, wanting to be on a par with Frank Cowper and the heroes of a century ago, but their hair must have been white at thirty-five: 'I have never had such an awful piece of steering,' wrote Cowper of Cuan Sound, a few miles north of this. 'The helm was always in movement, sometimes very slightly, and the vessel's head would remain in mid-channel. Then there would come a more violent rush, or the surging eddies would catch her stem, and away the old craft would sheer direct for the lurking mischief on the right, or the open destruction on the left.'

For us, matters were complicated by our inadvertently getting the jib stuck to windward, jammed on its winch; since we dared not risk tacking round towards the rocks of Craignish Point, we progressed through the Dorus Mor crabwise, effectively hove-to, hoping nobody was watching. Once through, we could free off the sails a little and make our way up Loch Shuna with islands rising around us like a dream: Shuna, Luing, Scarba, and Lunga in the distance, Torsa ahead. I had sailed these waters briefly once before on the St Kilda voyage with Christopher Thornhill: I remembered wild elation, terrible tensions when the engineless boat was swirled off-course in narrow sounds; Christopher's face, alternately white and pinched or pink and delighted, as he exhorted his crew and his boat out of danger and then played us rude songs on the accordion. I remembered this, but had forgotten what it is about the Hebrides which makes yachtsmen risk their dangers, tourists risk the rain, dreamers and saints and poets set up home here, and Highlanders keep their grim pride intact through generations of contempt and injustice. The sheer physical beauty of these islands does, quite simply, change everything. They are lands the world could be well lost for.

That western lands have always attracted saints and hermits is no accident. Deep mists fall here, and grey, grim silences enwrap the world; hidden dangers hem them around. Then on a summer's afternoon the darkness melts and this astonishing beauty is before you, behind the danger yet also a part of it; it is the beauty of a God who tests and torments before revealing himself. Distant blue mountains shade down to the sea; swathes of every green, of purple, of grey, rise from the water, coloured by moving clouds above as no harsh Mediterranean landscape is ever coloured. And there we were in the heart of this beauty, brown sails spread, singing nonsense. We jumped for joy in our little nutshell, and were kings of infinite space; free at last among the Hebrides.

Our goal was a tiny bay on the northern end of Luing island, protected by the islands of Torsa and Torsa Beg from every wind and called Ardinamar Bay. Not only was it snug, but it had a resident deity: a man in Crinan had told us that, 'A formidable lady named Irene keeps a book there and writes down every yacht that comes in. She has been at it since 1949. She usually tells you you've got in the wrong way.' Looking at the pilot-book directions, it certainly seemed a good place to get into trouble: gravel shoals, three barely covered rocks, and little indication of the way in except 'a splash of white paint on the wall and up a small rowan tree' as the Irishman had explained, which must bear two hundred and ninety degrees true as you run in. 'Irene McLachlan,' he said, 'has seen a lot of groundings. It is rare entertainment for her.'

Miss McLachlan's vantage-point, however, had lost some of its spice: the Clyde Cruising Club has put up two fine green beacons on the worst rocks. We picked our way in, gingerly, and anchored. On the shore, buttercups and bog-iris grew, red campion shone starry in the grass and a high spring tide lapped around the feet of big brown cattle. We trudged up the path and there, sure enough, barring our way, was a large and formidable figure: straight iron-grey hair, tartan jacket, broad ironic smile. 'And which of ye four is Grace O'Malley? Dear, dear. Come in. It's bitter, bitter cold.' As it was a mild evening, we wondered a little, but came in: the cottage room was dark, poor, carpetless, severely arranged around a big solid table bearing binoculars, a rope mat, a pile of leatherbound books, and Miss McLachlan's elbows. 'Well. Sign the book,' she said. 'The children too, if they're tidy with their letters.' She showed us the seven previous books. 'One lasted ten years, but you can't buy good visitors' books now.' There were yachts by the hundred, many faithfully repeating the visit over decades.

'A lot of them are fools,' said Irene severely. 'Fools. Two or three a week go on the rock, aground till the flood tide. Those people put up the beacons, but it's no good, there are too many fools. I wanted them to put up a big red sign saying KEEP LEFT. But they can't read, the fools. One boat said the perches were a great help, but didn't they have to go out on the other side of them . . .'

The children timidly stroked McKelvie the cat, who sighed in turn, as if despairing of human nature as much as his mistress. But the dark room, with its two-burner stove and ancient farming austerity, breathed nothing so much as happiness: obsessive happiness. Record-keeping, faithful down the years, had made a plain old farming spinster with a keen eye and a satirical grin into something approaching a tribal matriarch. Or perhaps she was more like a chipped old statue of the Madonna, with miraculous properties: one Clyde yachtsman trying to explain the phenomenon told us, 'It's sort of like a medieval penance: before you can finish your season's sailing with any luck, you *must* get into Ardinamar, and you *must* sign Irene's book to prove it.' Stockbrokers and merchant bankers, doctors and lawyers, advertising men and oilmen sit at her feet, anxiously seeking her approval; the wealthy with half-million-pound yachts and the frayed young in their old boats held together with optimism and patches all brave the complicated entrance and hidden rocks to tramp up the path that winds to Irene's door. They make her an honorary member of their yacht clubs, they miss their tide to wait if she is out, they plan their cruises around a visit to lonely Ardinamar. They are friends, but also supplicants: longing to be remembered and recognized. 'Och, I know them all,' she said, with motherly contempt. She showed us the CCC report of her annual tally: numbers down in 1987 from over five hundred to a mere four hundred and sixty-seven. The pages were falling apart. 'They don't bind these things properly,' she grumbled: obsessive, meticulous, friendly. 'Ye'd think they'd learn.' A happy cackle. 'People never learn. No-ooh sense. Take messages in bottles now: I pick up dozens. And can I ever read them? I can not. People are fools. They'll never learn to *dry the bottle inside* before they send it.' More pilgrims arrived in the little bay as we went back aboard: a consultant from Glasgow and his family. They rowed around quietly. 'Must see Irene,' they muttered. 'In the morning. Wouldn't want to disturb her.'

At the end of the long northern day, dusk was only falling at eleven o'clock: there was no light from the bare brown room at the top of the hill. The man pulled down his Royal Highland Yacht Club Burgee for the night. 'She's a member, you know. We made her honorary member at our muster, two weeks back.' He did not say so, but it was quite clear that the Royal Highland Yacht Club needed Irene more than she needed it.

In the morning, the Glasgow family walked up the hill with us, among the towering foxgloves and the stocky, dewlapped brown cattle that are Luing's main claim to prestige since its slate quarries closed. These monstrous creatures, half Highland, half Shorthorn, were the first new breed in one hundred and fifty years when forty years ago they were evolved for beef production. We took large detours around them. The lone bull, on his eminence above the road, looked like a child's drawing of a mammoth. Even the calves were huge, accusing-eyed, inquisitive things which one dodged nervously on the narrow roadway. They trampled off, over wild orchids, campion, periwinkles; overhead wheeled every kind of gull, and lapwings called triumphantly overhead as we breasted the hill and saw at last the Garvellachs, the Isles of the Sea. We bought the thirsty children a bottle of some fearful mixture called Crawford's Pineappleade, and walked back to Ardinamar in the watery sunshine.

Irene was sitting outside her house, binoculars and atlas on her lap: our trip round Britain had clearly inspired her to get it out and scan the nation beyond Luing. 'Ye came from here,' she pointed. 'Round, up, and here.' 'We did.' With her in the rough garden sat the driver of the Wee Highlander minibus tour, having decanted his passengers for ten minutes' scramble on the rocks. Bob, the Glasgow doctor, signed Irene's book with due formality, and glanced down the hill. 'We'll be off soon,' he said.

'There's no' much water,' said Irene, drily.

'Ah, we'll be fine,' said Bob. 'It's neap tides.'

'It's no' neaps 'til Thursday,' said Irene, with serene certainty. 'Ah well, we'll see you again.' She raised her binoculars to scan the horizon, and dropped them, turning her heavy, humorous face with its shock of white hair towards Paul. 'Suffolk,' she said. 'Ye come from Suffolk. Now I had a Suffolk Punch mare once. Fifty years ago. From Prettyman's stud, she was. Her name was Orwell Demoiselle. We called her Blossom.' The link with home, so unexpected, took our breath away. 'We sail out of the River Orwell,' we volunteered excitedly, 'and round Prettyman's Point, in the river. And we keep Suffolk Punches, too.' 'Woodbridge, that's where she was from. She came to Oban in a beautiful lined horsebox, then over on the vehicular ferry.' We jumped with excitement. 'Our boat was built at Woodbridge.' Abruptly Irene terminated the conversation, raising her glasses towards another sail on the horizon. 'Ah well, it was fifty years ago. In the thirties. Not worth thinking about it now.'

But we did think of the brown mare Blossom, coming as we had from the flat watercolour lands of the east, hot and bothered in a horsebox, swaying on a ferry and decanted suddenly into this rocky, sloping land half a century ago.

154

Bob left just before us. As he rounded the point in the narrow, rocky channel, he strayed a fraction to the south, and struck his keel on a rock. We saw it happen and thought he would bounce off; but the fast-ebbing tide stuck him further on each second. We got our anchor up and edged past him safely, offering to take a rope; he preferred an inward tug, so we thought – wrongly, alas – that a large motor-yacht on its way in would be faster help than for us to take a long turn. The motor-yacht, however, seemed in a bit of a panic, shouting at us to get out of his way, although we had far less water and held the right of way; he then thought better of attempting the narrow entrance with a yacht stuck fast in it – although we had just come past safely – and motored off in high dudgeon. Poor man. He would have to come back, now, and sign Irene's book another day. We circled a while helplessly, watching Bob attempt to pull his boat off: we could do nothing to help without grounding ourselves, and he would float off in an hour or so quite safely, so we reluctantly turned away.

The worst of it for Bob, as he cursed and hauled in his dinghy, was the thought of the satirical old lady up on the hill, noting every move. 'They never get off,' she had opined, 'until the tide lets them. Teach them a lesson.'

We sped on up the Firth of Lorn with a fair wind and blue seas. The children, sulky at leaving their small friends of the morning, whined about harbour; we conferred, and decided that tempting though the wild anchorages were, we would try to find them real harbours: secure, inhabited, lively places. We dropped the anchor for the night in the wide bay of Salen, but there was nothing to keep us there. Tobermory, best of the Hebridean harbours, was ahead, and before breakfast on Sunday we had brought *Grace O'Malley* to rest some thirty feet from its pink and yellow and blue and grey houses which skirt the harbour like a postcard photographer's dream. The church bells were calling, and the famous white legend GOD IS LOVE blazed in new paint from the harbour wall. It was written there in the last century, as a thanksgiving for the return of the full fishing-fleet after a bad storm, and nobody has ever admitted to repainting it. Yet pristine it remains from year to year.

The children took more interest in the thousands of jellyfish floating around the boat, the first prey they had been able to snare with their nets all trip. We feasted our eyes on Tobermory: walked its neat streets, peered longingly into the Sabbath-keeping shop windows, and realized from hasty subtractions of our own, and large proud banners in the street, that 1988 was Tobermory's year: two hundred years since it was founded by the British Fisheries Society to help feed the large and problematical population of Mull. 'The seas,' wrote a landowner, 'abound with fish, the Highlands with hard-working and good people. It will be our business to bring these two to meet.' Ullapool, Wick, Tobermory grew from this resolve; one of the few constructive and humane efforts of the dreadful era of Highland Clearances. I had been reading in my bunk at nights various grim, factual accounts of the days when villages were forcibly emptied to free the land for lucrative sheep, and the later nineteenth-century period when the Englishmen came and bought great houses and cleared out even the shepherds to make room for red deer. The house-burnings, the eviction of women and children without shelter, the ships waiting off the beaches like rubbish-skips to take the surplus people away to a rough and often hostile New World; these things came alive here on Mull. The moment of one 'flitting' was described two hundred years ago by Mary Cameron of Unimore:

> The officers of the law came along with it, and the shelter of a house, even for one night more, was not to be got. It was necessary to depart. The hissing of the fire on the hearth as they were drowning it reached my heart.

Her mother-in-law was carried on her son's back in a creel, she walked behind with little John and Donald; neighbours carried furniture:

> I thought my heart would break. We sat for a time on the Hill of Cairns to take a last look at the place where we had been brought up. The houses were being already stripped. The bleat of the big sheep was on the mountain. The whistle of the Lowland shepherd and the bark of his dogs were on the Brae.

Mary was lucky; she got into a sweatshop in the Glasgow cotton-trade. Others took the compulsory ships to Canada, to hack a living out of the great forests. Some died of shock and over-exertion; the strong survived to found dynasties of nostalgic Scots, singing the 'Canadian Boat Song':

156

From the lone shieling of the misty island
Mountains divide us and the waste of seas –
Yet still the blood is strong, the heart is Highland
As we in dreams behold the Hebrides.

Having visited the Highland Games, the Highland tartan mills, and find-an-ancestor services, I had formerly shared the southerners' mockery of Americans and Canadians who root anxiously through the tweed-shops for their clan tartan, or wear the fearful uniform of tartan trews; but I never shall mock again. On the forbidding coast of Morvern, opposite Tobermory, there lies a cleared village, bleak foundations of a murdered community. You can see it from the sea. Even two hundred years after such a flitting, the most remote descendants are entitled to their sentimental tears and their claims that this is 'home'. More, anyway, than the fat English cats who come up after the deer.

My reading had not put me in the best mood for a visit to Torosay Castle, a Scottish-baronial pile fifteen miles down the coast from Tobermory. But this Victorian mansion stands at the end of an endearing miniature steam railway from Craignure, and the children were due for a childish treat: so we puffed unsteadily down after the little locomotive (trying not to hear, in its steaming, the hiss of those dying fires) and wandered around Torosay for an hour avoiding the eyes of dozens of deer-heads, skeletal or furry, which stared down from every wall. For once, I dodged the children's historical questions about whether the people who lived here were clan leaders and wore kilts, and if not why not: the Vikings' imperialism was long enough ago to have lost its sting, but the evictions of crofters, by their own lairds first and then by English grandees with a taste for stalking, still spread a great discomfort over every amusing Victorian detail of Torosay. The lovely, empty landscapes should have been lovely, inhabited landscapes still, if there were justice.

To be fair, Torosay's owners seem not to have been involved in clearance. I rather warmed to the late David Guthrie-Jones, MP, for his painstakingly lettered captions all over the house: 'Your presence does much to keep the place alive . . . we don't do conducted tours, which in my view are hell for both guides and guests . . . take your time, but not our spoons.' There was something amiable about his messages, still gathering dust two years after his death, all signed D G-J. The best was on the staircase: 'These stairs lead only up to private flats. They carry portraits of six generations of the Jones Family. By all means come up and look at us if you wish, though I should warn you that bar my wife (the lowest picture) we are a pretty plain bunch!'

Back in Tobermory harbour we found a Brixham trawler, one hundred feet of old working sail, beautiful and solid. It was *Lorne Leader* of Lowestoft. We stared enviously at her hugeness, her immaculate decks and vast pumps; she was homely and business-like as only a real working ship can be. Next to us a tall, shaggy blond Viking was staring out at *Grace O'Malley* with equal interest. It was *Lorne Leader's* owner, Don Hind, who had just deduced that if *Grace O'Malley* was here, so were we. We had mutual friends: Christopher Thornhill again, and his wife Valentine who is Rose's godmother, and Michael Devenish who had sailed the first leg of this very journey with us. To meet a friend so far away was like a homecoming.

Don was a Glasgow merchant seaman and then skipper of training ships; he and his wife bravely bought *Lorne Leader* to save and cherish her. She pays her way with charter parties around the Hebrides, in which the rawest holidaymaker learns, perforce, to pull up several tons of mainsail. While his latest party roamed around the town he gave us tea and a tour of his preternaturally neat ship, and later he rowed out to ours with his cook Edward and half a bottle of Laphroaig. They spread the islands before us; talked of crazy Rhum and fertile Muck, of cheerful Canna and gloomy Eigg and the wonders of the Cuillins of Skye: these men sail endlessly in the stretch of waters between Kintyre and the Outer Hebrides, finding new anchorages, new castles, headlands, hidden bays, deserted villages; new pleasures every summer. We realized how little of it we would have time to see, but their enthusiasm was inspiring.

'It's best now – May – early June – ' said Don, 'when the flowers are out, the animals and birds, the seals and puffins have their young – everything is alive. There's no place like it.' They knew the pattern of the birds and the pattern of the ferries, the complex network of Caledonian MacBrayne which links the net of islands. They told us stories of small isles where the ferry skippers sit and carouse twice-weekly aboard their ships with all the islanders, passing on the gossip, while the tourists roam the deserted lanes and heaths thinking there are no inhabitants; of scandals and feuds and jokes between the differing islands, Catholic Barra and South Uist, Presbyterian North Uist and Harris; about the rows over Sunday ferries from non-Sabbatarian to Sabbatarian islands. This was their home, their watery, windy, glorious patch of sea; we saw it through their eyes and rejoiced in it. Don had his chartering down to a fine art, running 'theme weeks' for birdwatchers, musicians, historians; he had none of the professional's weary contempt for his punters.

'It's grand to be with people who have saved up and come because they really want to and they love it. A change from doing training cruises for kids on probation, which I used to do. I ran out of steam on that. You must never believe all this stuff people give you about the sea suddenly reforming difficult kids. They stay difficult on the boat. You name it, I've dealt with it: fights, drugs, drink, aggression.' He shuddered at the memory.

'Mind, there is something. When you've been in a bit of wind, in the North Sea shipping lanes, getting a sail down, relying on the man in front and the man behind to look after you, you change a bit. The main thing it did, when the probation officers and social workers came too, was to make the kids and the officials each see that the other was human. Nobody was in an office in a suit.'

As they rowed off, Edward suddenly called across the darkening midnight water. 'There's a poem. Do you know it?'

> I've sailed the seven seas
> And travelled every way
> But there's nowhere near as beautiful
> As Tobermory Bay.

In the morning, they were gone. We heard them on the radio once or twice, but never caught up with their wanderings again.

19

Mull is a huge tattered leaf of an island separated from the mainland only by the narrowest of sounds, the sunken glen of the Sound of Mull, and accordingly the most sophisticated of the Hebridean islands. Tobermory is its northernmost outpost; cosy and pretty with its colour-washed houses and the frowning pile of the West Highland Hotel looming over the whole like a Hitchcock castle. I grew most attached to the ornamental cherub on the fountain (presented to the burgh in 1843), and stopped to gossip with the man who had been commissioned to repaint it. 'It doesn't work, ah no, though they say that it once did. I painted it – see – even the fingernails are coloured.' So they were: very startling peach too, for a cherub. We came to expect the placid sound of the clock chiming the hours on the waterfront. We drifted through the forest path around the bay to Aros Loch, where fearless wagtails came and shared our pork pie crumbs, and bright waterlilies covered the freshwater lake: it was like, as Paul put it, a little bit of Berkshire in the Highlands. We had spartan showers at the guesthouse on the front, and shopped at Browns, the 1830s ironmongers which stocks everything, provisioning for the bleak coasts that lay ahead.

On the second evening I joined a handful of tourists in the Masonic Hall. It was a sinister setting: dark blue walls, pseudo-Gothic lettering, cabalistic symbols everywhere and a baleful stuffed bird. The windows were blacked out with ICI agricultural black plastic as if to camouflage some dreadful rituals. We, however, were met by nothing more ominous than a chap with an accordion and two schoolmistresses: this was the weekly slide show organized by the redoubtable Janet MacDonald, Gaelic teacher at the island's one High School, to introduce visitors properly and decently to the island beneath them. She welcomed us in Gaelic, and Fiona her colleague sang Gaelic songs ('Although, I fear, I am from Aberdeen'). Sandy with the accordion played Mull tunes, and the silent man in charge of the slides revealed himself as Miles, modern-Gaelic poet, and read a complicated conceit about 'The Scholarship of Worms'. As the fine western rain fell outside in the late dusk, I sleepily picked up snippets of the talk: about Rankine the piper who used to practise his secret, unsharable tune by standing behind a deafening waterfall, about the girl involved in the theft of the Stone of Scone in 1952, 'who later became a domestic science teacher at our school. We're proud of that'; and about the dozen sad, abandoned villages from the Clearances of Mull. Miss Mac-Donald practises an engaging piece of amateur archaeology in these villages: 'If you go to one of these, try to find the spot with flat stones and a good view and shelter from the wind, then you know that was probably the gathering-place of the village. Then dig down a few inches, and you will find old pipes and whelk-shells by the dozen. You can imagine them there, can't you, smoking in the evening and eating whelks, throwing down the shells.' Of all reflections on the Clearances, this one struck home most poignantly. Calgary Bay, the sweep of sand to the south of us, was the last calling-place for the emigrant ships. Muilleachs, Mull-ites, still don't like leaving their island. Janet MacDonald, afterwards in the corner, was casually commiserating with me on our failure to find a teenage babysitter for an evening ashore. 'Ah, you see, the girls all go to school in Oban during the week once they're fifteen. I remember it: the hostel looked out over the sound, and I could actually see Mull from the dormitory. It was terrible to go away.'

Perhaps it was their contented, celebratory Muilleach pride in their home which, overnight, precipitated me into the worst fit of homesickness I had had in all our thousand miles of travelling. We awoke in drenching rain and strong south-westerly wind; the seas would be too big to sail comfortably around Ardnamurchan, the most westerly point in the British mainland, which lay between us and the Small Isles and Skye. The thought of big seas brought effortlessly to mind the gloomy words of the Clyde Cruising Club pilot about Cape Wrath. The Cape had begun to loom over us, much as Land's End had done, and Bardsey Head, and the Mull of Galloway, only worse:

Great care must be taken in planning a passage around this major headland. It is totally exposed to north and west and frequently subject to very strong winds which build up a huge and dangerous sea in a very short time. Even in calm weather a large ocean swell is often present . . . once a yacht has left

Loch Inchard she is committed to the long and exposed passage until she reaches Loch Eriboll on the North Coast . . .

The pilot continues in the same cheerful vein about the MoD firing ranges which force small boats five miles offshore, the dangerous race off the next headland to the east of the cape, and so forth. This, coupled with the equally doomy prospects of the Pentland Firth (which contains two tide-races, the Duncansby Bore and the Merry Men of Mey, both fierce enough to get a special summa cum laude mention in Rachel Carson's *The Sea Around Us*, combined to give me a yearning towards the Caledonian Canal which by-passes the lot. I came to understand why so many round-Britain voyagers find themselves irresistibly drawn into the canal, even in fine summer weather. Reading an ancient, rather stained copy of the *Scotsman* I discovered a special bargain five-day tour to Orkney: coach and boat from Edinburgh, all comforts guaranteed. I may have made the disgraceful suggestion to Paul that we could nip through the canal in three days, do the coach-trip to Orkney instead of sailing there, then send the children home by train and sail straight home. We would be back six weeks early for a lazy summer in Suffolk. His reply was to push the button on the cabin tape-player and fill the air with the lugubrious sound of his favourite tape of the moment: the Star Accordion Band playing 'Keep right on tae the end of the road'.

> Keep right on tae the end of the road,
> Keep right on tae the end.
> Though the way be long let the heart be strong
> Keep right on round the bend . . .

Outside, another warm front whistled through, with wet south-westerlies, driving mist, and odd passages of sunshine. I snivelled a little, yearning for a nice soft sofa and a brainless evening with the television, but went ashore to ring the Met. Office, who spoke blithely of thirty-knot winds. 'Mind you, of course, you'll be finding that's not exceptional in Scotland, not exceptional at all.' I did not want to sail round Britain any more.

Luckily, to our rescue came *Aeolian*, a handsome classic 1950s yacht flying the Royal Cruising Club burgee. She anchored near us and the usual series of delighted hails identified her owner as Bill Spiers, the one and only Stornoway member. He and his son

Richard climbed aboard for a drink that night and shamed our misgivings with their cheerful accounts of nipping to and fro around Cape Wrath to the Faeroes, Shetlands, the Norwegian coast, going through Force Tens under storm trysail, lying to two anchors in westerly gales, and general intrepidity under sail. They had spent the previous day, while we mooched around Tobermory waiting for the wind to drop, beating hard for fifty miles on the way back from St Kilda. All this was quite matter-of-fact, and not remotely boastful in tone: despite Bill's artificial hip and Richard's temporarily paralysed arm, this simply was the way they sailed their boat. They revelled in their wild northern waters. The same headlong enthusiasm appeared in every activity: they told with roars of laughter how, on a Round Britain race, a group of racing yachts had turned up in Stornoway with ripped spinnakers in a storm, asking for the sailmaker. 'I said, "there's no sailmaker, what's your problem?"' In the end, 'We sent them all on their way with usable sails. My wife and I mended the lot. We also had seventeen people sleeping in the house.'

Personally, I daresay I would have sent them on their way with a brief lecture on not flying racing-sails in gales out of pigheaded competitiveness; but Bill was a nicer man. Life on the northern tip of the northernmost Hebrides clearly sharpens human sympathies. We all resolved to meet again the next night on the mainland shore: far up Loch Sunart in an almost landlocked inlet called Droma Buidhe.

Inspired by *Aeolian*, we managed to leave Tobermory, cross the windy sound, and anchor under sail alone in Droma Buidhe; unfortunately, Paul then glanced at the echo-sounder and realized that we were in too shallow water, and we had to move: eighty feet of chain came up, back-breakingly, and were re-laid; the lunch burned; this was followed by a tantrum from the children and a total, utter, and apparently final collapse of confidence and optimism on Paul's part. It had been my turn the day before; now it was his. He banged the chart table until the needle on the barograph flew up and down, leaving an indelible trace of his fury (he stuck it in his journal afterwards). 'Go home!' he cried to the children. 'You are quite appalling' – and they were, indeed, giving him adequate excuse for saying so, whining and fighting and making wounding remarks like 'I'm glad you two parents are arguing again, ha ha.' Paul decided to opt for the Caledonian Canal or, even better, for selling the boat in Tobermory and taking the train home. I was not too perturbed; both of us, if we are honest, admit to moments in our sailing lives when we could not decide between selling the boat, putting the children into care, or getting divorced; whichever, really, is the quickest route out of the claustrophobic trap of a boat in bad weather, seems at the time the best option. I was quite optimistic about the trip by now, though, and reckoned that Paul would come round.

The shore soothed us all. The sun gleamed through the wet beech-leaves in the silent, tiny bay; orchids and bog-iris, cowslips and daisies spread a carpet under our feet, and above us a hill rose, threaded by a clean, merry little burn. We saw that the custom of the local boats was to pick out their names on the grey rock or green grass in clean white shells from the beach. The children ran to and fro collecting them, then Paul climbed the hill with Nicholas to drink from the stream, and somewhere between shelling out the M of *Grace O'Malley* and discovering a clump of delicately veined white-and-purple orchids, I felt better. We lay on the rapidly warming grass, sheltered from the whistling wind, away from our claustrophobic little cabin and its family passions, and let the children run loose for a couple of hours. Back on the boat, Nicholas did his school reading without a murmur of protest, and Rose – having spilt the rubbish-bag all over the cockpit – amazingly began to tidy it up again.

Paul informed me of this, coming suddenly below with a happier face than I had seen on him for days. 'Rose is picking up the tins,' he said, as if some miracle had happened. 'She is actually doing something useful. She might be a good little shipmate, mightn't she, one day?' If this seems like unreasonable astonishment, it should be remembered that Rose, for all her wayward charm, had been contributing for some time nothing but senseless giggles and importunate hugs to the family weal, while on the debit side she shrieked, fought, created fusses, and ripped up bits of paper to throw all over the boat. Nicholas was altogether a different thing: he tried to learn to steer, switched instruments on and off, and asked pertinent questions. He was an adult in miniature, while Rose was a large, overgrown, overbright pet. It is the difference between three years old and five; ashore, in roomy houses with plenty of visitors, it gets blurred. At close quarters, it is overwhelming. Nor would we, on shore, have been quite so aware of Rose's hobby of morbidity. Just as you were grappling with a knotty tidal calculation, a little figure would appear beaming at your elbow and say: 'This is about a girl called Eileen who was lost and gone dead in an explosion, and someone shot her and wounded her to death. My bear Jingle was wounded and strangled to death by my other toys . . .' If you didn't respond in the right way, she would scream and bite you.

Having a clear recollection of how difficult Nicholas was at three, I had accepted Rose's foibles with equanimity. I always knew she would grow up into a rational being one day. Paul was realizing it only now, at that great moment when she picked up the tins and put them back in the bag.

Bill and Richard brought their boat alongside, under anchor, for tea; Richard dutifully scanned every page of the children's scrapbooks and accepted a lucky ship's bear for the chart table. Both of them joined us for supper. The children decided it was a party, and insisted on making our dignified guests play pin-the-tail-on-the-donkey; 'I always wanted a wee girl,' said Bill fondly, hugging Rose. The family, extended thus briefly with an honorary grandfather and an uncle, began to seem once more a secure and pleasant unit instead of a steel-jawed trap. Before bed, I pulled out the charts to try and decipher the next piece of coast, and revelled in Christopher's wonderful old pre-metric Admiralty charts. There is nothing so splendidly reassuring as a heading like,

LOCH SUNART
SURVEYED BY LIEUT-COMMR. W. I. FARQUARSON, RN
Assisted by the Officers of HM Surveying Ship 'Beaufort' 1934–7
Loch Teacuis from a Survey by Capt E. J. Bedford, RN 1864
West of Auliston Pt. from a survey by Capt W. F. Maxwell,
RN 1905–6

These charts are not yellow-and-white and clean and clinical, like the new metric ones: they are dense and grey. The small landscapes sketched on the border to assist pilotage, and the painstaking contour lines above and below the water, are visually appropriate in Scottish waters: the very look of the contours echoes the grey, complex, imposing look of the mountains. When the rain came on again at evening, they rose around us in this lonely, sheltered bay like a Victorian engraving in monochrome.

20

On a grim and drizzly morning, with a sharp west wind, we left the shelter of this tiny loch to round Ardnamurchan Point and open up a new landscape: the Small Isles and the Cuillins of Skye. Ever since some gung-ho yachtsman had told Paul that 'It's Ardnamurchan which sorts the men from the boys,' he had been gloomy about it: if there is one thing which peace-loving yachtsmen like us detest, it is any attempt to sort us from the boys. But we motored grimly on towards the point, bucking the headwind in the interests of getting a good sail once we could turn north. The wind, perversely, died right out after half an hour and left a big, sloppy, impossible sea behind it. I used to think that after a strong wind, it would be rather pleasant to hear a forecast of 'light variable' winds; but in fact, to sail through the rough water left behind by a blow is a miserable business unless you still have enough wind to hold the boat steady. The heavy boom slams to and fro, the sails flap, the speed drops to nothing; it takes a very firm resolve indeed, a purist or a man running out of fuel, to resist the lure of the ignition key. We duly switched on the engine again and engaged in a barely good-tempered philosophical argument about whether it was, in fact, really as despicable as it feels to motor a sailing-boat when you could make snail-like progress under sail. I did some gloomy arithmetic below decks, and worked out that so far we had spent just over two hundred hours under way, and logged ninety-eight engine-hours. However, when I remembered the Crinan Canal and the Menai Strait and the number of short hops we had done, it seemed more reasonable. After all, if you sail two hours from harbour to harbour, you may well clock up forty-five minutes' engine-time manoeuvring around in the two congested harbours either end.

They were fruitless statistics, but they kept me out of the rain. Reluctantly, I went back on deck: the Small Isles, Rhum, Eigg, Muck, and Canna were before us, dim shapes in the mist. No four could be more different: Rhum tall and shapely, its peaks like miniatures of the unseen Cuillins of Skye behind; Canna straggling; Muck flat and fertile, farmed assiduously to its very edges; Eigg a mad volcanic jagged shape. All had their appeal, and we sadly vowed to come here again and cruise them properly; from the sea all we could do was look, and read, and consider the usual bloodthirsty legends of Highland history. On Eigg, the Macleods – slighted in some way by the Macdonalds – drove the whole Macdonald population into a sea-cave in an onshore wind and asphyxiated them with burning straw. The awful thing about this particular legend is that one cannot cast civilized doubts on it, nor frankly disbelieve it as an exaggerated feudal legend; they actually found the bones only last century; heaps of them, still in the cave.

We could afford a night on one of the Small Isles, so we chose Rhum. Rhum has an even more chequered history than most of these troubled Highlands and islands: Neolithic man settled it, Vikings came to name its peaks and steal treasure from its monks and hermits, the eighteenth-century Laird of Clan Maclean ruled it, chasing its Catholic tenant-farmers into his Protestant church with a gold-topped cane (they called it yellowstick religion on Catholic Canna); famine stalked it, potatoes failed; finally the fifteenth Maclean, following the habit of the time, decided that clan loyalties came a poor second to folding money, and leased the island to the miserly Dr Maclean, his cousin. Dr Maclean did the dirty work: in 1825 he gave the islanders notice to quit and make room for eight thousand blackface sheep. A shepherd of Rhum, John McMaister, recalled 'the wild outcries of the men and the heart-breaking wails of the women and children, filling all the air between the mountainous shores', as the people were chased on to the ships for Nova Scotia – at the beginning of winter, too. The ships were, with dreadful irony, called the *Dove of Harmony* and the *Highland Lad*. Dr Maclean had a fine house for himself – its lodge house is now the post office – but it fell into ruin when the price of mutton fell in 1839, and the man himself was bankrupted. He retired, history relates, 'an alcoholic, to a medical practice on Tobermory'; which seems hard on Tobermory. Only a pair of crumbling gateposts now stand as memorial to his infamous memory.

Rhum, with its ruined cottages, depopulated shores, and wild unkempt forests, fell into English hands: the Marquess of Salisbury in 1845, then a mill owner from Lancashire, John Bullough, who fancied the deer-shooting. His son George was given the island in his will, and proved to be one of those amiable Englishmen, nutty as a fruitcake, who undertakes projects in such places as these. He built the absurd Kinloch Castle out of red sandstone from Arran (disliking the perfectly good Rhum granite); shipped in soil from Argyll, planted very English trees and hedges, and filled his house with bizarre bronzes, a Steinway, and an ornate orchestrion, to synthesize music for his shooting guests. He brought in hydro-electric power for his mad castle, and insisted that the laundry be built five miles over the mountains at Kilmory, so that his wife need not see linen hanging out.

We have, by chance, a clear account of what the palmy days of Bullough were like for the few remaining Rhum natives. Archie Cameron, in *Bare Feet and Tackety Boots*, relates his poor boyhood as a ghillie's son, distinguishing the freedom of the days when the Laird was away from the anxious humility of the 'Season' when the grand London folks came up. He is a cheerful man, full of relish for the amusements of poaching, sucking cods' eyeballs for sweet-meats, stone-throwing competitions, and making toy boats from the flat leaves of the bog-iris. Although he was expelled from the island at seventeen for a tiny misdemeanour (daring to complain at being fined £1 for borrowing a boat), Cameron is remarkably loyal to the Laird and Lady. His ire is reserved for the factor ('Factors and midges, the curse of the Highlands') who abused his authority and kept the islanders under an iron heel; not once does he kick against the basic injustice of Sir George's ownership and the entire lack of prospects for the lower orders on the estate.

The Edwardian splendour of Kinloch, somewhat foxed, remains: the castle is a hotel where guests can sleep among relics of Sir George, down to his very hunting-boots. As we slipped up the loch to anchor in clear glassy water, cloud poured off the mountains and fog hung around the red turrets of the castle and its tangled woodlands of alder and rowan, pine and beech, all planted on Sir George's imported soil. Midges crowded round us as we rowed to the deserted shore; Rhum is famous for midges. When Bullough built his pile, he brought workmen up from Lancashire and insisted they wear the kilt (Scotland has this odd effect upon the romantic Englishman). The story has it that the Lancashiremen, unim-pressed, negotiated a special kilt-wearers' midge allowance.

Since the Nature Conservancy Council own Rhum now, it belongs, I suppose, as much to the midges as to anyone; they have their place in the chain, along with the Manx shearwaters, razor-bills, divers, curlews, and deer. Experiments with early-colonizing post-ice-age plants, with deer population and other arcane natural history specializations go on all the time in large areas closed to the public; in the tiny post office (eccentrically open at 8.30 p.m., a true island shop) bearded figures in oilskins loomed in from the mist to buy crisps and tins of beans. Instead of lords and ladies from London, the island is given over now to naturalists from Cambridge.

We awoke earlier than usual to a rare morning: sun around the peaks of Rhum, sparkling blue-green water, seabirds' creaking calls around us and a light south-easterly breeze just lifting the flags. We were quite alone in the anchorage; without waking the children we hauled up the sails. Seals called from the rocks at the entrance, warning us off (quite rightly, as it turned out; there is a reef at the entrance of Loch Scresort which on a sunny morning one could easily forget). We tacked out, enjoying the sun around us all the more because we could see a line of fog ahead. It obscured the Point of Sleat which guards the entrance to the narrow sound between Skye and the mainland, and we sailed towards it across six miles of increasingly foggy sea. Nicholas took on one of his fits of enthusiasm, sitting on the inboard end of the bowsprit saying, 'I don't want this sail to ever end' – music to a parent's ears.

Grace O'Malley, suddenly alive under her topsail and decorated by gleams of wet sunshine, came to seem a wonderful boat again and our voyage a wonderful undertaking. The grandeur of the Cuillins might still be evading us to the north, but there were enough peaks and cliffs rearing ahead of us, shadowy and menacing, to bring even Rose to temporary silence. That afternoon we glided up to a mooring under the shelter of Isle Ornsay, and saw, gaping across the Sound from us the awful jaws of Loch Hourn: the Loch of Hell. It is the wildest and most remote of the mainland sea-lochs, a place famed for sudden ferocious winds, inexplicable downdraughts, and colossal depths. We felt the chill of it even on this calm day; the cloud pouring off the mountains seemed like the steam of Erebus itself. Our stocky little ship seemed tiny, inadequate to challenge any of it. Safe though we were on a mooring off the Duisdale Hotel, lying opposite Loch Hourn was rather like sleeping in a room with a strange Alsatian. The hotel, one of those

Scottish hotels which seem to have been designed with Agatha Christie houseparties in mind, welcomed us to afternoon tea on a clipped green lawn and to hot, hot baths – our first for three weeks; but whenever we raised our eyes from scones, croquet-hoops, bathmats, or other reassuring evidences of civilization, Loch Hourn's mountains mocked us on our lonely mooring.

There is no doubt about it: Skye is not cosy. The next day, sailing slowly up the Sound towards the narrows of the Kyle Rhea and Kyle Akin, the chasm around us grew deeper and more shadowy; the water alternately plagued with gusts coming down from the mountains themselves, and with calms so deep it felt as if we moved with hanging, wrinkled sails on some invisible current of an underground lake. We saw no other yachts; we could have believed that *We were the first that ever burst Into that sunless sea*.

However, in the shadows of Loch Alsh, Paul spotted a naval ship, HMS *Intrepid*, and had the satisfaction of stationing me on the stern-deck to dip the ensign to her; the ship dipped back, its men perhaps cursing us, perhaps grateful for the small diversion on a routine job. And we burst out of the sunless sea of Loch Alsh again, to see the humped shape of Scalpay island ahead, high Longay, flat Pabay; and the long, jagged mound of Raasay stretching fifteen miles away to the northward, a rag ripped off the Skye mainland. The Cuillins unveiled themselves, to the shoulder at least, with a show of cloudy modesty; at the moment when we first glimpsed them, the topsail shuddered and suddenly pushed us over sideways with one of the unpredictable downdraughts for which the region is famous. They are dangerous to yachts because, unlike a normal wind blowing sideways at you off the sea, these come from diagonally above and actually become a stronger force on your sail the more you heel over, not a weaker one. We took off the topsail. The light in this grey weather was extraordinary, a threatening luminosity beyond the mist rather than any manifestation of daylight; the landscape around us – or rather, above us – made us feel as if we had somehow sunk into the grey-and-black depths of the contours on the old Admiralty charts; we were inside the Victorian engraving, and yearned to see something coloured.

It seemed utterly impossible that out of this desolate landscape could come a town, let alone Portree. Approaching the promontory Ben Tianavaig from the south, we had no evidence of any human life; we might have been in the Lost World. Then, as we edged around the cliff, civilization burst rudely upon us. An aerobatic plane whizzed and zoomed across the mountain-faces leaving trails of smoke; a helicopter buzzed us overhead, and as the piers became distinct, so did a faint wailing of bagpipes. The boat secure in the bay, we tumbled into the dinghy with our inevitable bag of laundry, and rowed ashore at speed to find out what on earth was going on. Kilted pipers roamed the streets and skirled deafeningly from pub doorways, drinkers lurched around on the pavement giggling in accents from Newcastle to cut-glass Southern English (orf to the crorft for the summer). A magnificent Highlander, dirk in his stocking, plaid pressed to a nicety (ah, did Prince Charlie's men really roll themselves in sodden plaid to lie in ditches, hardy and hale?), stood like a rugged statue outside the bank; he was discussing suspension problems with a fellow-enthusiast at the vintage car display. Bewildered, we sought guidance at the Tourist Office. 'It iss Skye Week,' said the young man pensively. 'It iss ending today. It's a sort of ruse, ye see, tae extend the tourist season. Puts some people off, attracts Certain Others.' We remembered that it was Saturday, and spent a hectic hour putting our washing through the launderette and shopping at the supermarket. We had been warned of the implications of the Hebridean Sunday, and noted that the Skye Evangelical Bookshop was the most prominent building on the harbour front. Portree might be in carnival tonight, but Heaven help breakers of its silent Sabbath tomorrow.

We were right: on Sunday morning all was quiet except for the rustle of best hats going to church, and a strange, devout wailing music from the Gaelic service at the Free Church on the hill. We got Sunday papers, but only from a hotel and with a certain furtiveness; I actually hid them under my canvas smock as we walked past a group of rustling churchgoers, who were looking at my trousers with undisguised contempt. Not one ice-cream could we buy the children all day. I was rather pleased: we had been in plenty of places along the South Coast where every vestige of local culture or preference is subordinated, if not prostituted, to the tourist trade. A joyless Sabbatarianism may be rather a negative manifestation of local religion and culture, but at least it denies the altering, smoothing power of money.

And the children even understood about the ice-creams, because they had understood that Skye was a foreign land. We had taken them to the concert in the Gathering Hall the night before, to see jigs and hear harps and massed bagpipes. It was an uncompromising concert: we had secretly hoped someone would sing the 'Skye Boat Song', but all we got was mournful Gaelic laments and the harps and the pipes. The children were overwhelmed by it: Rose danced in the aisle, Nicholas sat solemn and respectful. We had had a lesson about Bonnie Prince Charlie, about the '45 rebellion, Culloden, the flight over the sea to Skye, the decline of the Clans and the clearances; and Nicholas, making a great effort of imagination for which I respected him very much, said, 'Scotland is sad about the English fighting them so hard, isn't it? Is that why the songs are sad? Because Prince Charlie went away to make room for sheep?' Well yes, I admitted, in a way.

Prince Charlie, however, took second place to a wonderful discovery the next day. Paul had gone off to climb a mountain on the understanding that it was my turn to do it at the next harbour; and the children dragged me up the hill, ostensibly to 'find the grave of Flora MacDonald'. I happened to know it wouldn't be there, since we were ten miles south of that particular shrine; but Rose was so morbidly keen on graves, and Nicholas so romantically struck with Charles Edward Stuart, that it gave some purpose to the expedition. After a stiff climb, we discovered something even better: the neatly stacked remains of the Skye Week Piano-smashing Competition. Pianos are wonderful when dismembered into piles of soft hammers and cunning little felt pads, black and white keys, tuning-knobs and bits of ancient varnished beading. We pillaged the heaps and took some bits back to the boat. Nicholas spent the afternoon banging a varnished board with old felt hammers while Rose attempted a Highland jig. The confusion in their minds was something, I felt, that future history teachers could sort out at their leisure. Did Prince Charles smash pianos, Miss? On Flora Mac-Donald's grave?

The Sabbath dragged on, with a keen, uncomfortable easterly breeze. We whiled away the hours cleaning the boat's nastier recesses, then climbed the tartan-carpeted stairs of the Portree Hotel for another bath, and a good meal in another hotel dining-room. Rose kept up a piercing commentary on her internal economy: 'My prawns are chatting, they're saying (silly voice) "Hello, Rose, it's nice in your tummee." But my scampis are very quiet, they're trying not to wake the baby prawns who are asleep just near my wee-wee-tubes . . .' I tried to quash this by very quietly reading them *The*

Railway Children, while Paul looked wildly around the hotel dining-room, pretending not to be with us.

We did not realize it at the time, but many of our problems must have been due to sheer fatigue. Living aboard a small boat is hard work even for an adult crew; when two members are making their full share of work and doing none of it, the load is doubled. We hauled every drop of water aboard in cans, kept children's beds sweet and clothes and toys in order, cooked and washed up and ran a cautious eye over rigging and sail-eyelets and the thousand minutiae of a sailing-boat; we never got to sleep before midnight, and were often disturbed by children or by the boat, and then each new day started with half an hour's worth of stuffing away bedding into bags. Every meal meant pumping up water, every wash meant boiling a kettle; the small efforts mounted up into substantial weariness. And it never grew properly dark: the long northern hours of daylight have many advantages, but they can compound exhaustion. It was light enough to read a newspaper out of doors at eleven thirty every night.

We should not have set out on the Monday at all. We thought we would sail ten miles north to the island of Rona, a difficult anchorage to-find but a good jumping-off point for the trip further up the more exposed north-western coast. We tired ourselves out in the morning stocking up at the shops, and finally dropped the mooring and put up well-reefed sails to face what was, to our chagrin, a headwind of about twenty knots. As we came round the point, it became apparent that we also had a big head sea to deal with: and for an hour and three-quarters we punched hard on to it in the narrow sound, tacking to and fro with a violent pitching motion. Rose wisely went to sleep, but Nicholas began whining about how much he wanted to see his friend Matthew, when would we be in harbour, would I tell him a story, etc. During one of our violent tacks, I hit my elbow hard on a winch, which sent the most painful, paralysing shock through my right arm and brought me whimpering to the cockpit floor for a moment: the arm remained almost useless for an hour. Nicholas finally went below, and threw a crying fit; Paul tried to tack the boat alone while I tucked the child up, but he then jammed a rope and threw a fit of fury.

'I – cannot – carry – on,' he said. 'Not into a difficult new anchorage, ten miles up to windward in a sea like this, unless the children behave. I wish we hadn't come; I wish we hadn't brought them, I am sick of this trip. It was a stupid, bloody, impossible idea and I want shut of it.' In silence, we freed off the sails and coasted back downwind towards Portree. We had made a mile and a quarter of northward progress in almost two hours; in fifteen minutes we were back where we started. Beating to windward, especially in a gaffer which is not too strong on this point, is a heartbreaking business. The Met. Office had told us the wind was set northerly until it died away at the end of the week: we felt trapped, pinned in this stern little port, claustrophobic in our little cabin. The log showed that we had travelled over one thousand miles on this voyage; we all felt that it was enough.

I took the children ashore in the gloomy grey afternoon, bought them an ice-cream and went into the dour Evangelical Bookshop to get them a new story tape I had seen of 'Daniel in the Lion's Den'. A shelf loomed at me with titles like *Withhold Not Correction*, *Spare the Rod and Spoil the Church*, *God is for the Alcoholic*, and *Death, My Greatest Adventure*. Two quavering old ladies held the fort, searching the window bewilderedly for the book I had spotted (it was the only cheerful one in the place). 'Aye . . . can ye manage, Winnie? This wood is terribly hard to get drawing-pins in tae . . . right Winnie . . .' I began, reluctantly, to see the funny side of our situation. There was a sign outside the Evangelical Bookshop saying GENTLEMEN'S HAIRSTYLIST WITHIN; I wondered whether an evangelical haircut would help Paul's despair.

Back on the boat, sunk in gloom, he continued to wonder whether the trip should somehow be aborted here, and if so, how. Sometimes it helps to separate the children; I dropped Nicholas back aboard, and took Rose off alone on a route-march along the bay. When we returned, I found relations still strained between father and son, Nicholas impossibly cheeky and unhappy, Paul aloof and gloomy, trying not to respond to his son's hail of insults and sneers. He made the effort to cook us all a good supper, then went ashore; ironically, the sun came out, glorifying the harbour and even revealing the far Cuillins at last. As the children sat in the cockpit eating toffee-apples on the rippling blue waves, any passing postcard photographer might have snapped the whole scene up as a carefree holiday idyll; for us, sticky and damp from the rough row out in the dinghy, our clothes unironed, two months and a thousand miles from home, it did not feel quite like that. I felt trapped: I could, I knew, jolly along the children around Cape

Wrath, past Orkney and down to East Anglia and home; but the journey was impossible without Paul, the boat's skipper, the children's father, and my only adult company. And he was reaching the point of despair.

Small children are, quite literally, maddening: tiny, isolated nuclear families, whether in slum flats or expensive yachts, are subject to intolerable pressures. It was ironic that I, who have never believed in tight nuclear families but filled my house assiduously with friends, nannies, nannies' friends, grannies, uncles, aunts, and passers-by, should have painted myself into this absurd, isolated corner merely out of the vain and romantic urge to make a voyage without harming my children by leaving them. We might well be harming them now: a cross, silent father, a mother prone to sudden angry slaps when she overreacted to their ceaseless nagging, must be compounding their unhappiness. That bad parents are better than a kind, even-tempered nanny is fashionable child-care philosophy, but then again, it might be wrong. Maybe we should have left them. Maybe we should send them home now. And we might have done, if it had not been by cruel chance that Virginia, still on the payroll and awaiting such emergency calls as this, was about to set off on her fortnight's holiday. If Paul could not continue under the pressure of fatherhood and gruesome Scottish weather, there was no answer but for me to go home alone with the children, leaving him to find a crew back.

21

Oute of these blake waves for to sayle
O Wynd, O wynd, the wedder gynneth clere . . .

No adversity lasts for long at sea, even emotional adversity. We awoke to a sparkling morning, although the north wind still blew keenly and the sound was as rough as ever; we managed to book the only hire car in Portree for the day, and carted the children off on a voyage of exploration over Skye. We roamed around doomy Dunvegan Castle and duly admired the tatters of the Fairy Flag and the dungeon, tastefully preserved with trapdoor and pit, right next to the Edwardian drawing-room. Depressing people, barons. We sat in a tea shop listening in a pleasant daze to swingtime renderings of 'Charlie Is My Darling'; then headed north into the austere Glendale region, where the grip of the Free Church is so strong that until the 1970s there were no licensed premises whatsoever, and whence the Elders still write angrily to the Queen when she is seen at Scottish horse shows on a Sunday. We spent hours in a lovingly reconstructed black-house cottage and its associated shebeen, promised one day to build the children their own shebeen in the garden at home, and discovered the most eccentrically delightful toy museum in a private house where the proprietress generously urged the children to hammer around on 1940s mechanical horses, wind up 1950s plastic film viewers, and play with the clockwork railway layout and the racehorse game. We found an old watermill, scrambled on rocks, and at last arrived at the newly founded Piping Centre. As a museum of piping, on the site of the MacCrimmon's home where piping began, it was informative enough; but we had difficulty controlling our giggles at the fact that the sound system was playing Scottish accordion music only.

The family atmosphere was lightening considerably; rather shamefully, it had taken a day out by car to make us feel normal again. A mile or so from the gloomy Piping Centre, we suddenly heard real pipes and stopped to see a young boy, outside his cottage in jeans and sneakers, practising with skill and unaffected devotion. As we stood and watched him serenading the troubled clouds above, we felt the first real stirrings of magic about Skye itself.

Back we came; that evening the Cuillins rose fully visible at last. Framed blue and distant in the bowl of green hills that set Portree, they were like gods, aloof and beautiful; then, like a pantomime effect behind gauze, they suddenly faded to leave nothing but a green bowl and an apparently clear sky above it.

That night saw the beginning of Paul's reconciliation with his maddening little children. It was Bonnie Prince Charlie who did the trick: Paul, who had been half-listening to my history lessons on the subject, suddenly announced that he would tell the children a bedtime story out of his head. He has always been good at this, producing tales of bears up mountains and the like; but this story was different. It went under the title of 'Nicholas and Rose and the Shining Armour', and began as the tale of two children who try to help a young king win back his throne. It was violent and alarming: the villain was a huge Highlander 'so fierce that he had *dead dogs* hanging from his belt'. The first episode, that night, stirred the children extremely; they hung on every word. Each night thereafter the story grew, with more and more ingenious plans being made by the children to foil wicked Highlanders, monsters, tricksters, and invading armies of Black Knights. The story did not end until the voyage did.

Wednesday dawned dull and cloudy, but calm; we motored northward in a thick mist, just making out Raasay and Rona before heading for Loch Ewe thirty miles northward. It seemed worth making progress after the long delay, but I did look rather longingly eastward up the luscious mouth of the Gair Loch, where the low green hills and yellow beaches made a paradisaical prospect after the austerities of Skye. Still, under engine on a glassy flat sea, just lifting to a long Atlantic swell, we all had time to play, and do schoolwork, and settle back into being at sea.

North of Skye, the rags and tatters of northern Scotland resolve themselves suddenly into a more solid, square-edged block of coast, open to the north and west. Yachts moving northward into these remote waters, the pilot advised, must be 'self-sufficient in spares and repairs', and prepared to hide from 'large and dangerous seas' in any strength of wind. Cowper pointed out that there is no land between here and the North Pole. Mind you, the same might be said of Cromer; and here there are the sea-lochs, deep and sheltered, to hide in. After seven hours of dull but useful motoring, still in a glassy calm we anchored in one of them, off the grey village of

Aultbea, next to the NATO jetty. We had had ample evidence of the British navy since reaching Scottish waters: helicopters buzzed us, submarines loomed in the distance, warships had to be dipped to ceremonially by Paul, always a stickler for etiquette (on my watches, I merely waved). That very morning we motored in the fog through the underwater weapons testing area in Raasay Sound: Paul, slightly less reverent about underwater weapons than about stately warships, had been flinging empty baked-bean tins overboard shouting, 'Track that, Navy!' But the most striking evidence of the naval uses of the Western Highlands was right here under our noses: as the sun at last struck through the mist at evening, we noticed that two of the grassy hills ascending towards the mountains above Loch Ewe were, in fact, not hills at all. Too regular, too symmetrical: a bit like Roman burial mounds, but subtly different. They were fuel bunkers, with pipes to the NATO jetty: nicely camouflaged for aesthetic reasons, no doubt. Less well-camouflaged was the usual assortment of dreary corrugated-iron semicylindrical huts which the services seem unable to do without. We decided to leave Aultbea very early in the morning.

It was flat calm again. We were once again, as in Menai, stuck in the centre of a large vague area of low pressure, in which the wind could blow from any direction at any time at the slightest shift of central balance; the Met. Office offshore desk had been tracking it well enough, but could never swear to whether a wind would arrive instantly or within a day, especially up deep, tricky lochs. In rather a bad temper, we motored for an hour, then saw wind ahead and prepared for the south-easterly as promised.

It was north-easterly, and light. Still, it was wind; I whisked up the topsail without a hitch for once, and we moved in stately fashion, at two knots or so, round the point and towards Priest Island and the major one of the Summer Isles, Tanera More. At two o'clock precisely, the wind died to nothing, left us drifting with slack sails, then abruptly came in from the opposite side: a south-easterly, which rapidly rose to Force Five and brought a rough swell from the loch south of us. It all happened so suddenly we barely had time to pull the topsail down. We discovered over succeeding weeks that this is a favourite trick of northern weather: sudden calms, followed by winds out of nowhere. The south-east wind was warmer; it brought sunshine, too; and we whipped easily into the deep, perfect shelter of the Cabbage Patch – the southern end of the bay at Tanera More.

Perfect natural harbours are rare: this one has one thousand nine hunded years of documented use. It was used by the Vikings who hid there from storms or from angry retaliatory parties of villagers from the plundered mainland; long before them, the Celts buried their dead here; medieval villagers used the islands as shielings, summer grazing for cattle brought across the two-mile sound by boat. Then the herring came, and a thriving fishing population lived, fished, cured and sold their fish here, shipping huge amounts to slaveowners in the West Indies. What the slaves made of a diet of salt Highland herring one cannot imagine. Then in 1900, the herring moved mysteriously away, and the usual island story followed; potato famine and wartime rationing made life in the end too hard for Tanera More, and the last island family left in 1931. The ex-island women were known on the mainland as 'pullets' because they lifted their feet so high, being used only to scrubland and bog.

But this is not another western island of ruined cottages, silent windy hills and undisturbed rabbits. There are still no roads at all, no flat paths, nor shops beyond a tourist tearoom, and no hotel; but when the tripper-boats go home at four thirty, and the naturalists go home for Michaelmas term, the lights still burn in a handful of houses.

'Our population just now,' said Melanie, the blonde, bubbling hostess of the teashop, 'is eleven adults and five children. The council pays for the school-boat every morning for the big ones.' The reason for this population lay around us in the bay: gigantic fish-farm netting pens, with bright pink buoys and blue netting garish against the muted island colours of grass and flower and pale-red rock. The Frampton family, London absentee owners of Tanera More, run one of the ubiquitous fish-farms which have taken over so many quiet Highland anchorages: half a million captive salmon leap, desperate and silvery, all day in the great pens, growing for eighteen months before being matter-of-factly harvested by lifting the nets and scooping them helplessly into baskets. Ecologists groan at fish-farms: the tin antifouling paint on the nets, the poisonous concentration of debris on the sea-bed, are killing rich areas of wild sea. But here on Tanera More, the human lights still burn because of it: everyone except the teashop girls and the naturalists is a fish-farm employee.

Landing on a shingle beach, the children and I heard childish shouting, and met two naked, jumping children of their own age. Their father, a friendly Lancashireman called Ken, invited me in for a cup of tea. Mhairi, his delicate, pretty Highland wife, at home with a crawling baby, told me that Ken had had the job, and house, for two months. Before that he was on the fishing-boats out of Achiltibuie; irregular money, not so good. And before that, he was in the North of England, unable to find a job or a council house. Here, in a good house and garden, with a virtually private beach and the wild glory of the island around, the family was learning to live island life. They learned to send Kevin, at six, all alone on the school boat in his lifejacket; to keep their car parked on the mainland for shopping trips, and to pick up what entertainment and company was going. The family came out to *Grace O'Malley* for a drink: the four children played on deck, the baby crawled around the cabin, and we sat talking about mundanities of island life: about the way television reception mysteriously stops on a line between their house and their nearest neighbours, so that you can carry a portable television across the line and suddenly lose reception, blocked by some invisible distant peak; and about how sick you can get of salmon, in their job. 'It's a good place,' said Mhairi, tranquilly looking out at her cockerel and chickens. 'You get a bit bored, but it's worth it.'

One other oddity came my way on this Summer Isle: on the 1908 chart we had borrowed from Christopher, PRIEST ISLAND TO LOCHIN-VER *Surveyed by Mr J. Jeffery Mastr. RN and Mr Cramer under the supervision of Captn. Otter RN 1848–9 and updated by Captn. Simpson of HM Surveying ship 'Research' 1908*, there was an inexplicable detail. A building just north-west of our anchorage was marked INN. When I asked in the teashop, the waitress said, 'Oh, there's a house there called the Old Inn, but it never was an inn, apparently. But there was a woman who was very old in the 1920s who lived there and brewed beer in great kegs. They say she ran an illicit still up the back on the hill.' Could we have stumbled on a subtle allusion here? When that old lady was a young, sly creature with a bit of a shebeen out the back, was there a spot of naval skylarking afoot? Did Captn. Simpson and the crew of HM Surveying Ship *Research* have a dram, and gigglingly mark INN on the chart? Did Captn. Otter, perhaps, even, have a drop with her old granny in the same spot? I fell asleep wondering, with the precise lines of the black-and-white chart engraved in my head.

22

The wind rose to a near-gale from the south-east overnight, giving Paul and me a troubled night thinking of our anchor; but the shelter trusted by the Vikings did very well for us too. When we eventually pulled the anchor up it was covered in wonderfully sticky, pebbly grey clay; the ideal holding material. We marched over the rocky island tracks towards the tearoom; but halfway we met Melanie, not serving teas but strolling along with her dog to pick berries in the remains of the garden built by the idealistic naturalist Fraser Darling. It was on Tanera More, in the 1920s and 1930s, that he made his once famous attempts to prove that the simple, ecologically responsible crofting life could be perfectly economic. 'It could,' said Paul. 'Provided you don't want any modern conveniences, or even the bus fare to Glasgow for the shops.' Melanie told us that it was far too rough for the tripper-boats, so her tearoom was shut. 'But there's yesterday's scones and things,' she said. 'And it's open. Go in and make yourselves tea, if you like.' We did, feeling rather like burglars, and sat in the empty tearoom enjoying Melanie's chocolate nut slices and admiring the model swordfish on the wall. Steve, the island boatman, wandered in and ate a bun and told us about the rigours of the school run in winter, in the small half-open boat which makes the journey to the mainland. 'The kids are all right, but if they play up it's hard to steer in the waves and keep them in order as well.' And so the day wore on with walks, long idle sessions on the boat reading or colouring, and more tea in Mhairi's house while Nicholas played on the beach with Kevin. There was a great comfort in having been caught by the weather, this time, in a place so well-inhabited and friendly: with eleven adults and five children on the island, we rapidly felt like just another cog in the small social machine; strolling around, meeting Dave and Steve and Melanie and Ken and Mhairi casually, sympathizing in a few small feuds, we settled in as temporary islanders. The forecast from London said that the strong easterlies were with us for five days more: impossible to round Cape Wrath into the teeth of a strong easterly. At least for us: we were sure that Bill Spiers would have tacked cheerfully all the way to the Pentland Firth.

On our last night on Tanera More, Paul cooked a fine treacle pudding. Later, I climbed to the top of the island and looked down on *Grace O'Malley* alone in the anchorage, far from home, with my children and my husband aboard her, united again, telling shining-armour stories together under the swinging anchorlight. I felt inordinately proud of them all: together we would crab on up this wild West Coast, taking each day as it came, trying to be optimistic and kind to one another, and often failing; we would get round Cape Wrath, conquer the Pentland Firth, and sail home southwards united. I sat for a long time alone on the hillside, smelling the damp, sweet couch-grass and the crushed flowers, and watched the black clouds overhead, accepting for once that we must take the weather, any weather, with as much grace and resolution as *Grace O'Malley* herself.

The forecast changed, and the weather did too: a damp westerly wind began to blow. We left the anchorage under sail, with both children still in bed and the rain pouring down. It was Paul's favourite kind of passage: damp Irish-misty rain, dim headlands and islands to grope around, a new course to set every twenty minutes: thoroughly interesting sailing, and only eleven miles of it. Our destination was Lochinver. A hundred years earlier Cowper had liked it a lot:

> The shelter is perfect; there are no tides to hurt or even hardly to speak of . . . It was here I first met the genuine E. coast fishing-boats, and I found the men wonderfully civil, well-informed and steady. The risks seem very great as regards making the trade pay, and if one is to believe what the poor fellows say, it is almost worse than the Stock Exchange. I felt truly sorry for them. Sinking their money as they do on some of the banks is very nearly as fatal as putting it on deposit in an Australian bank. I liked Loch Inver so well that I could have spent a week here or longer with much satisfaction. In the season it must be quite gay.

Feeling our way in through the mist, we made out its houses and then rank upon rank of fishing-boats lying alongside the pier nine or ten abreast. They had the typical, harmonious names that

Scottish fishermen give their vessels: *Fruitful Bough, Amethyst, Crystal River, Canopus, Ocean Star*. As we rowed ashore in the drizzle, hoping no more of this plain fishing-port than a few supplies, a night's shelter, and perhaps a bath under the baronial turrets of the hotel, Lochinver's first surprise burst on us: six feet from the dinghy, the huge head of a grown Atlantic seal, bolt upright in the water. It stared at us and snorted loudly. I had never been so close to a wild seal. It dived, a smooth grey hump; but reappeared nine or ten times, always from a different side of the dinghy, but always close, emerging from the oily water to snort again, and glare. The children were rapt. So were we.

It was soon to be the Sabbath again, and we expected no high jinks on a Saturday night in Lochinver; but at nine o'clock a skirling of pipes suddenly came over the water. Then silence. Then drums. More silence: then a command. It was clearly some sort of band practice in the long, empty fish-packing shed on the quay; I tumbled out, and without hesitation threw lifejackets on to the children, grabbed their boots, and rowed them ashore. Paul stayed for the weather forecast, preferring to hear pipes plaintively across the water. We three scrambled up a slippery iron ladder, across the crab-littered quay, and towards the shed. 'Perhaps they're dancing on swords,' said Rose, hopefully. I said no, they wouldn't be, it's just a practice; then the two children came to the entrance and –

'They ARE dancing on swords!' breathed Nicholas. Rose just stared. Under the corrugated iron and plastic roof, gathered around the fork-lift truck, pipers were playing and girls in kilts dancing. On swords. We watched them for an hour: old men, young men, girls and boys, with pipes and drums and immaculate Highland dress, skirling and battering and dancing under the command of an upright old man with a silver cane.

The crowd of loafers, tourists and locals might not have been there, until the leader turned suddenly towards us and said: 'This morning, at eight o'clock, the trawler *Golden Emblem*, which was built in Lochinver and fished here for thirty-two years, went south to Campbeltown – sold away from us. This tune, "Dark Isle", is a tribute to her and her skipper.' They played it, then swung into the traditional last tune, 'Scotland the Brave': remote, defiant, Highland to the backbone, doing it all for no one but themselves and their ancestors. Afterwards, the old man told me that this is the only pipe band between Cape Wrath and Fort William: 'The only one on the north-west coast. And most of the fishermen live in the East, bring the boats across to fish and unload. It wass the *Golden Emblem* that was our boat, locally built and manned. We were paying a tribute to her.'

We rowed back happy, deafened, and reeking of fish. The cabin was festooned with damp, clammy clothing and bedding, the heater was going full blast, and Paul had received a weather forecast of more harsh north-easterly winds and an unsettled outlook. I noticed a curious blip in the barograph-trace: he had clearly been banging the chart table with his fists again. Paul felt, far more deeply than I did, the weight of responsibility for bringing the boat and the children to this wild coast. I felt it too, in a way, but whereas Paul's instinct was to cast around for an escape, and feel frustrated at not being in control, I approached difficulties in a more calm and defeatist way. I had a Lowland Scot for a father, who repeatedly said to me in childhood: 'As you make your bed, so shall you lie in it.' It was his favourite proverb. As a result, I have never been able to let myself complain unduly, or openly, about anything that I have voluntarily let myself in for – childbirth, night shifts, windward passages. I find it consoling to say, as I did that night, 'Well, we always knew there would be low points.' Paul would reply, exasperatedly, that he didn't see that that made it any better when you were *in* the low points.

Still, we could plug on, making ten miles a day against the wind in the direction of the dread Cape Wrath and the shelterless northern coast. At least the bullying mountains of Sleat and Skye were behind us; as we got further north we were very much enjoying the low, granite-and-grass landscape of islands. It is more like Western Ireland, up here in Sutherland: boggy and low and wild. Cowper hated it:

'I have since learnt,' he says with a certain Johnsonian pomposity, 'that other people consider this district very grand and attractive. If rugged hills, piles of stones, an absence of all verdure, distant mountains, bleak and of no picturesque outline, and endless ramifications of coast, the sea strewn with rocks and the land studded with tarns, combine to form an attractive scene, then the N.W. part of Sutherlandshire is grand and attractive. The sky is generally overcast, and the prevailing local and mental colour is grey.'

Grey or not, it suited us very well.

The blip on the barograph had been caused by rage against the weather, not against the children. Paul had now taken over as their best parent, and the days were spent in discussion of what might happen that night in the shining-armour tale. This epic had now begun to take in Vikings and worse villains: 'This man was so HORRIBLE that he had a huge belly, so that he couldn't see his feet. So Rose tricked him by throwing custard on the floor so that he slipped and fell over . . .' On went the story, night after night, accompanied by squeaks of alarm from Rose and whoops from Nicholas, through complex plots in which Nicholas drained the castle water-tank with a siphon, Rose threw custard, and the Loch Ness Monster climbed aboard and steered the ship. They were, by now, at sea aboard the Good Ship *Clachan*. Paul's stories are invariably rather immoral and highly violent (in one episode, the children rescued a doomed haggis which begged them to get it away from its owner – and subsequently ate it themselves). The children relished it all as a nice rest from my high-flown heroic moral tales of Flora MacDonald, Minstrel Boys, lighthousekeepers' daughters and so forth.

Still forming in my own mind, private and treasured, was a sustaining sense of this voyage as an entity: a circle well on its way to completion. A pearl, to take out and look at in the prosaic days to come at home. If the North-west had given us no trouble, I would have been disappointed: the trouble was part of the pattern, another layer, a new sheen on the pearl. On the quay next morning, a lovely fresh north-easterly morning, I fell talking with an elderly fisherman. His was the only trawler-chimney smoking on this Sabbath morning; he was a Welshman, not one of the East Coast Scots. 'I've fished everywhere on the coast,' he said. He hailed lately from Port St Mary on the Isle of Man; he had fished off our home beaches in Suffolk; he had worked the seas off Cornwall, off Wales, off the Orkneys, and along the east Scottish coast for which we were bound. And his childhood had been 'on a Morecambe Bay prawner. Is that a caff-topsail rig you haff? Like my father's'. He seemed a good omen: a human embodiment of our whole circuit, another man who, like us, admitted he 'never got to know a place for more than a mile inland'.

We got the anchor up with considerable difficulty (it had wrapped itself round an old mooring-chain) and sailed out of Loch Inver. The seal stuck his head up again as we left. Then the wind hesitated and veered confidently to the north, increasing every minute; by the loch entrance we had reefed the sails, and were plunging painfully into a rising sea, towards the Point of Stoer. Rose turned green; Nicholas became whiny; the boat heeled over as far as she ever had before, and laboured up and down the coast in long tacks, first outward into the large Atlantic swell, then shoreward again into the short, confused reflected seas. Rose managed to be sick, then lay pallidly in her bunk, calling for the pot occasionally; Nicholas stayed on deck, damp and disconsolate, trying to find a good position to wedge himself in. The trouble with windward sailing is that it seems to shrink the accommodation of a boat: suddenly the big, comfortable cockpit is small and mean, and every tack means another set of toes or fingers trodden on, another rib elbowed, another temper shortened. Paul and I, left to ourselves, rather enjoy the odd thrash to windward, but with the children the pleasure is attenuated unless they stay asleep. The sun shone on us, though, and both children gradually emerged and began to enjoy the day. We showed them the Old Man of Stoer, an astonishing granite pillar with a hunched, grumpy head on it, and turned to leave it astern, with the sails freer; approaching calmer water we fell off one last huge wave which caused a bowl to leap right out of the galley shelf and the Nautical Almanac to vault into the sink, an almost incredible leap for such a fat volume. Then we were turning again, southwards, into Loch Nedd.

Loch Nedd had been recommended to us by a man in Tarbert harbour. 'I went in, and it was such good shelter I left my boat there all winter,' he said. 'Oh, if you get wind, please don't forget Loch Nedd. Really, don't.' So, since another six hours beating to Loch Laxford would have been legitimate cause for reporting us to the NSPCC, we had threaded our way through the rocks of Eddrachillis Bay to his favourite haven. And he was right: that nameless, passing acquaintance, how we blessed him. Loch Nedd is one of those miracles of Western Scotland, a long, crooked sea-loch which takes the wave-tossed sailor straight off the open Atlantic and the polar swell, and brings him within ten minutes into a still inland lake. The wind still blew Force Five or Six but Nedd's upper loch was smooth as a mirror, ringed with trees, crossed by paths of spongy boggy heather, beautiful as a dream. Inland birds sang, mellower than the wild seabirds who had swooped around us out by the headland; salmon jumped in the stream at the loch's head, and we were in paradise. The children poked around a wrecked ship's lifeboat on the foreshore, and shot their new potato-guns at imaginary foes; Paul and I lay on the sweet-smelling grass, forgetting the sea. There are Mediterranean harbours like this, with stunted olive trees not unlike the small Highland birches around us; but they are nowhere near so beautiful as a Scottish loch in the sunshine. Loch Nedd brought an end to Paul's nervous anger, to my gloomy musings, and to the children's worst behaviour of the trip. Here we cooked toad-in-the-hole and were tolerant and sweet to our children. Rose made an appalling mess with a bucket and toy boat long after her bedtime; Nicholas battered the ship's bell in a complicated private game. We drank quantities of whisky and smiled on their misdeeds, and refused flatly to listen to the weather forecast. Nothing could hurt us in Loch Nedd, and nothing could make us sail tomorrow for the north.

23

In the event, we stayed two days in the friendly arms of Loch Nedd, while a north-easterly gale mustered itself in sunshine and squalls, roared in overnight bringing dirty weather and drenching rain, then slackened into pervasive Scotch mist. We walked two miles to Drumbeg for an ice-cream, ate lunch in a dull little anglers' hotel to pass the time away, put our names down for fresh milk and bread on the shopkeeper's Tuesday run to Lochinver, and – as the second day dawned cloudy and black – pitched a camp at the head of the loch. This was Paul's brainwave: I had packed under a forgotten corner of Rose's bunk my small hiking tent and a miniature camping-gas stove. Armed with these, and the makings of tea, we took the inflatable up the loch and found a flat space among the bright yellow bog-irises and purple foxgloves to make camp. All day the children were delighted by the novelty of it, valuing the exclusivity of a tent far above the matter-of-fact homeliness of *Grace O'Malley*. In turn Paul and I walked the heights above, revelling in the sweep of the hills and the sudden glint of reappearing sunshine on the white water-lillies beside the Drumbeg Road. We patted the fat inquisitive sheep as we scrambled among them on the steep, birch-shadowed slopes above the boat, and wandered through the bare, deserted clearance houses; the impassability of Cape Wrath in these northerly gales was, at least, enforcing a better acquaintanceship with this odd, desolate, beautiful corner of Sutherland.

It is Scotland's Empty Quarter, where a village may be ten miles by sea but a hundred and twenty by road from its nearest neighbour; where bog and mountain, loch and pasture mingle confusingly. We read some of the memories of the recluses and twentieth-century crofters who have loved these places: Gavin Maxwell among his otters and flotsam furniture, a self-conscious, passionately escaping dweller on the banks of his loch off Sleat Sound; Mike Tomkies, red-eyed, watching wild cats in his *Last Wild Place*; and Rowena Farre, who wrote *Seal Morning* with rather less self-consciousness than either of those successors, and whose blithe childhood memories and delicate retelling of Gaelic legends entranced the two children when we had to hide for an hour in the tent during a particularly lashing rainstorm. Nicholas, indeed, began crying that evening at the sadness of the story about the Children of Lir who were bewitched into swans and only changed back aeons later into old, dying hags; but he asked for it again, sobbing, wanting to understand. The wind dropped throughout the second day, so to test the sea outside and to prevent ourselves from getting harbour-rot (although we met not a soul, we were beginning to regard Loch Nedd as home) we motored across Eddrachillis Bay in the pouring rain to a new anchorage five miles north, Badcall Bay. Despite the promise in our 1930s chart of 'Manse' and 'Doctor's House', there seemed no minister, doctor, or indeed living soul on the land; we anchored to sleep, and the next morning set out in a brisk east wind to get further North while the going was good. Since the nearest exit appeared to be Leopath Sound, at the northern edge of this rocky little pool, we flopped towards it in the faint breeze, and passed within a few hair-raising feet of two sluicing, sloshing rocks with white sucking foam reaching out to bubble round our keel. The children were, luckily, quiescent for this bit of the passage: feeling our way in, the night before, there had been an irritating sequence of non-sequiturs such as 'I'd better look at the chart – take the helm – Rose, in a minute – hang on, is that the one there? – where's the pilot-book? – look, take the helm again, I've got to find the corrections sheet in case – no, Rose, Daddy can't wipe you now – Nicholas, turn your own tape over – seriously, Paul, I'm sure that's only a fish-farm buoy – ' Rock pilotage with toddlers is a wearing business.

This passage soon became pretty wearing, too, since the east wind turned out to be northerly after all (it was blowing round the corner, as these things will in Scotland). What is more, it was blowing over a huge, confused swell left over from the gales. We motored towards Handa Island, once a well-farmed kingdom, run as a matriarchy with its own Queen: now a bird sanctuary disgorging an inexhaustible supply of puffins, gannets, and fat razorbills. Both children felt mildly sick, Paul reached the stage of not wishing to go below under any circumstances, and we merely endured as far as the head. The wind then fluked maddeningly round to the north-east, to greet us on the nose again; we stuck with the engine to thread our way through an intensely complicated group of rocks inside the Whale islets.

Since we would never get all the way to Cape Wrath in this huge sea with a light foul wind, we were edging as close to it as possible, so that when the sea went down and the wind was better, we would not have far to go before we turned eastwards. Most yachts hole up fifteen miles south of the cape in Loch Laxford, and indeed our *Sailing Companion* stopped there, at John Ridgeway's adventure school. But north of Laxford, better placed, is Kinlochbervie. This haven is a major fishing harbour, second largest whitefish landing port in Britain after Peterhead, and yachts are not – we heard – always allowed in. Reasonable enough: few things can be more irritating to someone trying to land eighteen tons of cod than a holidaymaking yacht parked against his quay. But just to the north of Kinlochbervie lies another loch, which backs on it across a narrow strip of land: Loch na Clais, or Clash. We could anchor up here in reasonable shelter, walk across the spit and possibly get water and gas; and still be five miles nearer the cape than if we had gone up Loch Laxford. Paul worked this out, and I concurred: but as we tore through the strange landscape in a rising wind, we were struck with a kind of awe. From sea there is no sign of either port: there is a red rock-headland, Ruadh Ruadh (charted 'Remarkably red'); there is a granite bluff, weirdly white in the mist; a distant mountain, appearing and disappearing with disconcerting speed; and a scatter of roaring, breaking rocks and islets. The one navigational mark, a light on the headland to guide boats to Kinlochbervie, was hard to spot: we might as well have been sailing up a cul-de-sac. In fact, as the mist whirled around us again and the rocks reared and roared, we might have been on another planet.

But Loch Clash was there after all; we anchored, and after the sense of interplanetary exile, we were rather reassured than otherwise by the sight of a crane on a raft by the workmanlike pier. A cheerful old chap in orange overalls came to help us ashore, and let us into his workshop to get fresh water from the tap: he and his mates were repairing fish-boxes, at a fast pace, ready for the return of the fleet. 'They're all oot the noo.' Indeed the port was echoingly empty. He admired our pair of diminutive sailors. 'Are they good crew, now? Mutinous? Well, all crews are that, mon.' Paul settled to the backbreaking work of filling the water-tanks, five-gallons at a time in a plastic can, while I took the children and explored this new scrap of land we had gained.

Kinlochbervie reminded me forcibly of somewhere, but it took Paul, panting up to the shop behind me after his second water-load, to put his finger on it. 'Mediterranean,' he said. 'Turkey.' And it was: the combination of romantic scenery and half-built piers, rock formations and rubble, clouds of white dust, builders, messy heaps of boxes and quiet, empty bays and islets was precisely like a southern Turkish resort busy trying to build itself while extending an unpractised welcome to the money-spinning tourists.

Or, in this case, money-spinning codfish. The new building in Kinlochbervie and Clash is of a first-class road for fish-lorries, new sheds, quays, iceplants; they are blasting away rocks, and erecting pavement and street lights and a bit of housing for fishery workers. Around temporary caravans, houses visibly grew: new gardens were shaping in this stony soil. There were all the marks of a boom: newly registered cars, bustle, a plaque boasting of an EEC regional development fund grant. A cheerful ex-nurse called Marie was running a craft shop on the quay: upmarket and pleasant, the usual mixture of Scottish sweaters, odd leatherwork, and bought-in fancy goods. The point was that she was doing well on minimal tourism – the road, after all, stops for good four miles after Kinlochbervie: this is the end of touring for the most determined. The money is there, and it is local. I almost expected the defunct Cellphone to spring back into life, detecting it. In ten years, Kinlochbervie may be quite a little town. The sad grace-note to this merry tune of prosperity would be to ask, for how long? The reason the east coast boats are here is that the North Sea is fished out. 'We find the Minches much better, now,' said a skipper in the main harbour. 'For a bit, anyway. We go out as far as Rockall.' The big boats, electronically and mechanically equipped to sweep the seabed with ruthless efficiency, have simply become too good, overtaking the recuperative power of the sea itself. They began to chug smoothly back into the vast main harbour and unload box after box, tube after tube, of glimmering fish.

I wandered back, marvelling at the scale of the new road; it would have done credit to Surrey. A group of young people came down to their boat on the Clash side to lay new salmon-nets, and spoke disparagingly of 'the enemy', the fish-farmers at Tanera More; adding some choice and colourful tales about the characters of various other fish-farming entrepreneurs which the laws of libel forbid me to retell.

The last thing we had expected in this dusty building-site of a harbour was hot showers and bacon breakfasts; but we had reckoned without the steely determination of the Royal National Mission to Deep Sea Fishermen. Here, beneath corrugated blue iron roofing, is their latest, most remote mission: a magnificent cafeteria, fishermen's television lounge, showers for men and women visitors, and that atmosphere of cleanliness and uplift which is only achieved in evangelical and alcohol-free premises where rough men suddenly mind their manners and carry their trays back meekly to the motherly canteen-ladies. I have always loved the Flying Angel, the Mission to Seamen, since my childhood in the diplomatic service: in Hamburg one of my father's favourite duties was to eat a huge, heavy Christmas dinner with all the displaced and beached seafarers in the steamy hut down by the docks. Even as a child, I was captivated by the practicality of providing hot meals, music, and clean shirts before preaching. The Fishermen's Missions had a stirring and equally practical beginning, during the nineteenth-century herring boom, when Dutch boats were selling gin and tobacco out at sea to the fishermen. Missioners set out across the Thames Estuary in boats of their own, with cheaper tobacco subsidized by W. D. & H. O. Wills. They also took tracts and hymns, but definitely no gin. There are tales of the two rival sets of boats cutting one another up, sneaking over sandbanks, taking risks to win trade and souls out there on the choppy grey water.

In Kinlochbervie, yachts are scarce enough to count as seafarers, and we were allowed to take showers at the Mission. I was glad of one; I had spent a sweaty, miserable hour hand-washing various essential clothes in a series of buckets aboard *Grace O'Malley*. This updating of the laundry was not before time: Paul, having run out of underpants, was wearing some of my stock of somewhat ex-iguous paper knickers. He came out of the male showers looking distinctly sheepish. A procession of huge Scottish fishermen had been going in and out while he was there. 'I had to pick my moment to undress,' he confessed. 'I couldn't be standing there in my paper panties, could I, when there was some chap just in from the Dogger Bank?'

At breakfast in the Mission, surrounded by brass plaques commemorating boats lost and men drowned, we half-noticed the television in the corner, silent at the moment, with Claire Rayner's image mouthing homely wisdom to a girl in a fluffy sweater. 'She's talking to us,' Paul said. 'She's saying, "Look, love, we've all suffered from north-easterlies. We all know what it is to have a slow-moving depression to the south of us. It's tough. But what you have to do is just tell yourself YOU CAN COPE."' We giggled, then abruptly the picture changed to a smoking oil-rig, and a young man in a sweater, pale as death, came dashing in and asked if he could turn the sound up. 'Ye've heard the news? The accident? In the North Sea.' The room filled up with a few more fishermen, harbour workers, packers: the women at the counter stopped serving, and for the first time we heard the ghastly news of the Piper Alpha oil-rig explosion: sixty dead so far, one hundred anf fifty missing, a handful in Aberdeen Royal Infirmary too burned to speak.

Of all the news that had filtered through to us via radio bulletins and the odd newspaper, this horror – heard here in this oasis of safe cosiness for working seamen – was the one which hit us the hardest. The North Sea was so close, this port so near allied to it, so many Aberdonians fished here: faces in the Kinlochbervie Mission were pale not – as far as we knew – from immediate fear for close relatives or friends on the rig, but out of pure empathy. Everyone in that room knew from close experience how cold the sea would be out there, how relentless, how appalling was fire on ship or rig. It was like a tragedy in your own close neighbourhood. Over the next few days we were to hear curt messages between coastguards, rescue boats, helicopters, on an otherwise silent VHF network; if we had been a day or so further ahead, we might have seen the distant awful flames of the exploding rig, far across the North Sea.

Sobered, we went back to the boat to prepare for the final assault on Cape Wrath. The forecast was, as London put it, for 'Nothing much from anywhere, and probably no fog to speak of.' We resolved to go for Orkney, whatever tedious motoring it involved; if we went to Loch Eriboll, the only near haven on the northern coast of Scotland, we might easily get fog-bound, and we were a bit sick of lochs, anyway. Paul readied the boat while I stayed ashore until the last minute with the children. It was a spectacular pebble beach, that: pink and blue and golden stones, flecked marble and granite, looking like a huge impossible nest of speckled eggs from which anything might hatch: trolls, dinosaurs, pterodactyls. I threw a few into the sea, and wished for a good passage. We were tired of thinking about Cape Wrath. It was time to sail round it.

24

The cliffs rose, ghostly and wild in the fine rain, ushering us up towards the Cape: Wrath, *Hvarf*, the turning-point, named by the Vikings who turned southward around it a thousand years ago. Monstrous towering stacks appeared one after another; then we saw the cape itself, huge, arched, surrounded even in this calm weather by heaving, uneasy Atlantic swells: a sleeping tiger. Rain ran down our necks and inside our oilskins; not a breath of wind rippled the heaving sea. It was both a relief and an anticlimax. Still under engine, we shaped a course for the spot fifty-five miles away where the narrow Sound of Hoy admits ships to Stromness, first and easiest port of the Orkneys. On we motored, on and on, windless, the sail idle above us. The sea was alive with birds, swooping pairs of gannets with yellow heads and wonderful tapered wingtips touching the glassy surface, bands of gulls, puffins by the bucketful: it was a fitting farewell to the rich and living seas of the west. For an hour, gloriously, we sailed close-hauled; then the wind dropped, and whenever it tried to blow it blew gently and from straight ahead, so we ignored it and rolled on under engine. The children played and fought and finally slept, numbed by the boring sound of the motor.

The long northern light was still with us, the sun high at nine o'clock, and we fell into a fury at the unctuous phrasing of the news bulletin about the 'worst ever disaster in the North Sea', when the newsreader read brainlessly the words, 'Now, with dusk falling, hope is fading . . .' Hope was fading indeed, and we bled for the families who waited white-faced in Aberdeen; but dusk was not falling in this latitude, not at nine o'clock. There is something peculiarly loathsome about journalistic cliché unsupported by geography, local report, or anything but the desire for a chilling phrase to add to the sensation.

We had seen Hoy, by now, towering in the distance, and took this as reassurance that mainland Orkney was somewhere in the thin fog behind it. By one o'clock in the morning we were craning anxiously for lights to guide us into Hoy Sound: the sea was still calm, but there was something unnerving about the great black towering cliffs and the solitary Old Man of Hoy in the dusk, accompanied as they were by a foolish bleeping noise from the Decca saying 'position suspect' and by the race-memory of warships and U-boats playing deadly games in Scapa Flow. At last a white light appeared, then others on the still invisible mainland shore, and finally the red leading light behind the white: we closed with the shore, and at two o'clock were tied up, heads hammering from the engine's relentless racket, slightly unsatisfied at having not sailed the distance but grateful for having arrived, at last, at our northernmost point. We fell into our bunks with a hot whisky each, and were rewarded for this by even worse headaches in the morning.

Stromness, however, was far from being the bleak little township we had expected. In the morning we came alongside the pier, where a cheerful harbourmaster reluctantly charged us a fiver for four days: 'It'd be free on a mooring.' We began to recognize the Orcadian version of a Scottish accent – a permanently surprised uplift, slightly Scandinavian, at the end of each sentence. We looked with pleasure at the crooked streets, and reeled with surprise to find within ten minutes a cosy, chintzy coffee-shop, a service wash for our vile bedding, fresh water, diesel near at hand, a bank, and shops selling exotic cheeses, untinned ham, and actual fresh bread on every day of the week. Our attitude – taken from my daily diaries – sounds rather silly in retrospect, as if we had left the most glorious unspoiled coastline in northern Europe to sigh with joy at the sight of a row of shops; but the pleasure of cruising lies in contrast. Kinlochbervie Mission one day, the vast Stromness Hotel the next. (One gets to the bar in this hostelry by going up in a curiously naughty old-fashioned concertina-doored lift, as if to an assignation.) The pleasure of Stromness is expressed by Frank Cowper: 'I realized we were quite in the world again.' We were indeed: after Aultbea and Kinlochbervie it felt like New York. Stromness is one of those cosmopolitan, sophisticated little port towns with no provincialism about them. Not only is it still the main ferryport for Orkney, but it had a solid eighteenth-century merchant tradition, and has harboured ships of many nations for a thousand years. There is a well where Captain Cook's ships *Resolution* and *Discovery* watered on their outward journeys.

We hired a car and drove to Kirkwall for our post, and paid a visit to the Highland Park distillery. Paul had had a yearning to visit a distillery ever since we crossed the watery border into Scotland a month before; we had reached the Talisker distillery on Skye (the whisky-man's Mecca) ten minutes after it closed. This time, we were in luck, and a winning young man in a pinstripe jacket, diamanté lizard brooch, spiked hair and single earring led us solemnly through the curious mixture of high-technology and peat lumps, ancient wooden spades and Customs-approved Spirit Safes, which is a malt whisky distillery. The children, astonishingly, followed the tour without a moment's restlessness, being particularly pleased at the news that during the war, with the distillery closed, troops were brought here for their hot baths in the vast wooden backwash tubs: 'Seventeen men in a tub, and the officers had the mashing tun because it was easier to get in and out.' We stroked the distillery cat, a whisky-coloured animal with the duty of keeping rats off the germinating grain.

It was Mr Churchill's fault that we had to hire a car. The Orkneys are a ring of stone, with the waters of Scapa Flow protected on all sides. Kirkwall lies on the northern side of the mainland island, and Stromness just inside the western entrance to the ring. A casual glance at the map – not chart – before we came had convinced us that from Stromness was but a short hop to Kirkwall, so we had asked for mail to be sent to Kirkwall. We had, to our embarrassment, completely forgotten the Churchill Barriers. In 1939, when a German U-boat broke in to Scapa Flow under the guard-ships and sank the *Royal Oak* and eight hundred of her sailors, Churchill ordered the Italian POWs caught in the North Africa campaign to be set to building barriers, great causeways blocking off the four eastern entrances to the Flow. It is, therefore, a good sixty miles' sailing, in fast tidal waters, to get to Kirkwall from Stromness, and only worth it if you are visiting the northern islands, which we had no time to do. Hence the hire car. Back on the quay at Stromness, I met Frank, a local fisherman who claimed to be the only man able to trace a straight fishing lineage back as far as records show in the same town and heard that he, too, was fed up with the Churchill Barriers. 'They're grand for the South islands,' he said, 'but it makes a long trip of it, in the fast tides, if you want to go out eastwards. Terrible seas in Hoy, terrible great seas in Pentland Firth.' Not, he said thoughtfully, that he really wanted to go out eastwards at all.

'But the fishing is not what it was. Overfished, the North Sea. The time was, we could go out and fill the boat with lobsters, crabs, anything. But it's overfished, almost dead now. Quotas don't help, because all they do is take the best fish and throw the small ones away, dump them dead. So we go further. They're fishing Rockall now. And how long will that last? Taking the best, and dumping the little ones dead.'

He seemed good-humouredly resigned to the disaster: the boats still bustle in and out of Stromness; fishermen still live in waterfront houses where washing flaps chaotically in the soft damp air; there is casual work around the harbour. Stromness is healthy enough, uncompromised by tourism, unpixified. Orkney fishing is not on its uppers: on the island of Westray, local prosperity is now such that houses rarely sell to incomers, thanks to the aggressive purchasing-power of successful fishing. But no fisherman denied to us that the fish is running out, and that the reason is their great seabed harrows and cruel purse-seine nets which kill indiscriminately. 'But what are we supposed to do?' they would say. 'It's a living.'

On Stromness's crooked, crowded main street my eye was forcibly caught by a slightly chaotic, hippy-looking shopfront with no apparent wares except a number of grotesque puppets and cut-outs, a shadow-screen, a smoking peat fire in the grate, and a bearded man in a permanent hurry. This was the Orcadia Folk Art Studio, and the children and I had barely put our noses into it before we were whisked into a basement by Andrew, the beard, and introduced to a variety of extraordinary puppets, mostly life-size: trollish little figures, fishermen, carpenters, and creatures with forbidding silver heads and gauze draperies representing the Finn Folk of Finnfolkaheem, the legendary land of jewels and golden sand at the bottom of the sea. 'And this,' said Andrew, laying his hand on a huge sea-serpent's papier-mâché head, 'is the Stoor Worm. A long time ago, the great Stoor Worm was a sea-serpent with a tail a thousand miles long, who wrecked countries and ate the sheep and cattle. A brave man called Assipattle rowed his boat into the Stoor Worm's mouth and set fire to its greasy liver with a lump of peat, and it died: its teeth became the Orkneys, the Faeroes, and the Shetland Isles.' The children's eyes shone: within the hour the legend had become so much part of their mental furniture that Rose had elaborated it and informed me that the dying Stoor Worm 'did a last big sickup, and that turned into England'.

Not unnaturally, this interpretation endeared us greatly to the Orcadian Folk Art lobby, and I went that night to one of their workshops. It was an odd occasion: under the blue-painted sky ceiling, among the draped nets and gauzy sea-cloths and disturbing grotesques of men turning to seals and creatures coming from shells, a dozen hard chairs were ranged for the passing public. Andrew and a fellow-musician sat tuning fiddles and exchanging penny-whistles, while a rather stern figure in ballet pumps introduced herself as Lyn, and announced that she would be doing some traditional dances. A large, slightly grumpy man named Arnie turned up and had to go away again and fetch his bagpipes; and a merry-eyed, bottle-nosed character with spiky grey hair and a distinct whiff of inebriation appeared and sat down heavily, determined to confuse the evening further by barracking from the audience. Every time Lyn began explaining about the importance of tradition and the rich Orcadian heritage of Pict and Gael and Viking, old bottle-nose would break in.

'Aye, but – I remember – ye said William Leslie's used tae be a grocer's shop, but it was an ironmonger's . . . nae, nae, that was his brother's, his brothernlaw's, he was kilt in the War – ' 'We are going to begin singing and dancing now,' said Lyn icily, and began, still hampered by an obbligato of folk-memory and unedited reminiscence from bottle-nose. Shortly, he began to do the fox-trot with a lady friend, before succumbing to the lure of the Royal Hotel bar opposite, and vanishing.

The young men sang pleasantly enough. Lyn talked of dance and drama traditions, and their relevance to the young, the unoccupied, the frustratedly creative unemployed groups who work with her from mainland Scotland. With sudden unexpected passion, she read a poem entitled *Dance to your Shadow*:

Dance to your shadow when it's sore to be living, lad,
Dance to your shadow when there's nothing better new . . .

But above all, Lyn herself danced. A dancing-teacher in a tweed skirt and pumps, at close quarters on a bouncy little wooden plank floor, is not the likeliest creature to inspire awe: but through my drowsiness as she leapt the figures of the dance, I began to see something of what she meant, and something verging on greatness in herself. The old folk dances of Highlands and Orkney have become tamed and civilized, diluted by courtly balletic influences in the sixteenth century and romanticized by exiled Scots into something cosy and remote. But taken in the right spirit, Fling and Sword Dance still hold martial, terrible overtones; the old songs ring true when they ring off the same stony hills that inspired them. As she leapt and sang and spoke, I began to accept that – airy though her projects might sound, teaching folk-dancing to the unemployed – it is a plain fact that a knowledge of the dances of past war, the songs of past struggles among a grand and desperate people might throw dignity and reassurance down on a new generation. A generation which has not been massacred or cleared: but merely left to wander in internal exile, cut off from the world of work and achievement. Dance to your shadow, when there's nothing better new.

As the night wore on and the lights burned brighter in the weirdly coloured windows, throwing odd lights on the wet pavement outside, she leapt and twirled like a dervish, neither man nor woman, fighting a fiendish duel at times with Arnie the piper. He huffed his bag full of terrifying noise and sent the cat scuttling for cover, then played hornpipe and jig faster and faster, trying to trip the dancer as she in turn threw in claps and leaps to distract him; it was an old duel, you could tell. When it was over, Arnie asked me rumblingly, pulling at his great belt, what I was doing here. 'On your own boat? Man, some people are well off,' he said without rancour. But when I humbly asked where I might find beaches off the main tourist tracks, he came alight, and led me over to the ancient charts on the wall. 'I was born here fifty-four years ago – now where was I quarried? THERE!' He stabbed an emptiness outside Kirkwall with a massive piper's finger. 'The cottage is still there, a ruin. Well, I went south – my wife's a Mackenzie – but she never settled south; I came back. I've been a pipelayer in the water service: I've walked every foot of mainland Orkney, up to my chest in heather, off the paths. People don't go off the paths. They've no idea.' He rumbled off some destinations to me, and slapped me on the back. 'I know each foot of this land.' This massive, romantic figure picked up his pipe-box and prepared to leave. 'Mind you, I'm a motorcycle instructor these days. Just one thing. Don't believe all this stuff about Scandinavian influences being strongest in Orkney. The Highlands count here. My wife's a Mackenzie.' With which mysterious emphasis, he vanished into the wet night.

Down the road, oblivious of their roots, Viking, Pict, Celtic, or otherwise, a packed bar of Stromnessians were celebrating pay-night at the Royal Hotel by belting out 'The Northern Lights of Old Aberdeen' to the accompaniment of a deafeningly amplified piano-accordion; and from the respectable front of the Stromness hotel came smashing glass and raucous singing of 'Happy Birthday To You'. The next morning, a number of the revellers were aboard the big scruffy motorboat inside of us at the pier. It departed, under the command of a man who was the spitting image of Professor Jimmy Edwards (whose death, by eerie coincidence, had just been announced on the radio). His passengers, oyster-eyed, were bound home for Graemsay. 'They were all a bit past going across last night,' said their commanding officer, twirling his moustache. 'Friday is pay day and that is a great day.' I was liking Stromness a lot.

Indeed, we were all liking Orkney a lot. It was odd to be among such fertile, arable flatlands again, gentle green hills with barely one rock per field; the very place-names, the suffixes of -*ness* and -*say* seemed to bring us back eastward again after the guttural Gaelic *Ruadhs* and *Eileans* of the West Highlands. We drove north to Skara Brae in the driving rain, to show the children the best Neolithic stone village in northern Europe, buried in sandstone for three-and-a-half thousand years until 1851; I did my best by telling them instructional stories about little Neolithic children helping to make pots, but my feeble efforts were nothing next to the sudden blaze of enthusiasm we met out there under the wet skies. On a soft green hillock between two astonishing little stone rooms – for they are rooms, with slab-stone dressers, beds, shelves – we saw a pair of bristling ginger eyebrows protruding from a blue water-proof hood, and heard a bark of pleasure at the appearance of children. Within seconds, Nicholas was being led around by the hand, Rose in respectful attendance, while this astonishing man lectured on the marvels of the settlement. 'Guard post. Here! Now would you be bored if you were on guard all day? Ye would? So ye'd write on the walls? Well, look what this laddie's done – scratched runes. Now what would ye keep in a clay pot like this? Drinks! Aye, water! And live crabs?' He leapt with agility into the low street between the houses, lifting the mesmerized children after him. 'DRAINS! I tell ye, these people three-and-a-half thousand years ago had inside toilets! There's people in Scotland, aye, and England, still waiting on inside toilets. But here, before those

Vikings turned up to ruin it all – !' he smiled disarmingly at two Swedes behind us – 'they had a drain which went through all the houses, making turns, draining to the dunes . . .' Breathless, we followed until, like a sentry in a Neolithic guard-post, he noticed an approaching coach. 'Coach coming. I must see them round. Thank you. My name's Alan. What's yours?' He was Alan Stewart, custodian of the Skara Brae Neolithic village, and it is a national disgrace that he has not yet got his own television show. He makes Magnus Pyke, Patrick Moore, and David Bellamy look like half-hearted exponents of their fields. It was the best virtuoso display of custodianship I had ever seen.

It fed the children's imaginations for weeks. We had learned, the hard way, a valuable lesson about small children. If things are difficult and amusements scarce, the answer never lies in offering obvious childish pleasures: new sticker-books, plastic toys, gimmicks, ice-creams, and roundabouts. We had tried all these, and got the same fractious, disrupted children we began with. The answer lies in the imagination: our children could be distracted and delighted, and their behaviour actually improved throughout the voyage by one infallible thing: new stories, opening new worlds. The Armada, the Vikings, Bonnie Prince Charlie, Paul's gothick adventure-tale, and now these wonderful people who built beds out of stone and lived in teeny streets: all of them had led to new games in a way that new toys never do.

Perhaps this is why we liked Orkney so much: so many people were willing, indeed anxious, to contribute their own input to our children's minds. The pinstriped lad in the distillery, Andrew among the puppets, Alan in the stone village, a passing lady who informed them that the Vikings had written rude words on a rock on Hoy when they found no treasures there. No sooner had we got them back to Stromness than Lyn Barbour at the puppet folk theatre took them firmly under her wing and supervised them in the making of puppets out of wonderful trunks of junk and papier-mâché grotesque heads: Rose made a mermaid, Nicholas a fisherman, and they spent the rest of the afternoon enacting some highly sexist, but folklorically correct, stories about Finnmaidens who try to lure human fishermen to their death and marry them, and how the Finnmaidens thwarted in this activity become hideous old Finnwives and are good only for spinning.

So was my head; Orkney was so joyful and self-confident, so full of more history than anyone can consume at a sitting, that you finish by being dazzled, able only to wander around the Corrigall farm museum patting the pet lambs and inhaling peat smoke.

25

We had neighbours by now at Stromness pier: four other yachts, a positive crowd after the remote waters we had grown used to. We had struck lucky, too: *Shearwater*, next to us, was another British family boat. The rest were silent male Danes and Norwegians, living in bleak squalid cabins and hell-bent on covering as many Neolithic sites as possible by land and sea before haring back to Oslo. *Shearwater*, what is more, had a crew of two amiable teenage daughters who, on being fixed by Paul's appealing eye, volunteered to babysit for an hour or two while we had a walk that night. Indescribable pleasure: we had not had a child-free walk together since Caernarfon five weeks earlier; and not before that for a month. We walked across the springy uplands over the town, thinking of the five thousand years' patient cultivation which had sweetened this thin sour peaty soil with seaweed and made it rich; we joined in spirit the protesters of Stromness in mourning and deploring the curse of uranium which lies under these fields. Inevitably, one day, some grasping and prodigal government will think it worthwhile overriding every local voice to dig the terrible stuff up.

Orkney is a dangerous place for dreamers. Seeing the small fields, ancient dry-stone walls, and old-fashioned human-scale farming, we entertained for a while the common delusion that we would shortly sell up down south and come up here to be crofters. The fiddler from the folk centre had set these yearnings brutally in perspective, though. I heard his voice again: 'Well, these people come up here and they've either got the Great White Settler complex, or the Good Life Felicity Kendal complex. They change things on their croft, get it all going, then we get a really terrible, terrible cold dark windy winter, and they can't hack it. And they sell up and go home, and leave the place in a mess for the next lot to change again. It's not good for the condition of the land. And they don't mix with Orcadians, except to suck up to a few old fishermen in the pubs who make up completely rubbishy local folk-tales in return for drinks.'

So we decided, after all, to remain voyagers: on the fringe, admiring, entertaining dreams but always moving on. There was nothing to stop us moving on now, anyway; Paul had at last achieved the haircut he had been wanting ever since he chickened out of the Evangelical Gent's Hairstylist in Portree. Now his curls, having been making him look more and more like Elizabeth Barrett Browning for some weeks, were efficiently shorn in an anonymous-looking barbershop in Stromness, where the sign, THE MANAGEMENT RESERVES THE RIGHT TO WASH DIRTY HAIR, indicated a no-nonsense attitude unknown in Vidal Sassoon's. With his briskly clipped hair, he certainly blended in better with the Stromness fishermen. My own hair grew longer and wilder, but I did not bother. There is, after all, only one small mirror in *Grace O'Malley*, and I was looking in it less and less often. There was too much else, I suppose, to look at.

So we were free to leave. On Saturday night it blew a near gale from the south-east, sending big seas right up the harbour to where we and *Shearwater* and the Norwegians lay alongside the stone quay. I woke at three to deafening creaks from the plastic fenders, and sluicing of water; going up to check the deck, I got the neck of my nightshirt soaked by a wave thrown up between boat and quay. It is the first time I have been soaked by a wave while tied up to a pier. The noise, motion, and pouring rain continued; I hopped up and down twice more, reassuring the children, kicking fenders back in place, adjusting ropes. Paul slept on, to my irritation, but then woke and redeemed himself by doing the cold wet job of doubling up the windward mooring-line. I failed to sleep again until after seven when, I am sorry to say, I was lulled into unconsciousness by a radio news report on the Church in Central America: it felled me like a sandbag. I could feel sleep coming at the first explanatory words, and vaguely wondered how my old colleagues on the 'Sunday' programme would feel about being used as a soporific. I decided that their Christian charity would prevail, and they would simply be pleased to be of use.

We all woke again to a bright morning, with the wind in the south-west blowing us clear of the pier. It was after ten o'clock when we stumped crossly to the coffee-shop for breakfast. But the day continued sunny, lifting our weary spirits; after a session of grovelling for the next lot of charts under Nicholas's mattress, and putting away the West Coast of Scotland in its case, we felt ready to continue. It was a pang to discard the charts of the northern Orkneys, fascinating Westray and North Ronaldsay, Eday and Sanday, and not to visit all the private, remote communities served by two ferries a week if they are lucky; but we had no time for a proper Orkney cruise. It was also a little lowering to be reading the prosaic English names on the charts for our next leg: Fraserburgh, Eyemouth, Humber Estuary; none of the crazy, surreal, fanatically detailed charts of the Kyles of this or the Ghairms of that; no more lochs, and very few remote anchorages without habitation. To go south and east meant going back to prose from poetry, back to solid Saxon from the lands of Celt and Viking; or so it seemed as I stuffed charts carefully away on that Stromness morning.

But we still had Scapa Flow ahead of us, and sailed in a very fresh south-westerly out to the point of Calva, then eastwards across the Flow.

It was one of those glorious and rare lifetime's sails: after our days of beating through the rain and mist up to Cape Wrath, and our long, teeth-rattling motor trip out to Orkney, we could have sung – we did sing, indeed – in exultation. Scapa Flow's flat waters, swallowers of battleships in 1918, shelterers of convoys and long grey warships in 1939, stretched out shiningly blue-green around us; we saw each island rise behind the other, from the Highland sea-cliffs of Hoy to the flat industrial platform of Flotta with its giant oil terminal – which looked oddly innocuous, even in this paradise. We saw standing stones high on the horizon, looking over their fifty centuries, and far away on our port side the tower of St Magnus' Cathedral, glory of the North. Then, as we opened the end of the southern islands, far away across the Pentland Firth we saw the north coast of Scotland and Duncansby Head, where we would turn at last southwards for home. The boat flew along under nothing but a reefed-down mainsail and one jib, reaching seven knots at times; the rudder thrummed with exuberant life, the tiller trembled in my hand. Nicholas asked for silver to throw to the Finnfolk for good weather; we threw them ten pence. At last, we rounded Needle Point into the sheltered bay of St Margaret's Hope on South Ronaldsay and picked up a vast mooring tied to a hideous red oil drum, clearly the property of one of the fishing-boats over by the pier. Ashore, the village was wrapped in silent Sunday calm; but a tractor drove past, and a young woman grubbed weed and moss out of the flagstones outside her grey cottage. We had at last sailed clear of the Free Kirk Sabbath.

The village seemed strange, its brick houses dropping to the water like a continental harbour, its streets crooked and stepped, chimneyscapes arranging themselves below us in the evening light. It seemed so untouched by the past five decades that it was impossible to believe that when these little shops opened on the morrow, they would not be selling the *Daily Sketch*, Fry's Five Boys chocolate, and Omo. A dog ran up to us, and a very old man, heedless of the Sabbath, ordered us to 'Thraw a stick for him – he'll gae tae the moon for a stick.' We did.

The timeless atmosphere of St Margaret's Hope was not dispelled next morning when the shop opened and the crooked streets began, in a desultory fashion, to bustle. We drifted around the tiny Wireless Museum, soothingly cramped with walnut veneer, sunburst carvings, and grey tin with black bakelite knobs on it. Paul looked dewy-eyed at a device called a Gramdeck, for playing tapes on a gramophone turntable. He had longed for one as a child in the fifties; I read avidly the 1961 edition of the *TVTimes* which lay around as window-dressing. *Ena and Martha take Minnie to the Out-Patients and hand out some of their own medicine . . . the honeymooners return to a surprise . . .* On the big horn gramophone, a 1912 record quavered out the long-dead voice of Willie Kemp singing 'The Smiling Orkney Isles': 'There's nothing but smiles in the Or-ke-ney Isles.'

In 1912 St Margaret's Hope was still an important place: it had been the finest port in the south of the islands, when the Water Sound between it and Burray was open. It was the home of the vanishing herring-fleet, a lobster port for two hundred years, a ferry terminal. Then the herring left, and when the war came blockships were sunk to keep invaders out of the eastern sounds into Scapa Flow: finally Mr Churchill set his Italian prisoners of war on Lamb Holm to building the barriers to seal the sounds off forever, and St Margaret's Hope had ended its career as a port of any importance. Jacqueline, our taxi-driver on a flying visit to Kirkwall that day, was a giggly, chirrupingly gossipy woman, a war baby with faint memories of all the talk about the barriers. 'Well, they were a good thing. I don't think there'd be so many of us still living on the south islands without the roads. They had to build the roads, you know – it was against the Geneva Convention to use prisoners for war defence work, so the government quickly had to say that it was a road they were building, not a barrier . . . so we got the road! But of course it was a barrier really, it was war work all the time, really . . .'

We stopped on Lamb Holm, and visited the touching Italian Chapel: two Nissen huts camouflaged with infinite love and care by Italian prisoners of war, painted with trompe-l'oeil brickwork and marble columns, with sanctuary lamps beaten out of bully beef tins and a driftwood tabernacle. Step inside the Nissen huts now, lovingly restored after the war, and you would think you had stepped in from the harsh Mediterranean sun, not the wet westerly gale that blew across Scapa Flow that day. They built themselves a bit of Catholic Italy, up here at the edge of the world: poor homesick boys, poor pawns of war. Almost more touching on the site of Camp 60 was the work that began it all: prisoner Domenico Chiocchetti's statue of St George and the Dragon, made of barbed wire and cement, brilliantly aping stonework. It seems chivalrous of him (unless he was ordered) to have chosen an English saint.

I asked Jacqueline, as we push-started her elderly taxi down the hill to the main road, whether Orkney has really changed very much since the war ended. 'Ah . . . we feel not,' she said. 'Well, a few changes. For the better, we feel.'

In Kirkwall, still waiting for the wind to drop, but waiting well-contented, I took the children to see St Magnus' Cathedral. Enough tributes have been paid to it, rose-red and intricate, less like a building than a gloriously rationalized section of sea-cliff; we watched the pale sun through its tall stained windows, and hunted for skull carvings on the florid seventeenth-century tombs. I took some pleasure in telling my bloodthirsty children, who played Vikings daily, the tale of young St Magnus of Orkney: taken on a raiding trip at his Earl's command, he rebelled. While his fellows attacked the Welsh ships in the Menai Strait, Magnus refused the command, and read and sang pacifically from his psalter. In the end, he got his head bashed in for it: but it was a treat to encounter a pacifist Viking at last, after the trail of blood and pillage and casual imperialism we had encountered all up the West Coast.

Orkney had been a transitional place for us: we were out of the Gaelic and into the Norse: back among fertile rolling hills after merciless cliffs; back in populous country after the ruggedness of the West Highlands. But between us and mainland Britain lay the

Pentland Firth: a daunting piece of water at any time, and not – the pilots all firmly advised – to be approached at spring tides or in any wind over Force Four. Unfortunately, we had winds of Five and Six, 'gusting Eight', as forecast; equally unfortunately, with every day we waited for the wind to abate we came a step nearer the spring tides. We walked and waited and rang the Met. Office, willing them to take away the wind; yet all the time I felt a tug towards Orkney, a desire stronger than anywhere else since Caernarfon. I could stay here among these islands, keep sheep that feed on seaweed, wait in patience for the winter boats. I knew this place would enter my dreams permanently. As Duncan John Robertson wrote, with an odd echo of the 'Canadian Boat Song':

> Where the dear green isles shine low and fair
> We moor in dreams beside familiar quays.

All the best island songs are about coming back, or dreaming of it. Never about actually living there.

Our waiting to cross the Firth came to an abrupt end: the wind in these northern latitudes, close to the centre of depressions, seems able to drop suddenly away to nothing in a manner surprising to southern sailors. After a night and morning of westerly gales, the wind fell to a near calm by four; a prudent telephone call to Pentland Coastguard made it clear that the currents would have flattened out the worst of the night's westerly swell, and that we could cross this tidal motorway in safety. We sailed off the mooring, and with a sense of destiny made southward for the islands of Stroma and Swona which guard (and intensify) the Pentland tides.

At first, we had little wind. We had motored around one of the great northern corners of the nation, and were deeply reluctant for sentimental reasons to motor around the second. But sentiment and sailing tastes take second place in waters like these, and rather than find ourselves in the full tide still lying upstream of the dreaded Pentland Skerries, we turned on the engine and proceeded southwards. I rather petulantly threw a silvery new fifty-pence piece into the waves for the people of Finnfolkaheem, asking for a decent wind and fair crossing; Paul said, 'Throw them a fiver and do the thing properly,' but Nicholas insisted the Finnfolk preferred silver, because Lyn had said so.

Ten minutes later, a south-easterly sprang up, moving swiftly more to the east to become a thoroughly pleasant breeze; the rain-showers cleared, and the sun came out in a torn, troubled, beautiful cloudy sky. 'Chuck them another quid so that we don't have to reef,' said Paul, but I was purely grateful. We began to see the reason for the reputation of the Firth: as the first of the easterly tides began to run, the wind kicking against it threw up an uneasy, boiling sea, and began to form larger waves. We did not care: Duncansby Head was close now, and we were well clear of the legendary Skerries and the Swelkie, where the Viking witches turn their salt-mill forever underwater at Loki's command, churning out the salt of the sea and causing an impressive whirlpool (the *Admiralty Pilot* calls the Swelkie a tidal eddy, which is less interesting but more exact). Around us the life of the northern seas visibly abounded still; puffins swam, shearwaters swooped, razorbills beat the sea with their wings; a couple of distant seals surfaced and once, fleetingly, the cartwheel-section of a glistening dolphin's back.

And so we passed into the North Sea again, the last of our seas, the home stretch: with five hundred miles still to go, we could already see plain evidence of home ahead. There were flat-topped cliffs instead of mountains, dark-blue seas instead of green, Saxon names instead of Gaelic. Duncansby Head passed close to us, borne on the accelerating tide: we saw its red sandstone arches and caverns, and then we were in Sinclair's Bay, looking towards Noss Head lighthouse. Rose, sensing something, appeared on deck in her nightdress as the sun began to lower behind the green eastern scene. 'In the distant distance,' she said, 'I can just distantly see the gleaming whiteness of Pattle's Farm.' And she began to sing one of her made-up songs, spur-of-the-moment songs full of every grand and momentous phrase she could conjure from carol, hymn, *Alice in Wonderland*, Armada stories and sea shanties. I wrote it down in the log:

> In the ranks of South Australia
> Spanish ships sailing the East coast
> Going West
> Sailors sailing sailing to harbour
> In the ranks of Beth-le-hem!

It went on for a quarter of an hour in this exalted strain, before degenerating as usual into a lot of bum-talk and horrible raspberries to amuse Nicholas. I felt privileged to have heard it, as one feels privileged to hear the seals singing on the rocks.

The evening, and the sail, continued beautiful: sunset over the cliffs, Noss Head ahead of us with its white lighthouse, *Grace O'Malley* twisting over the growing waves with obedient glee, heading homeward. I sat on the foredeck, then lay on the deck-planks gazing at the sun through her rusty sails, loving every inch of this boat, struck into wonderment by this voyage around our big island. Frank Cowper had such moments too: I quoted him to myself up on the moving foredeck: *It is a noble thing, this voyage around our coasts.* Even the back-breaking task of making up the children's beds in a considerable seaway seemed noble that night.

Any conviction that might have been growing that from here it was all downhill work was abruptly challenged off Noss Head. An unexpected tide-race got hold of us, and reduced our speed to a knot. *Grace O'Malley* dipped her bowsprit repeatedly under huge waves; seas broke over our foredeck. We twisted through it for an hour, unwilling to ask the engine for help, and finally dropped the sails a hundred yards from Wick breakwaters.

Frank Cowper came to Wick on the rather hurried final leg of *lady Harvey*'s voyage round Britain in the 1890s, 'and after taking a look at the unsavoury and untidy inner harbour, left about ten the next morning'. The herring-fleet must have been in at the time: Wick was one of the queen ports of the great herring fisheries founded in the early nineteenth century. Every summer more than fifteen hundred men and girls walked here from Sutherland, across the mountains from Kinlochbervie, Lochinver and the glens, sleeping rough. Most of them were dispossessed crofting families looking for work in the great summer herring fisheries. Relations between 'Wickers' and 'Hielanmen', despite horribly stretched accommodation, were reasonable, except for one famous riot – almost a race riot – on the hot night of 27 August 1859, when a brawl over a dropped orange ended in a gigantic knife-fight; but the daily scenes in the inner harbour, behind the quiet walls we saw that night, were very likely as indescribable as Cowper says. Photographs show a noisy, smelly chaos of drying sails, women gutting herrings at the rate of forty a minute, tangled nets, drunkenness and general gold-rush prosperity of a type a gentleman-yachtsman would have shrunk from as we today shrink from an industrial building-site. *Lady Harvey* remained anchored primly out by the old breakwater that night in the 1890s; ninety years later *Grace O'Malley* slipped thankfully between Bremner's stately piers to get out of the easterly swell, and motored all alone into the vast, echoingly empty mill-pond of the inner harbour.

For Wick still fishes – gulls, nets, fish-boxes, an ice-plant all testified to that, as did a couple of trawlers being painted on the slip. But the herring are gone now and the great days ended. And the North Sea itself is dying: we saw more boats marked WK for Wick working out of Kinlochbervie and Lochinver in the west, than ever we did in Wick itself. Ironically, it is the Highland ports which are in the ascendant now. We tied up in solitude against a private ladder, next to twenty other vacant berths, and drank a late mug of soup in the twilight.

More modern advisers than Cowper had told us to skip Wick, giving a fastidious shudder; and indeed it is not natural idyll material. But Wick is a comely, decent, grey-stone Scottish town, with manicured lawns on its clifftop, a neat lifeboathouse, and the remains of the old kippering sheds standing rather forlornly around the harbour walls. True, the town is disfigured by hideous boxy new houses; but this is mainland Britain, after all, where few towns escape the dead hand of the charmless contemporary planner. Wick still has dignity. And at its heart, to our delight, we found a remarkable museum. Masquerading under the gloomy appearance of the usual two-room civic museum, and the irritating title of Heritage Centre, Wick boasts the biggest museum in the North: the curator led us through room after room, narrow staircase after staircase, until we were in the lower room of a lighthouse, inside its very light, then in a high kippering-shed where the fish hung on special hooks. They are called tenterhooks, hence, some say, the colloquial phrase; although what could be less suspenseful than a dead herring I do not know. Another doorway, and we were on a busy fish-quay of the last century. It was a museum with a discernible life, an almost frightening sense of recent-ness about it: toys though they now were, every boat was rigged by a man who had done the job at sea, every net made by a woman who had done it as a child. The cooper's workshop had barrels made here only ten years before, and the lighthouse bore a poem by a local fisherman beginning 'As sweet to me as light of moon or star/Is thy bright gleam, old trusty friend Noss Head . . .' Downstairs, in a turn-of-the-century kitchen setting, there lay casually on the oilcloth table a little leather satchel. Even that has a recent story: in 1919, a boy called Willie Grant, aged ten, brought it back from school the day before he succumbed to the influenza. His mother kept it just as it was, with his schoolbooks and a cabbage-root from which he was making a whistle: many years later, the family gave it to the Heritage Centre. It was the peculiar power of individual memory and skill which makes a town museum great. This one was perhaps, for Wick, a desperate last grab at identity, but it was profoundly stirring: a display you could not skim over or ignore. The town lives largely now upon the Dounreay nuclear power station; two thousand five hundred people work there. The reactor has replaced the herring as the silver darling, the source of a decent living.

We walked to the castle ruins and on the way back we noticed an outcrop of the same slabby rocks which the Stone Age people of Skara Brae had found so handy for making dressers and box-beds. On the flat rocks below the road was a curious concrete enclosure, a pool with a white-painted bottom, and the huge painted word TRINKIE. What was a Trinkie? we asked an old man in a car, who could not believe we didn't know. 'Man, Trinkie is a swimming pool. Not many use it now: the weather, ye ken.' But we paddled, and some schoolchildren arrived to strip naked and plunge into the icy tidal waters.

Wickers still come tough.

26

Our depression was moving onwards, providing us with northerly winds. We had the Moray Firth to cross, whose great gaping jaws separate the prosperous bulge of Grampian Scotland from this remote John O'Groats' peninsula. It seemed imperative to move on before the depression shifted its centre. Accordingly, we woke at five the next morning to sail; Paul, however, hearing the drumming of insistent rain on the hatches and seeing the puddle in the cabin floor made by overnight leakage, moaned as he drank his tea and muttered some nonsense about there not being any wind anyway; then he sank back to sleep. I read my rather racy historical novel for an hour, got the heroine safe out of England and away from her remorseless Puritan enemies, and tried again. At six he was more amenable to the idea of leaving: although the rain still pelted down, we could not deny that the tell-tale streamers on the shrouds were indicating a healthy northerly breeze.

Outside, the wind was fair enough, although wind from dead astern is not the most welcome thing in a modern sailing boat. Square-riggers loved it, setting their yards precisely square; but without some slight sideways bias on the sails and hull, a fore-and-aft rigged sailing boat rolls horribly and unpredictably, and threatens every minute to gybe, bringing her boom and gaff over with a tremendous crash. The booms of gaff fishing-vessels were known, routinely, as 'widowmakers'. So through the day we concentrated in turn on the steering, braced ourselves against the wild rolling, and took turns resting below, wedged in a bunk reading or listening to the radio. The children woke, but took little interest in food or sailing; they had developed a strategy of conserving their energy, like husky-dogs who will lie still for days in snowstorms, waiting for their chance to run and frisk but not frustrating themselves by trying. Rose stayed determinedly in bed, surrounded by her toys, occasionally peering through the window above her at the tumbling, grey, foam-streaked horizon that tipped and tilted. She had seen it tipping and tilting before, and could not be bothered with it.

Once she appeared and ate a vast chicken sandwich and an apple, then went back to sleep. Nicholas got dressed, and came on deck once the rain stopped; only an incessant conversation about what he would have for his birthday and how he would decorate his promised new bedroom kept him happy, and I kept up a rather random series of answers to his queries, my eye glued to the compass and the sails as we rolled, increasingly wildly, down the wind. Heaven knows what I promised, in my 'Mmm – yes – that's a good idea' sequence of responses.

It was a long, dull, featureless passage, but a very fast one: we covered nearly sixty miles in ten hours' sailing. It was odd to reflect that this was possibly our last long passage with no coast to look at, the last great dent in the British coastline: Lyme Bay, Cardigan Bay, Liverpool and Morecambe Bays . . . I wished we had had the time to cruise more of these indentations in detail: just under our lee, for instance, lay the famous stretch of sandy coast known rather barbarously as the Banffshire Riviera, but we were leaving it unexplored. To compass the whole coast of Britain in one brief, uncertain, stormy British summer inevitably means such sacrifices. Cowper, after all, had taken four years in his explorations; E. E. Middleton's famous *Cruise of the Kate* was only round England, since he took the Forth and Clyde Canal route, utterly ignoring the Hebrides and the far north; Jonathan Raban had gone through the Caledonian Canal and left out the north, and so had Bob Bond in his little catamaran. The nearest equivalent we knew to our voyage, apart from the racing boats which whizz around Britain and Ireland almost non-stop in three weeks or a fortnight, was Mark Fishwick's circuit in *Temptress*, two years before: and he had told us it would not be a relaxing cruise; 'You're always moving on, or worrying about moving on, and wondering how far back you'll be set by the weather in the next week.' We now saw the truth of this.

On the Moray Firth crossing that day, I lay reading the pilot-books for the east coasts of Scotland and England, and realized with foreboding that our options were closing rapidly. After the splendid variety of anchorages and harbours offered by the lochy indented west, we were back in the situation of petitioners, cap-in-hand to Fate that she would let us reach every harbour at the right tide, without a strong onshore swell, and help us to find it among the dunes and low cliffs without hitting a sandbank. The comparative shallowness of the water near the coast was already coming as a shock: onshore seas break readily in shallow water, making eastern harbour entrances into death-traps in strong winds. In fact the general burden of the pilot-books seemed to be that if the wind came onshore hard in the North Sea, you might as well stick your head straight in a bucket of water and have done with it.

And so we tore down in a rising northerly to the north-facing coast of Banffshire. The seas were indeed breaking nastily as we spotted Fraserburgh harbour mouth; but luckily it faces east, so we hoped for some shelter behind the pier. With nothing but a reefed-down mainsail, we sped towards the harbour wall, looking apprehensively at the dunes close behind, and fearfully at the echo-sounder; we were in barely eighteen feet of water. Smartly enough, *Grace O'Malley* rounded up under Paul's hand, and I ran to get the mainsail off as fast as possible in the narrow outer harbour. From the cabin came squeals, bangs, and loud tape-recordings of 'Nellie the Elephant': the natives were restless. The sail once under control, we motored cautiously into yet another fine Victorian stone dock, and tied up near a Danish yacht, the only one we had seen all day in the lonely Moray waters. 'Wint strong, ja?' he said. Ja, we said. But we had made it. We persuaded Rose into her clothes, and limped up through the rain towards the welcoming arms of the Royal Hotel for high tea and a bath.

They refused the bath at first, clearly being unaccustomed to families of damp, streaming, scruffy tinkers waving American Express cards; they did not know how to place us. Then the manageress realized we were off a boat, and therefore had some excuse for looking so alarming, and she hired us a room and bath for an hour. Not before time: we all smelt rather nasty, as well. You can sail for weeks without more than a wash if the weather is nice; but spend one day in hot, sweaty oilskin trousers and jackets and you stink like a badger. If it then rains on you, adding dankness and oily wool to your bouquet, then a bath or shower is the only answer.

Paul's story that night took the children in their shining armour aboard the good ship *Clachan*, bravely through the North-West Passage where they met Eskimos, lumberjacks, and the Loch Ness Monster again. This imaginary voyage was beginning to be a crazy parallel to the real one; sometimes, as I fell asleep listening to their late story session, I could not be quite sure which of the voyages I had done that day.

216

We were, as became apparent at dawn, right out of the herring-heritage atmosphere of Wick and back into the prosperous business of 1988 Britain. The market began at seven thirty with crashing and shouting; the oil industry ships began whirring and roaring, doing their arcane duties, at eight; and the town was inordinately full of hairdressers, hypermarkets, and solidly prosperous retail businesses. The children ran and climbed on the dunes, but the wind whistled in hard from the north all day and stung their bare legs with sandstorms. I could see how Scotland became such a grand nursery of empire-builders, colonial administrators, and fearless explorers: they toughen them up young. Another woman near me, wrapped tightly against the cold in a huge purple cardigan, watched her heavily-wrapped baby and naked sons cavorting on the wild beach. 'The bairns are never feart of cold at all,' she said. 'I'm the wan that canna take ay mair by afternoon.' The accents we were hearing as we moved southward were broad-vowelled, almost stagy Lowland Scots, after the soft hissing Gaelic voices of the Highlands and the Scandinavian lilt of Orkney. None of them had had much in common with the standard 'educated' Scottish accent heard in Westminster, or the London theatre, or anywhere south of Berwick.

It was a lively town, Fraserburgh: young men shouted and joshed one another around the fish-packing stations; wives wheeled babies down to the quay in prams to meet their men, home for the weekend on a Friday night; children kicked tin cans around in the respectable grey streets. Depressing though it was to read in *Fishing News* about great catches of prawns being dumped dead into the Minches because the market had slumped; alarming though it always is to see the vicious harrows and beams on the big boats, ready to drag every piece of life out of the sea and dump half of it dead; gloomy though it is to know for certain that Fraserburgh and Peterhead will meet the same fate as the poor herring ports of old, we also clearly saw the opposite view. When you are on the spot, at the heart of a prosperous fishing-port, then the bustle and the baby-buggies and the general air of a purposeful traditional trade are powerful emotional arguments for laissez-faire. In the end, these arguments will lead to the death of the seas and the end of the prosperity (unless one of the sunrise industries sets all the fishermen to work making components for pocket calculators); but meanwhile, it would take a tougher politician than Britain has ever bred to put the brakes decisively on pollution and overfishing. The seabed, unfortunately, has no vote.

Not all the boats were in by dusk. At two in the morning after that Friday night, a fearful crashing of feet and loud cries awoke us overhead. The sound of huge, turning engines suggested that a fishing-boat was trying to berth against the wall inside of us; after brief thought, we both buried our heads in our pillows and let them get on with it. There were, after all, a full crew on the boat and we were just two poor tired yachtsmen. The harbourmaster had put us where we were, and we had paid our dues. In the morning, we found a degree of chaos on deck, ropes thrown overboard anyhow and a bronze fairlead ripped clean out of the deck; but we were secured to the outside of a large trawler. We had promised the children breakfast at the Fishermen's Mission before sailing, so set off across the huge machine's deck for the ladder: the trawler, however, was lying well away from the iron rungs in the harbour wall, and we were effectively stranded. Paul and I might swing like baboons from the huge mooring-lines and get ashore; short of rigging a breeches-buoy we could not get the children up to the pier.

We accepted this fairly philosophically: trawlermen, after all, are working in the harbours where we are playing, and we do not allow ourselves to resent anything they do to us, as a matter of principle. The fairlead could soon be screwed back on, anyway, and most of our ropes had survived. However, at that moment the assistant harbourmaster appeared, took in the sight of our children in little lifejackets standing forlornly on the big steel deck, and us balancing on the trawler's guardrails, and he flew into a passion of irritation. He clearly had a more robust view of the rights of yachts.

'Did he – did that *rascal* come inside of ye at two in the morning? Did he? When there was other berths free in the Broch? He knows well that this berth is for the wee boats. For the wee boats! That man is trouble!' Weakly, we smiled tolerant British smiles and demurred. 'Nae, nae, he's the most selfish man . . . he's trouble! Every time he comes in here!' By dint of pulling and hauling and stretching and calling up an associate, he manhandled the children ashore, still fulminating. 'The most selfish, selfish man – he knew these were berths for the wee boats! Did he do ye any damage? Did he?'

We felt very encouraged by this proof of our status, and adjourned to the Mission for our bacon rolls with a bit of a swagger. The Mission seemed to have a considerable following in Fraserburgh: seamen came in to leave gear, to leave messages, to eat, or drink tea; rows of baby spout-mugs testified to a keen wives' group, well-read thrillers in the bookshelf to quiet blameless hours spent by visiting crews. And when I was hunting for a skip to put our rubbish ashore, I asked two old men what to do with it. They gazed at me in amazement and said, 'Why, tak' it tae the Mission, lassie.' This seemed too much to ask of Christian charity, to take in a large bin-bag of smelly rubbish; but as I wandered ineffectually around hunting for a skip, the Mission representative in overalls firmly took control, and directed me to the spotless evangelical dustbins round the back. 'Nae problem.'

We, by contrast with the Mission dustbins, were an utterly filthy ship. A fine rain of dusty white fish-scales had been descending on our deck for two days; splashes of oil, soot, and mud had come down on deck and not been washed off by the rain, which had merely spread the stains into depressing muck and reconstituted the fish-scales into bouillabaisse. I had washed the cockpit down, but nothing – least of all the harbour water – would remove the taint. Rose, settling in her bunk the night before, observed, 'Mummy, my duster (her comforter) smells of fish.' Then, thoughtfully, 'Actually, everything smells of fish. So it doesn't matter.' There was something gallant about Rose sometimes: in the high winds which battered us in Stromness harbour, she had woken in the night and asked subduedly for a pink seasick pill: she thought she was at sea, and was quietly making her own small preparations for the sickness she had resigned herself to.

She had a pink pill that morning, and we set out southwards. The seas in the bay were large and confused: motoring through them, Paul went yellow and furious. Within half an hour, though, we were sailing beautifully on almost calm waters in a light south-easterly; we rounded Rattray Head without incident, although it was days later that some tourist booklet told us to 'Keep Mormond Hill a handspike high, and Rattray Briggs ye'll nae come nigh'; we looked out to sea and spotted an oil-rig, which prompted Paul to reminisce happily about his days as a young reporter when he was sent off to witness the sinking of the first ever rig in the North Sea. The world's reporters, he recalled, were struck with awe at the

219

unique majesty of the occasion, but only when they discovered that on the cruise ship chartered by BP the bar was to be free all week. Then the telex link broke down, and half the newspapermen found they didn't have to file a story anyway. The fair tide swept us on at a triumphant pace; we skimmed past Peterhead harbour, built by prisoners from the jail as the 'National Harbour of Refuge'; we thought it would be full of falling fish-scale dust and big rude trawlers, and sailed thankfully past. We spotted Slains Castle, which inspired Bram Stoker to write *Dracula*, or so they say; then a quite different castle, which our *other* guidebook said inspired Bram Stoker to write *Dracula*. It was interesting to coast past straight, low shores instead of forever rounding headlands; but we still found the shallowness of the water and the short steep seas unnerving after our Atlantic coastal journeying.

Then the wind betrayed us again, moving into the south; fed up, desperate to make Stonehaven before the tide turned full against us, we switched on the engine and indulged in the exhausting but effective practice of motoring hard to windward with mainsail and jib set, just filling the sails with the wind of our own passage, and so adding a knot to our speed. The self-steering could not cope, even with the topsail off; in turn we steered into the increasingly fresh wind and choppy seas. There was no option but to make Stonehaven, for we had passed Aberdeen. We suffered four hours of this teeth-rattling progress, with Nicholas and Rose blowing soap-bubbles in the cockpit and listening to a tape of Joan Greenwood reading *Alice Through the Looking Glass*. Greenwood's ginny, knowing, forty-plus Alice puts a whole new gloss on innocent old Dodgson's vision, and will forever be connected in my mind with headwinds. At last we turned thankfully in the dusk towards Stonehaven harbour, and got in with just enough water under us to tie up to a fishing-boat.

We thought it might not go out, on a Sunday. But although Stonehaven is the picture-postcard ideal of a fishing village, almost Cornish with its pretty double harbour, it is really a haunt of tourists from Aberdeen and inland. Aberdonians like sea-angling; six boatloads of them left at 8 a.m., our companion being amongst the keenest to go. I came on deck half-dressed to find him gaily tossing our ropes into the sea without fastening us to the quay at all. I gritted my teeth at him, and hauled the yacht into the quay. 'When are you back?' I asked. 'When I need to be,' he said rudely, and chugged off. We resolved to be of no help whatsoever when he got back.

We spent a day of rain and mist in Stonehaven. In the afternoon Paul took the children off to a wet castle along the coast while I cleaned the boat. This was a startling role-reversal, since Paul's favourite job as a rule is spring-cleaning the boat with nobody else aboard; but the trace on the barograph in the cabin showed one of its periodic needle-jumps. He had come aboard at lunchtime, taken one look at the fluff and fish-scales and old crisps and general filth under the floorboards and in the corners of the galley, and Bang! on the chart table; Jump! went the barograph, and another Great Wobbler had been made immortal. So I volunteered to clean while he castled; and I quite enjoyed the process of washing over and under the floorboards and dismantling the galley, cabin steps, and other dirt-traps. Nothing gets quite so filthy in a short time as a cruising yacht: in a house, dirt falls away through floorboards or is hoovered up – in a yacht, it has nowhere to go except through the bilges, and needs chasing into those. Fluff comes from woollen jerseys; dirt from quaysides; in our case, ripped-up bits of Mister Men sticker-books, plastic dinosaurs, and crisps added to the revolting layers. As I laboured, rain and sweat plastering my hair to my head, hauling huge floorboards and wet cloths in and out of the cockpit, a series of interested Aberdonians stopped on the quay to watch the idle yachting rich at play. 'Wha hae ye been doing, tae get sae dirty?' 'Does that boat go well in sea? I was forty year in the navy.' And occasionally, suspiciously, 'Are you Paul Heiney and Libby Purves?' One of them, I answered politely, and wrung out my cloth with an ingratiating scowl. Paul and the children came back at four, and unable to face the return of the angling boat, we cleared out to get nine miles further south on the last of the fair tide.

At sea, the wind had dropped away completely, leaving grey water and fog. We groped through it, seeing sea-cliffs solid with white birds, and countless puffins on the water around us; once or twice a cormorant on a rock would spread its wings to dry them, black against the white mist. A futile exercise, I would think: I had been trying to dry my last spare pair of cotton trousers by the same method for three days without success. Even when the rain stopped, a thick, humid Scotch mist remained, saturating the air. When we eventually reached the hamlet of Gourdon, the view of it from the sea was like a Lowry picture: a particular rank of new buildings has asymmetrical pitched roofs, like a Lowry factory, and from every chimney rose wisps of smoke. It looked as if this dim village was the very home of fog, its manufactory: the wisps of smoke rose to blend with the white clouds hovering at mast height. We tied up our wet boat, with wet ropes, to the wet quay.

27

Gourdon was a snug-enough hole to lie in for the night, among the stacked lobster-pots. But in truth we were now fed up with grey fishing-ports, with streaming harbour walls, the constant rain of fish-scales and grubby gull-feathers on to our deck, the choke of diesel and the slippery quays. The weariness went deeper than these externals: for a month, rounding Scotland, we had been reading and watching and thinking about fish: about the herring boom, its collapse from overfishing and from such uncontrollable outside forces as the Russian Revolution, which dried up the trade in salt herring. We had been thinking about Highlanders driven from their land and forced to fish, and fishermen driven ashore by shortage. We had thought about the dismal aftermath of the first gold-rush for silver fish, and had wondered about the new gold-rushes: shellfish, salmon-farming and – on a vaster scale – North Sea oil, which had just exacted such a terrible price on Piper Alpha. Apart from the shimmering, mythical interlude among the Stromness folk-musicians and the ancient builders of Skara Brae, we had been thinking far too much in terms of commerce: getting and spending and laying waste of lives. It was time to sail among some dreaming spires. St Andrews lay on our southward path.

We were a little nervous about sailing into St Andrews Harbour: it may be one of the most ancient seaports in Scotland, but it has barely any water in it. None, at low tide. The wind, however, was forecast light for a couple of days, and the sun shone as we eased out of Gourdon at seven, both children asleep. The brisk north-westerly breeze that greeted us outside the harbour was a mild surprise, since the forecast said south-easterly; but light-weather forecasts are rarely exact. Wind bends around coasts, gusts round headlands with sudden unexpected force, blows off the land at dawn and the sea at afternoon. In these northern waters it seems to have habits all its own: dying away suddenly, reappearing from a new and unreasonable direction. On many days it was impossible to make any strategic plan according to the weather forecast: only a tendency could be deduced, and after that we were as much in the hands of fortune as Cowper a hundred years ago; except, of course, for twenty-seven horsepower of biddable energy under the cockpit floor.

Which is not to say that we were disappointed in the Met. Office: when it comes to serious wind, not the capricious Force Two or Three variety fluking around the coast, they have comprehensively belled the cat. During that week of calm wet days and sunny flickers, we knew quite clearly that a strong southerly wind, probably a gale, was booked for some time on Thursday: it was as much a date in our diaries as Christmas or Wimbledon. We planned around it, sent messages to my brother and sister-in-law that their joining us might have to be put off, checked our harbours for southerly shelter, and generally treated this wind – five days away – as a well-expected houseguest. Next to such warnings, a failure to diagnose a freakish breeze over ten miles of coast is a small complaint indeed. Anyway, coming out of Gourdon I had furtively thrown ten pence to the Finnfolk, who obliged with sunshine and a fair wind all day.

Ahead of us lay the low, smoky blue hills of the Kingdom of Fife, and as we sped across the Firth of Tay my heart lifted. I never knew my grandfather, Purves the draper of Cupar, Fife; but from my father I knew how this small tradesman, a stern Lowland Scot who believed in education, had succeeded in sending all three of his sons and his daughter Dorothy off to St Andrews University, fifteen miles away, in the 1920s. 'They used to say,' my father would tell us, 'that St Andrews was the place "Where Poverty Walks in a Scarlet Cloak".' From half-heeded remarks of my father's I gained my first childish idea of university: a place where students went with their sack of oats for the term, poor, keen, and serious; where young men and women sat at the feet of great philosophers; where Sunday walks to the harbour in red gowns were the chief harmless recreation and one had to walk ten miles for a pint of beer in the strict days of Sunday licensing. All the brothers prospered: my father was the dreamer of his family who read philosophy, and went on to a higher degree at Freiburg in Germany, then to the overseas service of the BBC; then into an advertising agency and finally to his life's love, the Diplomatic Service. In the process, his native Scottish tones were softened to a courteous, ironic, English diction. His brother Roy was the engineer, energetic and curious;

Clifford the chemist emigrated to Canada and reached his own eminence at McGill University. Sister Dorothy worked for the BBC, and was the best of aunts: the sort who would have a teenage niece to stay, sullen and miniskirted, in London, and never ask where I went, trusting to a shrewd, humorous glance at the day's end. Dorothy is buried now, in a Suffolk churchyard under a simple headstone engraved with the arms of St Andrews University; twenty miles away in another Suffolk grave my father lies. Without hesitation, we engraved 'James Grant Purves, of Cupar, Fife', and embellished his grave, too, with the lion and book and crescent of St Andrews. Fife and St Andrews were perhaps more important to him than anything since; although he never spoke much of his youth in case he should become a bore. I came here with him once, twenty years before on a family holiday route home from Ireland: I remembered North Street, Market Street, and South Street fanning out in an orderly manner from the cathedral's ruined doors; and vaguely, I remembered the harbour with a great jagged tower above it.

None of which was any help, of course, in getting *Grace O'Malley* in without running her spectacularly aground on the shores of the Kinness Burn. Paul is better than me at these shallow-water manoeuvres in limited space: shrieking inwardly with panic, I peered up the narrow space between the piers, saw the inner harbour closed and dry, and realized we could not turn if we needed to. Paul and I exchanged one brief, comprehending glance, and made for the only bit of accessible harbour wall. It was the sloping side of the stone slipway. With about an inch under our keel, he edged us skilfully close to it: with an undignified leap and swing on a fish-hoisting device of some sort, I got myself up on to the slip and threw a rope round the crane to stop us. 'Fortune favours the Brave,' I muttered. 'Well, the sentimental.' And I looked around properly at this place which my father had won by study and I by sea.

It was quite clear that we had got away from the grey prosaic fishing-harbours. There were lobster-pots and floats on the quay, to be sure; but there were also two ladies with easels, painting the pots keenly in a genteel still-life style. The lobsterman who helped with our mooring lines, Tom, accepted this aesthetic presence with a kindly gallantry unimaginable in Fraserburgh fish-dock, and carefully stepped by so as not to knock the pots and ruin the ladies' composition. Ahead of us lay green turf and ruined towers, the remains of the largest cathedral in Europe (or what would have been the largest, had it not been for reforming Protestant zeal with sledgehammers). Out to seaward lay the ragged outline of the castle, and around us a harbour over a thousand years old, built and rebuilt since the Vikings' days always to the same beautifully engineered pattern. It is basic, but at high tides effective and remarkably safe. The time was that a hundred sailing-ships could lie here: today, we were the only sailing-boat among the small motor dories. Looking at a 1920s photograph of a basin full of little fishing smacks with brown sails, I realized that this was not a dead bit of 'heritage', but the accustomed view of my own father's Sunday walks in the twenties. And here we were, with our tan sails and our bowsprit, in the same harbour: Grant Purves's daughter and family, back to pay tribute. Paul took the children, and I ran off alone to see my father's city.

I had forgotten, from that one visit long ago, what a place of dunes and wind and empty, sandy spaces it is; and how powerful in this Presbyterian stronghold the great romantic form of the wrecked cathedral still remains. It explained a few things to me: how my father, who hated picnicking and sand in his trouser turn-ups and all such undignified frolickings with nature, none the less chose to live in Suffolk, among more dunes and windblown marram-grass and great wide bays like these. He hated religion, too, having suffered many dreary boyhood Sabbaths without so much as a book to read; yet in all his European and world travels he was always quite content, surprisingly so, among the stones of the cathedrals and abbeys to which my Catholic mother would drag him. Old grey stones and dunes were part of him, and he made them a part of me in turn. Not that this was his boyhood home – he came from inland Cupar. But St Andrews had been something more powerful than a home: a boyhood dream. It was to the university that everything in his childhood had longingly tended. I walked its streets again, for him.

And for myself. After the wild windy Highlands and their primitive mysteries, after the commercial bustle of the North-East, it was indescribably soothing to be here amongst cultivated roses in old university gardens; to be surrounded by libraries, by statues in niches, weathered tombstones, and leafy avenues where a solid, tile-turreted house might be labelled MORAL PHILOSOPHY, or LOGIC. A white-haired man rode by in a three-piece suit and cycle clips, eating an ice-cream cornet, and I recognized immediately the genus

Don from my own Oxford days. A pair of unkempt, thin, tweedy women in the teashop discussed museum curatorship with a passion and humour that took me back to the Banbury road twenty years before. St Andrews is a civilized city – insulting to call it a town – it is cosmopolitan, almost Parisian; its shops sell ormolu clocks and exotic vegetables, its air is carelessly aloof. Even up at the golfing end, where you find the Links Hotel and the Niblick Bar and bookshops selling fifty years' worth of secondhand books like *Tips and Hints on How to Play the Royal and Ancient*, there is dignity.

And from the sea, to make the cultural experience complete, we had spotted a red-and-white circus tent pitched on the West Sands: and it was actually open. We had been sailing for two-and-a-half months around Britain, and everywhere we stayed, there were notices about a barbecue last week, a fair yesterday, or an agricultural show in two weeks' time. Here at last we had coincided with an event. The circus was a great success: one of those bold touring enterprises in which the programme-seller reappears in cutaway sequinned swimsuit as Natasha the rope artiste, and the motherly woman on box-office keeps nipping off to do a novelty dog act while the advance booking queue stands bewildered on the beach.

The children were overdue for a day on a long sandy beach, and a juvenile treat like the circus. In the last month's difficult travels, we had become too isolated within ourselves as a family. Since the sociability of Tanera More, apart from the interlude in Lyn's puppet-workshop in Orkney, Nicholas and Rose had had hardly any outside contacts; Paul and I had had a few conversations with strangers on the quay, in shops, in occasional pubs, but there was no doubt that the Heineys were in the process of turning into a sort of Lost Tribe, cut off from outside influences and civilizations. We had all the symptoms: our own culture was developing. The normal concentration of family jokes and catchphrases had intensified alarmingly, so that conversations aboard *Grace O'Malley* were almost incomprehensible to outsiders. In an unconscious effort, I suppose, to introduce social variety, we had all developed a range of different personae and grotesque imaginary characters. Paul had become Florag, a ferocious Scottish cleaning-lady who scrubbed children's faces with pumice; I spent periods as Mrs MacSlappy, a similarly aggressive old nurse with real steel teeth. Rose was a series of animals, mainly cuddlesome, but sometimes indulged her morbid streak by being a 'coffin maker', or a surgeon treating her teddy for

'Eternal Bleeding'. Nicholas sought refuge either in banging his shield and sword for hours in solo macho aggression, or in planning wild, impossible construction schemes for the day he got home. 'If we arrive in the morning, I'll get on with building my schooner that afternoon . . .' In their minds, the castles, ruins, Vikings, and Armada ships had become more real than home or school; their companions were Bonnie Prince Charlie, saints, knights, and Finn-folk. Mad fantasy games built up between the two of them with great intensity. 'I'm Saint Maggus,' Rose would say. 'I'm gutting herring, forty a minute, till they cut my head off.' 'Ahaar, but I'm King Philip of Spain, and I'll kill you with a spiked flail,' Nicholas would reply. In the Christian bookshop in St Andrews, the two of them were squabbling in the corner while Paul paid. The assistant said in reproving, motherly fashion: 'What are you two quarrelling about? It's surely not important?' The children, with a killing look, informed her that they were arguing about precisely where in the orchard at Pattle's Farm each of them was going to build their own private cathedral. There is no answer to that, especially in an evangelical bookshop. We hoped uneasily that the children would somehow snap back into normal social ways when we got home. Meanwhile, a mile of firm sand, a sunny day, and a little circus at dusk would do something to normalize them.

St Andrews dealt kindly with us; *Grace O'Malley* rose and fell on four tides alongside the old stone slipway before, reluctantly, we set off in another early morning breeze to get southwards before the depressions marching across the Atlantic brought the gales we were promised. That day was another rare gift: one of those days which keep sailors hopefully in thrall to their pastime through weeks of drizzle and rough water. We glided down to Fife Ness, then tore across the Firth of Forth, surrounded by puffins, gulls, and flight after flight of noble gannets, white shapes of speed and grace with black-tipped wings skimming the water. As the afternoon wore on the wind dropped; we moved more slowly towards St Abb's Head, the coast still glowing translucently green and gold around us. The service of remembrance for the victims of the Piper Alpha oil-rig explosion was broadcast; it was the last act of the tragedy which we had first heard of in the Mission at Kinlochbervie three hundred miles before. We listened quietly to the singing, grieving, praying voices across the sea from Aberdeen, with the gannets dipping and wheeling around our little ship.

28

Eyemouth was our port of refuge from the expected winds: we got in at half-tide, its long narrow piers rising around us like a ravine. Inside was a bewildering crush of trawlers, a racket of fish-marketing and welding, a noisy funfair for Herring Festival Queen Week, and – mercifully – a gesticulating harbourmaster pointing us to an unlikely but reasonably comfortable perch on the very end of the middle pier. It seemed a happy enough spot to be: our aversion to fish had faded in the healingly philosophical atmosphere of St Andrews, and we smiled again upon the tender, sentimental names of the last Scottish trawlers we would probably see: *Children's Friend, Golden Hope, Valhalla, Radiant Way, Bright Ray, Golden Quest.* I spent the evening trying to persuade two excited children to get behind their bunk-curtains so they could not see me wrapping presents; 20 July 1988 marked Rose's fourth birthday, and even in the roaming exile of our voyage, marked it must be. We had rather sneakily taken advantage of our children's infantile innumeracy to put the birthday off until this galebound day, and to get the sail across the Forth done in fine weather. It had, in fact, been a particularly jolly family day at sea: the children had much enjoyed Paul's sudden frenzy of housekeeping. He chiefly threw obsolete items of bakery overboard following one of his overbuying fits: the seagulls got, in quick succession, several stale 'butteries', half a loaf of inedible pumpkin-seed bread from Wick, and a packet of absolutely disgusting, but apparently traditional, things called Bere Bannocks from Stonehaven: they smelt vile. He also celebrated his discovery of a posh cheese-shop in St Andrews by throwing away a huge lump of plastic cheese which had lasted since Kinlochbervie. Then we discussed Firths, and the Forth, and the children invented a chant: 'We thought it was our fourth Firth, when we crossed the Firth of Forth, but it was our fifth Firth.' So it was, Firth of Clyde, Pentland Firth, Moray Firth, Firth of Tay, Firth of Forth.

Eyemouth, as it happened, was in the throes of Herring Queen Week, an ancient festival of the town. 'It always rains in Herring

229

Queen Week,' said the marine electrician proudly. We had missed the boat procession, but various disco nights, three-legged races, and other jollities were discernible on the fringe of the town's life during our two days there. Despite the rain, youths dressed as bananas and St Trinian's girls prowled the streets three-legged, and real girls sang aloud in the chip-shop opposite the Masonic Lodge where Robbie Burns was made into a Royal Arch Mason. But Eyemouth is a fishing town, with only a light, dignified gloss of tourism. Indeed, it has a problem: the fishermen want to extend the harbour, which would destroy the sand beach. Whether fish or tourists will, in the end, do the town most good is under hot debate.

We marvelled for the last time at the Scottish national talent for things public. We had noticed the excellence of the children's playgrounds from Portpatrick onwards but the Scottish municipal firmness of touch was never more apparent than in the Eyemouth swimming-pool. Modern it might be, squirting Jacuzzi bubbles and providing rafts and balls in the toddler-pool; but there was none of that Anglo-American nonsense you get in the south-east about 'Leisure'. Instead of putting up soupy notices like 'The only rule is, Enjoy!' (spotted in East Anglia, of all places), the city fathers of Eyemouth firmly adjured patrons in large black print not to spit, dive-bomb, indulge in horseplay, or fail to wash their feet. Lifeguards male and female prowled the sides of the pool, and the flooring was of agonizingly – but safely – rough non-slip concrete. There was no flashy mosaic in sight. As a result, although the pool was so crowded with big children and teenagers that down in southern England I would not have dared to take my small non-swimmers in, here I had no qualms. The dour lifeguards would sort out any duckers or splashers. Scottish municipal leisure provision is thirty years out of date in its atmosphere, and all the better for that.

There was an odd farewell to Scotland for me. You cannot visit Eyemouth without sharing in the remembrance, still green after a century, of 14 October 1881: Black Friday, the day of the great gale. Eyemouth had fifty fishing-boats then: the same number as a century before, and the same number as today. It is a balanced, classic fishing community, with a harbour exactly sufficient to its needs and a sea with – up to now – more or less enough fish for them. Fishermen in autumn, though, are always anxious men: the

230

weather worsens and money must be caught before the real winter. On that Friday in 1881 there had been a week of gales when suddenly the day dawned – as the Revd David McIvor recalled later – 'cloudless and blue . . . the sea as a great expanse of almost restful water'. Fishermen were uneasy, though: one boy recalled that 'the glass never was sae low'. They must have been, with hindsight, right in the centre of a depression, between two sets of gales, much as we had been in the West Coast when we had an idyllic blue day in Loch Nedd before the northerly gale. They had no professional forecasts to rely on, though; and the Eyemouth fleet, encouraged by one another's example, put to sea: so did Burnmouth and Cove. From St Abbs, only one boat went out, from Berwick, none.

At noon the storm struck, a northerly gale of unprecedented, legendary violence. From Eyemouth alone, thirteen boats went down; from the immediate vicinity, Cove and Burnmouth and St Abbs, thirty-two were lost. A hundred and eighty-nine men died, sunk or washed overboard from boats with the same tender names as the modern fleet: from *Beautiful Star* and *Radiant, Guiding Star, Press Home, Forget-me-not* and *Two Sisters.* The local newspaper reported the disaster in stylized Victorian prose, but the enormity of the horror comes painfully through; most of the boats were washed ashore:

> It is impossible adequately to describe the feelings of those on shore, as boat after boat approached thus within hailing distance, within a few yards of the haven of refuge, only to be broken or sunk on the treacherous rocks of that rugged coast. His would have been a heart of adamant which could without a pang witness those scenes.

All this I read in the town museum on that rainy day, thinking with a shudder of the other October gale, the 1987 hurricane which had devastated our house and garden and left me with an abiding uneasiness about high winds. Then I turned into the last room of the museum before going out to find the family; and there, on the centenary tapestry of names and crews lost, I found evidence of an older family of mine. Still detachedly sad, I was reading names and ages of the men who died in 1881. I came to the *Myrtle* of Eyemouth, and saw: 'James Purves, aged 51', and on *Two Sisters,* the only St Abbs boat, the skipper: 'Charles Purves, 55'.

I never heard of a Purves yet who was not a traceable relation:

but with my father and aunt gone and my last uncle gone to Canada, I had nobody to ask about Charles and James: were they great-great-uncles, far cousins, or who? I had never heard of their dramatic deaths; Paul, from further south, had a relative who was believed in family legend to have perished in the great gale of 1881, but I had heard of no fishing Purveses. Down on the quay, where I bought a model trawler carved by Bobby Patterson (there are seven Pattersons on the roll of 1881) I asked if any Purves kinsmen still fished here; not here, I was told, not for years. There were several Purveses in local boatyards, and on the war memorial a naval cadet who died . . . I got no further, but walked on down the damp grey quay, past battlements of fish-boxes, to where *Nimrod*'s crew worked with netting-needles, and *Radiant Way* loaded ice. A fleet of fifty boats again, as it was on the morning more than a hundred years ago when Charles and James my kinsmen sailed out on to a blue sea for the last time.

Bing Collin, the young electrician who had come to chat and admire *Grace O'Malley* at the quayside, reappeared in the morning, just as we were ready to leave. 'Present for ye,' he said laconically, and tossed down several packets of fish. 'And – ' he motioned to a grinning associate beside his van – 'you'll need this.' A huge plastic bag of fish-ice fell ten feet on to the deck with a crunch. We were immensely touched by the thought, and particularly by the sack of ice; we lashed the lot down on the foredeck, and tried to thank Bing. 'Ah, no. Come back. Come back. Eyemouth's great. Only ye came in a bad week. In Herring Queen Week it always rains.'

29

It was a grey, quiet day; a light north-easterly wind enabled us to sail quietly from ten until four, ghosting down towards the low outline of Holy Island. Mist began to shroud it towards the day's end; we motored in, cautiously, to the harbour made by the swing of the sandy bay. A rock beacon, a buoy, leading marks to be brought into line, a beacon to be lined up with the church tower, all preoccupied us until we came under the shelter of St Cuthbert's tiny island of Hobthrush. Here the saint, finding the isolation of Lindisfarne not quite enough for him, would retire to be cut off one more degree from the world by the rising tide (Holy Island itself was, and is, cut off from the sinful mainland for eleven hours a day). We felt a sense of freedom at being once more out on a mooring, remote; we rowed ashore and took the path to the village through the ruins of the Norman priory, currently full of champing sheep. We had not thought much about the border, except to draw the Scottish lion down from our spreaders that afternoon, but as we came into the quiet village we realized that we really had come back to England. In fact, this was our first step into England since we had sailed from Mousehole over two months before: Wales, the Isle of Man, and Scotland lay between. Very little of coastal Britain is English at all, especially if you count Cornwall as an alien kingdom. But in this stone village Englishness met us on every side: lazy, rural, pretty Englishness. Wafts of overpowering floral scents of pomander and Old Englysshe soap assailed us from the door of the National Trust shop; flat Midlands accents and heavy Geordie vowels marked the tourists' hasty departure across the flooding causeway; and we spotted our first Porsche since Salcombe, complete with high, clipped voices and leather jackets carelessly slung on the back seat. After a series of remorselessly workmanlike fishing harbours Holy Island's twee front came as something of a shock. But the tide rose, the people vanished, and by dusk it lay around us with more dignity: low sands and high castle, priory ruins and low stone crosses, much as they had been for centuries. 'It's a different island when the tide is up,' said the village shopkeeper fondly. We inspected the castle and the priory, but were more taken by the practical and pleasant sheds made by the lobster and crab fishermen on the beach: these were the black humped shapes of old herring-boats, upended, tarred and canvassed. Inland from the castle (a medieval stronghold adapted with real *Country Life* taste by Sir Edwin Lutyens) we found a walled garden created by Gertrude Jekyll. Paul tried to explain to me why. 'Jekyll and Lutyens,' he said. 'Were the – were the . . .' he cast around desperately. 'They were the Abbott and Costello of their day. Did everything together.' The garden was a dull one, relying rather too heavily on the pale, frosty, boring plant known as Lambs' Ears.

Another gale was due in a day or two, and Paul, looking around this bleak scene in the rain, was restless and unimpressed. He had not had the Catholic upbringing that I had, and did not shiver with inward awe at the name of Lindisfarne: St Cuthbert's and St Aidan's isle, the fount and origin of British Christianity. Here in 634 Aidan brought his monks; from here he taught gentleness and the fear of God to all Northumbria. Here Cuthbert the shepherd boy became a mad, holy hermit on Hobthrush; from here he retired to a cell on Farne Island, windowless but with a hole in the roof to contemplate the heavens. They brought him back as bishop, but he flitted to Farne again to die in solitude among his seals and seabirds. Here the Lindisfarne Gospels were devotedly illuminated, to lie now a thousand years later in the shamefully undevotional surroundings of the British Museum: on these shores the book was shipwrecked and lost, but revealed – the legend says – fresh and good as new by a freak low tide which revealed it on the seabed, 'in all the beauty of pages and writing within, as though it had never been touched by water'.

Through all the teashoppery and National Trustery, I felt the old shudder of recognition, uncompromising holy voices calling out of my convent childhood. The tawdry crucifixes and plastic shrines provided in the village shop for real pilgrims seemed more appropriate than all the craft shop's displays of ornamental Celtic crosses, Lindisfarne brooches, and earthenware St Cuthbert mugs to adorn the homes of the tasteful but godless. The declining North-East provided its own strand of sad, drained souvenirs too for visitors in Porsches: endless toys and ornaments made out of old bobbins from the dead mills; miniature brass miners' lamps to remind us of the dead mines; booklets of Geordie jokes to remind us of the days when the North-East had something to laugh about . . . Through it all St Cuthbert never left me; as I wandered with the children among brisk National Trust ladies selling prettily wrapped heritage chocolate bars and lyrical coffee-table books about Lindisfarne by middleweight TV presenters, I thought only of monks in home-spun, cut off by the tide, making their Gospels as a sign to all Europe of God's work.

I had, however, to keep these romantic thoughts to myself. The children were plainly fed up. The almost constant rain over the past three weeks, and the sudden cancelling of a longed-for visit by my brother and sister-in-law with their new baby had made them bored, tired, and quarrelsome. Nicholas had conjunctivitis, and was sore-eyed and angry, talking constantly of 'The Great Day' when we would decorate the boat and sail home up the Deben; Rose had dimly perceived that her birthday had been a rather paltry affair after all, with no children and no jelly. Paul too was fed up with travelling: on the second morning on Holy Island he suddenly erupted again, with a force that would have sent the poor old barograph needle flying had the fury taken place on the boat.

'I am sick of this bloody voyage. There is no pleasure in it for any of us any more. I am sick of pointless bloody castles and museums and beaches and rain, and I just want to get the hell out of it and get a roof over our heads again.' We were in the dinghy at the time; he rowed violently into a rock, and bashed it viciously with the oar. 'I am fed up, the children are fed up, so we are now all fed up. I want to go home, home, home!' I have learned, in ten years' cruising with Paul, to stay silent at times. It was not the moment to say how much I was enjoying being here in this crescent of sand, with the foghorn sounding and the sheep munching and the benevolent spirits of early monks around me. I squelched into the water and removed the children from his ambit for an hour. That was all it took: he walked off his bad temper very rapidly, and bore the children off to Bamburgh Castle in the afternoon in high spirits.

Indulging myself one last time, I sat alone on the Hobthrush, St Cuthbert's private isle. There is a rectangular stone chamber, open now to the sky and full of scented clover: there is a high wooden cross. People had left flowers to wilt at its foot, and a fish, silver and stiff, lay in offering. On the shore a coachload of pilgrims sang 'How Great Thou Art', while the tide came up over the slimy stones and the gold sand, cutting me off like the hermit, on a tidal island at the edge of another tidal island. Peace came dropping slow.

At six Paul and the bickering, whining children returned to represent my worldly burden. Since the weather forecasters were now becoming really insistent about the south-westerly gales, we decided to spend an hour at anchor in the Kettle, inside the Inner Farne island, then make an evening passage with the tide towards the guaranteed shelter and easy landing of Amble Braid Marina. Two or three days cowering in the Holy Island anchorage with waves breaking over the bow, unable to get ashore, might have taxed even my religious sentiments.

The low, rocky Farne islands lay ahead of us; the evening had cleared the mist and we could see, among the wheeling clouds of seabirds, the Longstone Rock where Grace Darling lived a modest life and performed her legendary rescue.

I had thought I knew about Grace Darling, heroine of Farne, the Longstone lightkeeper's daughter who rowed to the aid of the stricken *Forfarshire*.

> 'Twas on the Longstone lighthouse
> There dwelt an English maid
> Pure as the air around her
> Of danger ne'er afraid.

But I didn't. She was a heroine in her day, like Flora MacDonald a century before. But Grace was a victim of the popular press. The ballads are disgracefully wrong:

> Said Grace, 'Come help me Father
> We'll launch that boat,' said she
> Her father cried, ''Tis madness
> To face that raging sea.'

Even during the great furore of Grace's celebrity, when theatrical managers were inviting her to perform her rescue at the Adelphi, for £50, or at Batty's Equestrian Circus in Edinburgh for less – even then, the plaintive, unheard voices of her family tried to set the record straight. William Darling, lightkeeper, regular rescuer of shipwrecked sailors, would not have bowed to pressure and performed any unseamanlike act for his pretty daughter's sake. In fact, she was not especially pretty, being rather solemn-looking, made to pull an oar rather than flutter a fan. It is true that Grace saw the wreck and bravely agreed to go as a second oar with her father; but only because her brothers were away.

> One murmur'd prayer 'Heavn guard us!'
> And then they were afloat
> Between them and destruction
> The planks of that frail boat.
> Then spoke the maiden's father:
> 'Return or doom'd are we'
> But up spoke brave Grace Darling
> 'Alone I'll brave the sea!'

Well, it was not a matter of murmuring a prayer: it took the efforts of Grace, her father, and her elderly mother (another forgotten heroine) to launch the heavy coble into the high seas; far from alone, Grace pulled for over a mile to reach Harker Rock, under orders from her father. As for the romantic ending, in which the ballad says 'A crew of nine all told' were saved, that is not so either: the *Forfarshire* drowned over forty men, women, and children, and on the wet rock where Grace Darling and her father William landed, Mrs Dawson was holding in her arms the bodies of her two dead children. It was a nasty business; unromantic, grim, deathly. Grace Darling was not called upon to be 'spirited' or 'dashing' as the press made her out. She was a decent spinster daughter, who in an extreme hour did as her experienced father told her, pulled a heavy oar in heavy seas, and assisted in one of the hundreds of lighthouse-men's rescues of the period. William Darling made a second trip, aided by survivors on the other oars, while she stayed to help the stricken Mrs Dawson and the other passengers.

Grace seems to have resisted press efforts to make her a heroic bimbo; in the four years more that she lived, she modestly refused the Adelphi and the circus, put up reluctantly with medal-ceremon-ies and constant visitors, refused postal offers of marriage, and finally died of tuberculosis in her sister's care in 1842. Her repu-tation – according to her family – distressed her rather than otherwise, because of the imputation that her father would not have gone without her urging. We saluted the Longstone and its present keepers as we passed, and paused at the Inner Farne for supper, surrounded by birds. A lone seal swam around, glaring at us. The warden would not let us land, because 'the seabirds won't settle on their nests. I have to close at six'. We watched them settling from the boat, then very gently, so as not to shatter the peaceful horseshoe of still water with the fumes and racket of an engine, we hauled up the sails and ghosted out.

It was eight o'clock; so far had we come south, so much had the season advanced, that eight o'clock felt like evening again instead of early afternoon. In a troubled, magnificent sky the sun set; we sailed at first, then motored in a large unaccountable swell towards the south. The swell must have been driven up some by some storm wind south of us. The sky, the swell, the very smell of things would have made us uneasy, even without the clear and unequivocal forecast of exceptional gales. But the peace of the evening was so far undisturbed: in turn, Bamburgh and Dunstanburgh castles rose golden ahead of us and fell astern as black ragged shapes against the sunset. As real night came, Nicholas appeared saucer-eyed from his bunk, and begged to stand his first night watch: we taught him how to scan the horizon for a lighthouse, how the Coquet Island light shone red over one sector of the sea, white over another. He drank it all in, gravely, and gazed at the shore lights of Craster and Alnmouth and finally Amble before he slept. *Grace O'Malley* became a black shape in the night waves again: once more, after our long weeks in the almost eternal northern daylight, we had to do such things as standing on the foredeck, anxiously looking out for an unlit buoy on our track, and trying to make out the flashing red and green lights of Amble harbour piers among the sodium shore-lights. It was odd to be on a true night-passage again: it was part of our homecoming to the south and to winter.

Amble harbour, however, proved nightmarish. As we passed inside the dark piers, Paul said, 'Good Lord. Its end has fallen off.' And so it had: the shape of the pier-end in the night showed a large crack, where it had subsided and fallen away. Then, searching for red lights, cardinal marks, piles and so forth, we threaded through unaccountable sticks in the water, and found ourselves avoiding a quite unannounced and unlit giant black python on the dark water: some sort of dredging-pipe perhaps. Eventually Paul decided we were heading the wrong side of the breakwater, and doubled back; he is very good at these night approaches to strange harbours, and battles on, deducing and reasoning coolly and daringly in circumstances where I, if in command, would see no alternative but to drop the anchor and burst into tears before drinking half a bottle of Scotch and waiting for daylight.

Eventually we found our way into Amble Braid Marina, and made for the first pontoon we could see. The wind was already rising. The night-duty berthing-master hurried down the pontoons and hailed us in a warming Geordie accent. 'Aye – ye can lie a canny way along, there on that one – aye – canny – '. Satisfied with his decision, the friendly man waved us good night, and stepped smartly backwards straight off the pontoon into the water. It was not funny. *Grace O'Malley* was already moving away towards her new berth, so I dropped the rope I was holding and jumped the gap to the pontoon to grab the spluttering, startled man's arms and hang on. In chilly northern waters like ours, it is so rare for anyone to enter the water from a yacht marina pontoon or dock that it always spells emergency: a middle-aged man, falling in the dark into a cold, muddy, deep basin, is not funny, ever. I hung on until Paul managed to back the boat on to the pontoon and throw a line ashore to hold her; then he came with a rope to tie under the man's arms. This done, we all began to joke, to hunt (successfully) for his floating hat, and to heave him at leisure back up on to the wooden planking. Then the clocks struck midnight in the invisible town, the berthing-master squelched off uttering grateful sounds, and we had arrived in Amble.

30

We awoke late, to the most gratifying of all yachting sounds: a whistling gale heard from the security of a harbour which we had cleverly got into before it began. We examined our surroundings: Amble Marina is a freakish place, as smart and modern a marina as any along the South Coast. It was the fastest-built yacht harbour in Britain, being financed partly by the district council and partly by a grant from the EEC Regional Development Fund in the North-East: 'They knew,' said a neighbouring yacht broker thoughtfully, 'that they'd get no money unless they got on with it quick.' It lies in what was a silted-up coal-ship dock in this prime coal-carrying port: eighteen months before we came in, it was a mudflat. Ten per cent of the town opposed it, but they were vigorous: the tenor of the argument being partly conservationist (it is possible to make a case even for the most coal-stained mudflat) and partly an expression of distaste at 'rich southern folks' coming in yachts to disrupt the plain people of the region. In the event, to everyone's surprise, most of the resident yachts are from Newcastle, and several of them (one of the staff confidentially assured us) are Newcastle millionaires; there is, he murmured, 'an awful lot of loose money' hanging around in this depressed and shocked region. Indeed, my Cellphone had detected it and started to work again.

It was a pleasure to be on a river. The children and I strolled up along the Coquet, admiring its deep muddy red colour; its course is only a century-and-a-half old, having changed violently in the early 1800s. One stormy night the Coquet decided to join the sea at Amble, and turned it into a coal port. We followed the broad stream up towards the towering shape of Warkworth Castle a mile away, and never minded the wind or rain. Warkworth had a nice inland feel to it, with its plain honest castle on a meander of the river, and the Coquet winding on through deep woods into the heart of Northumbria. After lunch we followed the river upstream again, breathing in the scents of wild fennel and mint and thyme, crushing abundant leaves in our fingers, rejoicing in the smooth, waveless current alongside. We crossed in a brown varnished, ancient rowing-boat with an equally brown and antique ferryman, and walked right through the rock-face into the odd little hermitage carved out of solid rock in the fifteenth century; we walked back, happy and slow, Rose trailing behind sniffing plants and talking to herself. The blustery squalls which out at sea must have been lethal were nothing much here: shaking branches, fat drops of rain.

As Nicholas and I reached the castle, and turned through the grass moat (my mind a little numbed by his monologue about how he would, one day, build a Viking ship of his own in the garage and sail away with a real radar set) I suddenly missed Rose. I had seen her two minutes before, not less, maundering along just behind us; I looked round and turned to a pillar of salt, for she had gone. Below us in a deep declivity the brown river still ran fast to the sea; above us were woods, around us strangers. She had been, by chance, wearing her bright yellow buoyancy jacket; I decided to enlist every quiet Sunday stroller in a search-party, brandishing the twin of her jacket: 'A little girl – about four – in a coat this colour?' I accosted old ladies, young girls, children, men: nobody had seen her. I ran around the moat, Nicholas puffing behind; climbed the wall, peered down into the swirling river cutting; my heart hammered: Rose drowned, Rose under a car, Rose with a stranger . . . I have never mislaid a child in a public place before. More and more strangers were enlisted, and all rallied nobly to the challenge, shouting ROSE! and combing the castle mound. I cursed my complacency, negligence, wickedness. Nicholas was on the verge of tears, but had sense enough to say sharply to me: 'You must listen, Mummy, as well as shout. In case she might answer.' After a quarter of an hour, a moustached young man, who had instantly abandoned his own wife and children to hunt, panted up to me: 'She was on the pavement down the road. She's on that bench.' I ran back up to the bench where, very sensibly, he had told her to wait – no man of discretion would ever tell a child to follow him anywhere in these wicked days – and found a morose little figure very pleased to see me. Some ladies had looked after her, she said. Not bad strangers, because they didn't ask her to go anywhere, just to wait. We walked home, in a soothing web of tales of my being lost as a child, of Uncle Mike's being lost, of endless lost but sensible children, and had a long coin-operated bath in the marina Ladies'.

We were rather enjoying being in our first yacht marina since Troon six weeks before. The clatter of halyards and the tinkling of rigging were familiar, and it was not unpleasant to feel again that yachts are common and normal things, rather than silly little objects that get in the way of fishing-boats. And it was a treat to do revolting jobs like the bilge pump and the lavatory seals with the certainty of a hot shower afterwards without having to beg a seaside landlady for it. We shopped in Amble, took the bus to Alnwick, and tried to get haircuts; I walked along the harbour and listened to the grumbles of the fishermen about their rapidly silting harbour, and the new dredger. 'Theeay bought it cheap from the west coast. Meeght as well send your kiddies out with buckets and spades.' It was good to see cobles with their high sterns used everywhere for fishing-boats; the wooden coble yard in Amble is almost defunct, but the brave traditional east coast shape has enough devotees to make fibreglass cobles quite the rage for leisure fishermen.

And all the time, the wind blew. The lifeboats all along the coast were out; a yacht was towed in during our second day in Amble, and the news reported gusts of seventy-seven knots at St Andrews, the windiest Scottish summer gale ever recorded, and the worst July weather for fifty years. We read forty-seven knots of wind over our deck inside the marina, and it was barely possible for the children to stand up in exposed places; Paul was nearly tipped overboard while measuring the wind strength with a pocket anemometer. It was a sunny gale, though, and in the end we became quite used to the wind, moving through it as through a new element, barely believing that it could ever stop until the world stopped whirling and the clouds flying. It lasted three full days: we heard news of railway lines in Scotland blocked with driftwood, of great trees down, of yacht rescues in places we had been through weeks or days before; but we lay placidly in Amble, took walks, washed our clothes and hired rowing-boats to meander up the Coquet in peace. We grew used to Amble and its strange contradictory views: looking upriver, cobles and smooth river and the eminence of Warkworth Castle make it a place of timeless English beauty fit for the guidebooks; downriver lies the ugly sprawl of bad modern housing, the chaos of the old docks, the air of rusty deprivation which make it part of the modern North-East, where one man in eight has no hope of work. Britain: the beauty and the beastliness.

On the fourth day, the wind still howled, but less strongly. Shuddering slightly at the prospect, we decided to use the remaining south-westerly wind to dash south-eastwards before the next bit of trouble struck. The Met. Office, in tones of reluctant honesty, had broken it to us that another depression, fierce and low, was on its way on Thursday; Wednesday was the only day they were prepared to guarantee free from gale-force winds. This placed us in a quandary: wherever we got to in that day's sail would be the place where we were trapped for two, maybe three days; the options before us were Blyth, fifteen miles; Hartlepool, forty miles; and Whitby, sixty miles. We had to be in Whitby to meet friends on Saturday; and, with hand on heart, Paul had to admit that whatever the fascination of the industrial North-East, neither Blyth nor Hartlepool docks struck him as the best possible spot for a rainy imprisonment. So Whitby it was; with the added advantage of a broader course to steer off the wind, as we cut straight across the bays of Tyne and Tees.

He was right, but I was frustrated. I had wanted to go to Blyth, if only to meet George Chapman. Mr Chapman's works had been much in evidence in Alnwick gift-shops: he is a canny old shipwright who had the bright idea of hanging around the Blyth shipbreaking yards when the redundant warships came in, amassing a store of teak and brass scrap from HMS *Ark Royal*, and others: over succeeding years he patiently made these bits into miniature cannon, binnacles, wheels, and other doll's-house items of naval equipment, each with a plaque showing the master ship's name and origin: the result is a line of pretty little artefacts selling like hot cakes to old sailors, naval widows, sentimentalists like myself, and small boys with glowing eyes, their lump of warship safe forever in their tracksuit pockets. I thought Mr Chapman a fine example of entrepreneurism in the face of declining industry, and was assured by a slightly awed shop assistant that he was also 'a reet character, we should saay'. But I waved to Mr Chapman as we sped past Blyth's chimneys in the sunshine; then saluted my cousins in Newcastle as we passed the smoggy Tyne. The pilot-book here actually warns of 'lessened visibility due to industrial smoke', and the coastline off the Northumberland and Durham coalfield has advanced four hundred feet in the last century due to sewage and coal-dust dumping; we cannot be accused of sentimental cherishing of nature in this spot. I have always had a secret soft spot for

Geordies and Geordieland, though; Brian Redhead and I used to sing choruses of 'Keep your feet still, Geordie Hinney' during dull 'Thought for the Day' tapes when we presented the Radio 4 'Today' programme together. I played it now, badly, on the penny-whistle as we passed Newcastle.

The coast was certainly forbiddingly smoky; as we reached the Tees it grew even less obviously alluring, but here again I pined. Of the two places I had firmly determined to call at during this voyage, one was Orkney and the other was Hartlepool: if Hartlepool seems a strange destination for a pleasure-lover, be assured it was not. I had been to see HMS *Warrior* in Portsmouth, but long before that I had spent a day with the men who restored her in Hartlepool. I had been in Walter Brownlee's chaotic office, riffled through Victorian files and plans, heard passionate debates about the right sort of doorhandles for the boilers, and talked with middle-aged, delicately skilled shipwrights about what it meant to have a job, and such a job as this, dropped in your lap again after ten years' bored idleness. It seemed only decent to go back again to *Warrior*'s old empty dock, now that those men's jobs had been towed away towards the south; besides, there was a limited happy ending to the tale, because the Hartlepool team did so well that they are now building replica ships for developers, and have the contract to restore *Foudroyant*, a frigate which has been a familiar sight in Portsmouth as a sea cadet HQ for years. I pined for Hartlepool, but still we sailed on by at a vigorous six knots under a reefed mainsail, twisting and churning through the rough seas.

The wind showed little sign of dropping towards dusk, but we were at least sheltered by the approaching bulge of the North York moors. In the late sun, the high moors shone pale green and purple, as if lit from within. A flurry of foam under our white bows showed that we were sailing far too fast: we would reach Whitby at dead low water and would not be able to get in. We shortened the sails more, but still sped on towards Yorkshire; past Staithes, where Paul, as a child, still saw women in black Sunday cloaks and bonnets; and Port Mulgrave, built beneath a cliff to take ironstone from the tunnels direct from mineworkings. Finally we saw the glitter of Whitby, just after dusk. With the children almost asleep, I tried picking out 'On Ilkley Moor baht 'at' on the whistle, but was quelled.

It is an oddity of sailing voyages that each harbour makes a different impression on approach each time, because the character of the passage beforehand – savage or sleepy, bright or threatening, dull or cheerful – stamps itself on the harbour. Whitby, after a light, glittering, windy day, with high wild gale-clouds underlining the need for shelter, appeared both welcome and distinctly daunting. A huge yellow moon veiled with black was rising over the floodlit abbey ruins on the hill, and gulls rode dark on the waves around us, sometimes swooping like bats across our deck. It was an hour after low water, and repeated earnest calculations at the chart table had assured us that, with luck, we would just about float in with a smear of mud on our keel. We would still have to wait three hours for the swing bridge to open and let us into the upper harbour where yachts lie, but we felt an uneasy hurry to be inside. The wind was getting up. Under the vast, shifting moon we motored very slowly in; a strange, awful cry from some late seabird startled us, the great tower of the old lighthouse rose unlit ahead of us like a giant's black finger; the cold bit into us through jerseys and oilskins. As we tied up with cold, clumsy fingers to a fishing boat, we looked up and saw horror-comic lettering flaring high above us on the quay: THE DRACULA EXPERIENCE.

No wonder it felt so creepy. Whitby, having long ago joyfully annexed the entire life and work of Captain Cook on the grounds that he served his apprenticeship as a Whitby collier, and having milked dry the picturesque potential of its old whaling history, has lately taken over Dracula as well. Bram Stoker obligingly set two chapters of the book here, driving a ship ashore on Whitby beach with a dead man lashed to the helm and the bloodsucking Count disguised as a black dog. In the morning, we took our morbid children round the Dracula Experience with much nervous, high-pitched laughter as mannequins sprung out of boxes or groped from lichened recesses in the wall; snooty although I had been about the Dracula hype, our eerie approach the night before across the sucking mud, and a later walk around the town, convinced me that Bram Stoker knew what he was doing. Whitby, then as now, must have been a curious, unique blend of the pleasant and the slightly sinister.

It is a naturally creepy place. The tall, grand merchant houses, dark alleys, and air of ancient, careless, seaport cosmopolitanism convey a mixture of quaintness and threat. We toured a sinister old house converted into a waxwork museum of showground freaks, like fish with beaks and the Mule-Faced Woman. The Human Caterpillar (a sad armless and legless Oriental, apparently modelled in spam), the Siamese Twins, and a model of Fagin were paraded before the allegedly more sophisticated and compassionate eyes of the newest generation; and I have to report that the children loved it. They also deeply appreciated the scabs and sores on the models in the 'Great Whitby Plague' exhibit; although I felt the effect of the plastic sores was slightly lessened by the fact that the underlying human figures were slender and mincing creatures clearly left over from the shop-window-dressing industry. They were high-street dummies. Charlestown had had the same problem: when a town waxworks runs out of design money, it seems, you get 'Scenes of Medieval Life', or 'A Traditional Fisherfolk's Cottage of the 1870s' being inhabited by creatures with high cheekbones, long finger-nails, slender necks and pert little noses; they look like a lot of *Vogue* models slumming it in sackcloth. Tearing Rose away from the effigy of the World's Fattest Man, we emerged blinking into the drizzle, only to be confronted by shop after shop crammed with mourning brooches in genuine Whitby jet, 'as supplied to Queen Victoria and the Pope'. Oh yes, Whitby is creepy all right.

But it is a healthy, British creepiness; a holiday shudder. Even the fortune-teller's notice in the tent on the front said rather snappishly: 'Predictions on love, marriage, career, or any Reasonable Question answered'. Madame Lee, clearly, had had trouble in her time with unreasonable questions: tykey, cheeky enquiries such as, What do you fancy for the four forty? or, What Price Scargill Now, Mother?

Two more depressions were tracked to the west of us, crossing the country fast; the barometer fell, the rain continued to lash down, running rapidly down the precipitous alleys of the old town; our friends' son, Nicholas's bosom buddy, Matthew, was poorly and their visit therefore delayed anyway. We were comfortable enough in the tiny marina (more EEC money, we observed, although Yorkshire practicality had built a car-park four times as big as the marina). We had a peaceful time on the pontoons, despite the gloomy remarks of our neighbour, a local yachtsman. 'You'll not be let to face that way,' he said. 'Peter, the boss, he likes all his boats facing t'same way. Tidy.' Peter turned out perfectly affable, even when the rain wiped out the entire weather forecast he had just written on his blackboard, and never even suggested we move.

But every little community needs a few villains, and a local huddle of yachts, all wet and matey around the floating planks, is a community after all.

Damp but undaunted, we settled down to another few days galebound in Whitby. Time, anyway, to perfect 'Ilkley Moor' on the whistle; to walk among the high tombstones in the evening with gulls wheeling below and the wind screaming round our ears; and to follow the bedraggled donkeys and the deaf donkey-man down to the beach, for rides in raincoats while the red flag flew and the waves crashed violently on the hard sand. I had plenty of time to talk to the roundabout man as the children whirled. He had travelled too. 'I were at Skye. I were a construction supervisor. Built the nuclear sub base at Applenoss.' Another old man in a stuffy little shop lectured me on the marvels of Whitby jet. 'It's wood. Fossil wood. It's warm, it's light. You can't fake it. It keeps off evil spirits.' I bought a rough-carved Yorkshire coble to go with my Clyde Puffer, Eyemouth trawler, and *Resolution*-in-a-bottle; then hesitated in the back streets, outside a little kipper smokery, at the sight of a whisky bottle (still labelled) containing a wild approximation of a clipper ship in balsa-wood and cut-up notepaper. To the true collector, provenance is all: the kipper man told me his Dad had made it, so I bought it for £4. Then I climbed the one hundred and ninety-nine steps to the abbey and the church once more, and stood by the graves of John and William Storr, lifeboatmen of 1861, looking down at Captain Cook's statue and the gallant bulwarks of Whitby harbour. I saw the fishing cobles chugging efficiently in, the swirl of brown water where the River Esk deposits its load of silt on to the shifting banks outside; and distant, green-grey acres of the North Sea under the cliffs where James Cook first learned to navigate. Our voyage around the coast, so nearly over, began to mean something new: it had been a voyage around perseverance, around gallantry, around the eternal, humble give-and-take of humanity with the sea. Harbours, havens, lighthouses, lifeboats, were all part of the reaching out into the unknown, and cautious guarantees of the homecoming.

There is something indescribably gallant about an East Coast harbour: few natural features assist its safety, as they do in the rocky west; nature throws up sandbanks, treacherous longshore currents, anything to cause trouble. But the harbours creep seawards, not always with the arrogance of the great industrial shipyards but more often with persistent, under-financed, local determination to catch fish, to take trade, to give small, insignificant towns a maritime backdoor. I saluted it all.

Beside me, a gloomy-looking couple got out of their car, and stared at Whitby harbour walls far below us, reaching out to the wrinkled sea. 'There's noothing to see,' said the wife, peevishly. And the husband: 'Nay, noothing much. Coom on, Donna.' Their child, about ten, continued to stare at the sea, enjoying the unaccustomed eagle's view. 'Coom ON!' They dragged her back to the car. I had thought I revered the sacred status of the natural family; but found myself fleetingly wondering what the legal penalties would be for abducting a child from its family for the afternoon, and taking it round a museum or two, lecturing it on environmental and historical topics, and returning it thoroughly stirred up and subverted to amaze its pudding-like progenitors. Severe, probably. Donna and her parents got back into their car and bumped away, Donna still trying to look at the sea with some hopeful mental process going on in her head. Three more children walked ahead of me down the cliff path, boys at that sickening macho, brainless stage of adolescence; one of them threw his plastic lunch-wrapper over the cliff, another his Coke can. 'You are a pair of litterbugs, and you ought to be ashamed of yourself!' I said rather squeakily, my urge to boss other people's children still not slaked. They stared, bovinely, and stumped on in their inanely threatening boots.

Suddenly, despite the kipper-man's father's ship, despite the good humour and beauty of the town, I was in a furiously bad temper. These dreary Philistines had too many counterparts in places high enough to know better. There were too many ministers, industries, councils, and bureaucrats ready to say, 'There's nothing to look at there, throw the rubbish in it, use it for the nuclear waste, route the slurry pipes across it. Stop staring, get back in the national car and drive on aimlessly in the name of progress.' The newspapers that morning had broken the news of a virus killing the seals in the North Sea; they were washed up on the shore, more and more of them, made into victims after thousands of healthy years because their resistance was lowered by human filth. Britain pumps more untreated sewage and industrial waste into the living sea than any other civilized nation. There is, after all, 'nothing to look at out there'.

31

At last the wind eased; it was eight days since we had fled south from Holy Island to Amble to escape the coming blast, and during the whole week there had only been one day fit to sail. Three days in Amble, three days in Whitby, were making the children highly reluctant to sail at all. As we coasted towards Flamborough Head and Bridlington, another thirty-five mile passage, they slept on, then woke excessively cross, even to be out in these gentle winds on this flat sea. Recovering, they listened with cynical caution to our encomia of Bridlington. Paul spent all his childhood holidays there from Sheffield: his great-great-grandfather and great-great-uncle were ferryman and fisherman at Brid, and we have their pictures, whiskery and dignified in Sunday suits, hanging in photograph frames in the hall at home. As Flamborough Head appeared, Paul became more Yorkshire in tone, deeply nostalgic; the wind, which had been light and vacillating, became a purposeful brisk westerly as *Grace O'Malley* shot down under her white topsail towards another of our children's ancestral homes. A cry of emotion from Paul brought all three of us on deck at one point. 'That's THORNWICK!' he shouted. *Thornwick*? What? 'The pleasure-boat round the bay. Mind, we never went on *Thornwick*. We went on t'*Yorkshire Belle*. Or the *Boy's Own*. The accordion-player were better, on t'*Boy's Own*, we thought.' What about *Thornwick*? '*Thornwick* cost five shillings. *Thornwick*,' he said with ancient remembered scorn, 'was the one you went on if you really thought you were summat.' We contemplated the boat in the distance (it turned out to be called *Flamborion*: 'Some upstart newcomer,' said Paul; later still it turned out to be *Boy's Own* under a new name). His eye roved further over his old horizon. A hideous white 1940s building rose from the coast as we rounded the Head. 'That white thing,' he said. 'That is the Expanse. Expanse Hotel. We used to look at that and marvel. We stayed at Mrs Wilkie's boarding-house. You paid extra for use of cruet.' So the Expanse, I murmured, trying to grasp the nuances, was where you stayed If You Thought You Were Summat? 'No, you WERE summat, if you could afford the Expanse.'

We turned to windward and tacked for a couple of miles, strenuously, in memory of those great-great-uncles who had brought out their fishing-smacks in such laborious style; then we rather guiltily switched on the engine. They probably would have done the same, if they'd had one.

Alongside the fish pier, more rewards: the watchkeeper who saw us in had known old Teddy Trufitt, Paul's great-great-uncle. 'Mind you, that's going back a bit, old Teddy Trufitt.' Paul was six years old again, looking over the crowded, pretty harbour where the old Yorkshire one-design racing boats were gliding into their old cradle moorings (ninety years old, many of them: the same rich folks' yachts that Paul used to watch with his Nan's hand clasped stickily in his). Trawlers prepared for the Monday morning trip, crowds of tourists milled on the harbour and the beaches in the lowering sunlight. Bridlington is not as pretty as Whitby, not as quirky, not as self-conscious in bragging of its sons; it is more downmarket. It is not as famous as Scarborough. But as I took the children scampering along the front, to the harmless child-sized amusements, I felt the happiness of the place. There were grannies with new babies and girls in strappy shoes, sweating Dads and running children; this is the resort for Sheffield and Rotherham and Doncaster, for the sort of people who come back year after year to build up a patina of happy holiday memories. Brid is a highlight, and it has been a highlight, for thousands of people over a hundred years. 'Most of t'visitors,' the lady in the Blue Lobster told us, 'are regulars. They know they'll not do better.' Not in the sweaty, gritty Mediterranean, not in the flashy south.

A black horse, showy and well-cared for, stood with a landau just above the quay. Mr Bellerby ('I'm retired, really, you know') drove us competently around Bridlington, as Paul had never been able to afford to drive as a child. My husband's eagle eyes were everywhere. 'That's Vernon Café. Terrible, what they've done to it,' he would say. On questioning, it turned out they had changed the sign. A baker's shop in Richmond Road where he used to stay had become a hairdresser's. But: 'That's the United Reformed Church where my Auntie Aga used to sing in the choir.' (I knew about Auntie Aga from his mother: 'Her that lived at Nafferton. She never trusted winter sunshine. Said it were treacherous.') He remembered his Uncle Jack, taking him rowing inexpertly round the harbour and being roared at by the skipper of the incoming *Yorkshire Belle* – 'He said Pull your Port Oar. We didn't know what he was on about. And there's the Sailors' Bethel. On Sunday nights we would stand outside and hear the wonderful singing.' Worn out with memory, the children yawning, we set out for the Royal Yorkshire Yacht Club, whose members, buzzing happily around their boats in the harbour, had jointly and severally urged us to go and wash there even though the clubhouse was closed for the night. Paul went back ahead of us, and the children and I crept from the darkened building, locked it up, and followed with dragging, tired feet.

The southern dusk was with us now: nine o'clock saw the streetlamps on, the illuminated bulbs above the prom showing up against the dark sea. Suddenly we all felt as if the end of term had come, the end of our Summer's Grace. We had less than a week to home; our next leg would take us across the Humber and over the Wash to our own land, the round bulge of East Anglia. The children looked around wonderingly at the dark little town; 'Other children don't go to bed in a harbour,' said Nicholas, as we turned from the glow of houses towards the lonely line of sodium yellow lights along the quay. 'Other children don't sleep on water.' They negotiated the lengthening ladder, with skill and understanding. 'Isn't the tide low already?' said Rose knowledgeably. On unwise impulse, I asked them if they had enjoyed their voyage, now it was nearly over. 'I don't want it to be over,' said Nicholas. 'Except for seeing Matthew and my Manta Force.' 'Well, we can always sail around Britain again,' said Rose with optimistic firmness. 'When I'm big enough to be bothered, we might.'

I sat up until two, to watch the startling progress mudward of our poor boat. The ground is so soft in Bridlington harbour that we were quite unable to lean her against the quay: instead she flopped away from it into a deep, oozy hole made by the last few nesting trawlers, and lay rather helplessly at a daft angle until dawn, with frequent yawning visits to the ropes from me. Paul dreamed, content with the same contentment I had felt in St Andrews: there is nothing quite so satisfying as regaining a scene of your childhood in your own boat, coming full circle home to Teddy Trufitt's ghost, and the approving shade of grandmother, grandfather, and Mrs Wilkie at the boarding-house.

Yawning at eight thirty in the morning, we were roused by a shockingly cheery hail from the quay: a thin, blond, wire-spectacled lad who looked the quintessence, the Ecky-thumpessence, of the old Yorkshire comics: thin plastered fair hair, round glasses. He wanted to use the crane above our berth to lower a new buoy which his boat was contracted to lay on a gas pipe out at sea. We hauled ourselves out of the way along the quay, made tea, and decided that leaving Bridlington on such a fine day was out of the question. So we built imperial sandcastles on the beach, indulged the children on the council amusements and ate fish and chips. It rained for a while, but even when lowering bagsful of disintegrating curd tarts down twenty feet of wet slimy quayside we stayed contented: Paul had found many traces of Trufitts in archive and lifeboathouse, and everyone on the quay would pause in their work to discuss precisely whose Uncle George it was who used to talk about old Teddy Trufitt, and where Warehouse Road used to be where he lived in the twenties; nobody could actually remember anything particular about Teddy Trufitt, but that, in Yorkshire, probably redounded to his credit. The Clitheroe Kid appeared, cheery as ever, as the tide came back up at six, and with a great sangfroid supervised the swinging of several tons of steel buoy over our stern again.

A lone figure on the end of the quay watched attentively: Mike Peyton, the yachting cartoonist and best, bitterest eye for an impending disaster or contretemps afloat. He was just up from Maldon in his boat *Touchstone*. 'Looking for material,' he said happily. 'There's a cartoon in this.' The buoy swung over us safely, children agape, and Peyton departed, thinking wistfully of entanglements and flying objects that might have been. I idled on the quay, reading about the building of the South Pier in the 1840s. One day of particularly low tide involved two hundred men being summoned to work on a Sunday: they were all brought to court and sentenced to the stocks as Sabbath-breakers, but the queue for the stocks grew so long and unruly that the sentence was abandoned.

Mike Peyton came aboard for a drink that night, and revealed that he was off round Britain, too, via the Caledonian Canal. As he was going in the opposite direction, we offered him our complete set of pilot-books – some of them rather specialist ones that Paul had only got through assiduous writing-off to club secretaries in remote places. He accepted the loan, with a rather embarrassed laugh. 'Err . . . the thing is, I'm already using all Jonathan Raban's charts . . . borrowed them off him.' Peyton was clearly doing well out of the offshore publishing industry. The Raban charts were particularly interesting, he said. 'Full of pencil marks like "Shop-soiled cliffs".' We had a postcard from him weeks later, thanking us for the books but complaining that they had slowed him down; he entered one small esoteric harbour purely because he could not resist the pilot-book's injunction to steer for a patch of bird drop-pings on the cliff. Perhaps he carefully, in his neat draughtsman's writing, amended his borrowed charts to specify more closely the type of soiling on the cliff.

32

The next morning a hail from the deck woke us. 'Are ye reet, *Grace O'Malley*? Mr 'Einey?' It was someone else with news of Teddy Trufitt. 'Tell yer how he died. It were a big thunderstorm, on the ebb; the tide just kept coming in and didn't go down, and there were this tidal wave. After the war. A tidal wave inside the harbour. He were an old chap, tried to row against it in the ferryboat and strained his heart. He died a while afterwards.'

With which dramatic full-stop to the tale he wished us well, and departed.

We set off southwards towards the sandy flatlands where we would find home. We had been through a baffling time with the pilot-books in Bridlington, as bad as our early sessions with the Scottish charts; but whereas up there it was a matter of choosing which way to go, here the problem was finding anywhere at all where we could get in. From Bridlington southwards there is nothing for thirty miles until Grimsby; Grimsby involves going eight miles up the Humber, which at spring tides you can only do on the flood; you need an ebb to get out again, but if you do have a falling tide on the Humber, you will miss getting into the next haven – Wells-next-the-Sea in Norfolk. If the wind is onshore and strong, you can't get into Wells anyway; and there is nothing else for thirty-five miles until Lowestoft, which is the first all-tide harbour on the open coast since Peterhead four hundred miles to the north. The alternative idea of going right up the Wash to Boston involved tidal calculations of such intricacy that we gave up; as Paul said, the moral is that once you get to Bridlington you either have to stay there or else go back round via Orkney again.

Eventually we gave up Grimsby with only a slight struggle. We had a fair westerly wind for the sixty-mile passage, and on picking up the tide-tables again from the corner where we had thrown them, it turned out that we could carry eight full hours of fair tide if we made straight across for Wells. The wind swung north-west, and we flew down the coast; saying farewell to Flamborough,

254

passing lower stretches of farmland and dunes, looking out to see the Amoco gas terminal and its retinue of fussy little ships. We crossed back into our own eastern hemisphere at noon exactly, over the Greenwich meridian; ahead of us lay familiar scenes. Clouds of black smoke rose from the stubble-burning, USAF jets whined and screamed overhead. The two things we liked least about East Anglia were making themselves felt. Spurn Point passed, with its lonely lifeboathouse: as night fell, we were off the mouth of the Wash.

This maze of sands, leading to the fenland where Hereward still walks the watery coast at nights, has always seemed ghostly to me from the land: it is a hundred times more ghostly from the sea. Flashes of mysterious eldritch light from military bombing-ranges split the sky; bangs and whines broke the peace of the night. A bloodstained red moon rose in the east. We saw the lights of Mablethorpe and Skegness, and around us the flat silky water glowed with phosphorescence. The wind dropped away, and we motored doggedly on; at 3 a.m. we anchored somewhere near the Wells fairway buoy, and settled down in a huge rolling swell to sleep while the tide rose.

Crashing and rattling of stowed gear, clanks from the galley, tapping of halyards, grinding of chain, and the occasional bomb entered into our dreams. Ill-rested and disorientated, we lurched on to the rocking deck at nine, reassured the waking children, and spent twenty minutes of misery getting the anchor up. Then, at last, we made our way into Wells-next-the-Sea.

We had thought that the voyage around Britain had introduced us to most kinds of harbours: deep lochs, sandy holes like Bridlington where we had seen police-horses trotting at low water right between the piers; fishing-harbours, yacht harbours, tourist traps, locked basins, creeks, fast rivers. But we had never been anywhere quite like Wells. Dynamically, hydraulically, and socially we were quite adrift. Wells is a marsh harbour: there is no river feeding it, and its tortuous winding channel and dock are, when the tide drops, effectively no more than a sand-pool left by the sea. So instead of a relatively steady drop and rise, Wells gets – as the harbourmaster gleefully informed us, 'three hours' flood tide, nine hours of ebb'. The usual rules-of-twelfths and rules of thumb are no use at all. That night we observed with fascinated horror that with high water due at eleven, by nine fifteen nothing whatsoever had happened; the sand lay dry, quiet and bare. Of course nothing can happen until the tide creeps high enough outside to burst over the sill of the pool and fill it up; we sat apprehensively like spiders in a dry bath, waiting for the tap to be turned on.

When it does flow – or ebb – in Wells, it does it with striking force. Paul actually got trapped aboard the boat, alongside the little coaster we were moored to, because the force of the ebb pushing our bow off was too great for him to haul himself in. We were alongside the coaster because these were spring tides, and at spring tides Wells forgets that it is a seaside resort and yachting harbour, and remembers its real identity as the northernmost seaport of East Anglia. A cloud of dust hung over the quay; cranes and lorries roared and rattled around the five small coasters taking advantage of the high tides, and the only way a yacht could moor was alongside them, sinking down at low water some ten feet below their rusty, ladderless sides. The children, however, were very pleased. 'Mummy!' cried Nicholas. 'Are these ships – are they *importing*?' I wished that I had had such a vivid, crane-hissing, clanging, rattling introduction to the dire school subject of commercial geography.

We felt a little sheepish at having believed the idyllic rural ravings of the guidebooks. These had led us to arrange for the Stevens family, Caroline and the children's longed-for friends Matthew and Charles, to meet us at Wells. They arrived, peered gamely over the two huge rusting decks separating us from the quay, and began climbing. Caroline was wearing immaculate white Bermuda shorts and a pale peach sweatshirt; luckily, she is a girl who can take a joke. The children were possessed by joy at meeting again, so that a few banged knees and rusty clothes meant nothing.

The harbourmaster had said, in his cheerful way, that we should have to shift away 'for a few minutes' that night when the tide came up, so that the coasters could all change berths. We sat through the evening, tied up to the *Island Dart* of Rochester, staring nervously at the blank sand and waiting for the tidal rush. The wide bowl of bright sea-lit Norfolk sky hung above us; the sun dropped; peace lay over little Wells. Then with a flurry of weed and a whirlpool of sand, the tide came back. We rose within half-an-hour back to a level with the big ship's waterline, and in the darkness we cast off into the sluicing tide to find somewhere to wait 'for a few minutes'. In the end we tied up to another yacht, a highly disgruntled couple from Whitby who had already broken one boat's bowsprit today in the tide 'and never seen anything like it. I am sure I will get a communication from his insurance company, and mine will reply in kind, but I said to him, I am unwilling to risk my boat in this tide, I told him. We were on our way to Holland but I doubt if we shall ever get there. I told him, before he insisted on leaving the berth . . .' Beyond him was a shrimp-boat, where the crews were energetically boiling up their catch in a huge vat on deck; the smoke rose in the darkness like an emanation from hell, the smell was all-pervading. Caroline sat fascinated, while the propellers of the three large ships manoeuvring in the gloom sent tremors and churning waves upstream, stretching our ropes to the limit, and said, 'Wow, I've never been cruising before, I didn't know it was like this.' In vain, we told her that we had never seen anything quite like it either. The children slept in their overcrowded bunks, eight little arms thrown casually around and among the furry toys, Nicholas and Matthew huddled together after three months' separation. After an hour's threnody from the cross Whitby couple about tides, ships, harbourmasters, bowsprits, and Holland, we got back at last alongside the *Island Dart*, to sleep.

At 7 a.m. the cranes began to unload her. A hail of hard little pellets rattled like gunfire on our deck; I poked my head out of the hatch and was rewarded with a number of soya-beans down the front of my nightshirt. Work had begun. I reflected that what with the fish-dust and the soya, we could make a nourishing soup by now if we boiled up our rigging in the winter. It was with some thankfulness, though some affection too, that we escaped at high water into the comparative peace of the open sea.

In this peace, with a fair wind and all four children happy, we edged around the curving coast of Norfolk: Blakeney, Sheringham, Cromer, Happisburgh rose alongside us, church towers aloft, houses hidden behind the dunes, tall beacons to guide sailors, and in Happisburgh the great mound of sailors' mass graves. This coast is lethally dangerous: the Haisbro sands claim ships every year. Indeed, the week after the 'rationalization' of lightvessels took the Haisbro lightship out of service, yet another ship ran on to those sands. There are no havens for nearly forty miles when a storm comes up over Norfolk. But today all was quiet and balmy; we had fast sailing, we had a fair tide. We passed Newport and Caister, Great Yarmouth and Gorleston; we were possessed with the idea of going on all night, making Woodbridge on the dawn tide to complete the voyage with the sun rising. But at nine the wind dropped; Paul was tired, our chart was out of date, the buoys off Lowestoft were puzzling; we dropped main and topsail, and motored into Lowestoft Harbour. A policeman on the quay shouted – not very convincingly – 'HELLO BOAT!' Hello, we said gruffly. 'ARE YOU EXPECTED?' he shouted. No, we said, more gruffly. 'WELL, ARE YOU KNOWN AT THE YACHT CLUB?' Yes, we said, wondering whether we were. It turned out that Princess Anne was coming to Lowestoft in the morning. We turned in and slept.

The next day we sailed southwards for the last time, towards the River Deben where *Grace O'Malley* took shape in Robertson's boatyard eighteen months before, opposite Sutton Hoo. We had sailed from here in spring, to fit the boat out for this voyage in the River Orwell; we wanted to return quietly to the Deben and call the voyage complete when *Grace* was back in her first river.

At three fifteen, with the sunshine upon us, we rounded the Deben Fairway buoy in a choppy sea, freed off the sails to go upriver, and tied balloons and flags in the rigging for Nicholas's long-awaited 'Great Day' celebration. *Grace O'Malley* had sailed round Britain. It had taken us ninety-nine days; we had covered just under one thousand seven hundred miles; we had said we would do it, and we had. We knew that mundane, earthbound work was waiting for us, and that the voyage would fade into the light of common day. We knew that in real life, there are no Finnfolk. But like a retreat, like a long dreaming sleep, like a love affair, the summer's grace had enriched every moment of mundane life that would follow it. You cannot be cynical or indifferent, flippant or dismissive on such a voyage: you cannot leave the coast and forget it as you drive impatiently inland to the motorway, because you are wedded to its moods and you lie at its mercy. In return, it gives a great deal back.

When we got home to our house and garden on a soft summer's evening, we walked around its wide spaces and comfortable rooms with a sort of disbelief. We did not think we really lived here; we thought that perhaps the owners were kindly letting us have a bath and a meal, and that when the evening ended we would have to go. We would walk back through the night to some damp dockside, climb down an iron ladder to our waiting boat and sail on again in the morning.

We stayed, though. That night in the children's own bedroom Paul finished the story of the Good Ship *Clachan* and the Shining Armour. It ended with the hero and heroine, Nicholas and Rose, standing proudly before the young King and being knighted. They had earned it.

STATISTICS

(All mileages are in nautical miles)

TOTAL MILEAGE BY LOG: 1688 nm
AVERAGE DAILY MILEAGE: 17 nm
AVERAGE SPEED: 4½ knots
AVERAGE LENGTH OF PASSAGE: 31·25 nm
AVERAGE TIME ON PASSAGE: 7 hrs
NO. OF DAYS SPENT ENTIRELY IN HARBOUR: 45
DAYS AT SEA: 54
HOURS UNDER SAIL: 210
ENGINE HOURS: 180 (including harbour manoeuvring)
MILES UNDER SAIL: (calculated) 1050
MILES UNDER ENGINE: (calculated) 638
LONGEST PASSAGE: 140 nm (28 hrs) Ipswich–Brighton
LONGEST PASSAGE WITH CHILDREN: 110 nm (20 hrs)
  Mousehole–Milford Haven
HARBOURS VISITED: 57
  Anchorages: 13
  Moorings: 12
  Alongside town or village quays, afloat: 11
  Yacht marinas: 7
  Alongside drying quays: 6
  Drying out on legs: 4
  Locked basins (inc. canal): 4
MOST EXPENSIVE BERTHING FEE: Camper & Nicholson's
  Marina, Portsmouth: £13
CHEAPEST BERTHING FEE: Free – no charge was made, or
  mooring was lent, in all anchorages and in nine
  harbours (seven of them in Scotland). Average
  harbour charge was £4–5
LONGEST PERIOD WITHOUT A BATH: 20 days
  (Fishguard–Isle Ornsay)

GRACE O'MALLEY

THE BOAT

Grace O'Malley is a Cornish Crabbers' Pilot Cutter 30, a centreboard gaff cutter designed by Roger Dongray, with a GRP hull moulded by Cornish Crabbers of Rock, Cornwall, and a wooden deck and interior built by Robertsons of Woodbridge, Suffolk in 1986/7. Her overall length is thirty-eight-foot, thirty-foot on deck, twenty-four-foot waterline. Sails consist of gaff mainsail, jackyard topsail, roller-reefing staysail and roller-furling jib. The engine is a Yanmar twenty-seven horsepower diesel.

MAIN EQUIPMENT: Avon Redcrest inflatable dinghy; Sestrel main compass; NAVSTAR Decca navigator; LOKATA RDF and SSB radio; Brooks & Gatehouse log and depth sounder; Zeiss barograph; Walker impeller log as backup; Autohelm self-steering gear.

THE WOMAN

The original Grace O'Malley, or Granuaile, was Queen of Connaught in the sixteenth century, captained her own ships, and is reputed to have driven off Turkish pirates with a blunderbuss on the morning after giving birth to her son at sea. She kept the hawser of her favourite vessel tied to the leg of her bed, they say, through a hole in the wall of her castle at Rockfleet which you can see to this day. As a very old woman in her seventies, she sailed to England and up the Thames to Greenwich to complain personally to the elderly Elizabeth I about her treatment by the governor of Connaught, and won her case. Her story is told by Anne Chambers in *Granuaile* (Wolfhound Press, Dublin) and – more lyrically – in Sean Davey's song-cycle of the same name.

BIBLIOGRAPHY

It would be impractical to list all the books, pamphlets and publications which we carried with us on *Grace O'Malley* through the summer, but apart from pilot-books, these were the books which gave us most general pleasure and information during the voyage (OOP denotes out of print).

Sailing Tours (3 vols), Frank Cowper, Ashford Press Publishing.
The Yachtsman's England, Frank Carr, Seeley, Service (OOP).
The Yachtsman's Weekend Book, Seeley, Service (OOP).
Island Farm, F. Fraser Darling, Bell (OOP).
Coasting, Jonathan Raban, Collins Harvill.
The Cruise of the Nona, Hilaire Belloc, Century Hutchinson.
The Cruise of the Kate, E. E. Middleton, Grafton Books.
The English Channel, Nigel Calder, Chatto & Windus.
Against The Wind, Douglas Sutherland, William Heinemann (OOP).
Bare Feet and Tackety Boots, Archie Cameron, Louth Press.
Illustrated Guide to Britain's Coast, AA Publications.

INDEX